VISITOR'S GUIDE: CZECHOSLOVAKIA
World Traveller Series

CZECHOSLOVAKIA

VISITOR'S GUIDE
CZECHOSLOVAKIA

Andrew Beattie

MPC

HUNTER
PUBLISHING INC

Published by:
Moorland Publishing Co Ltd,
Moor Farm Road West,
Ashbourne,
Derbyshire
DE6 1HD
England

© Andrew Beattie 1991

British Library Cataloguing in
Publication Data:
Beattie, Andrew
    Visitor's guide to Czechoslovakia.
    — (World traveller series)
    I. Title   II. Series
    914.3704

ISBN 0 86190 438 9

Colour origination by:
P&W Graphics Pte. Ltd, Singapore

Printed in the UK by:
Richard Clay Ltd, Bungay, Suffolk

Published in the USA by:
Hunter Publishing Inc,
300 Raritan Center Parkway,
CN 94, Edison, NJ 08818
ISBN 1-55650-492-6

Cover photograph: Charles Bridge,
Prague (*International Photobank*)

Illustrations have been supplied as
follows: Čedok (London) Ltd: pp
67, 79 (bottom), 119 (both), 123, 130,
150, 162 (both), 171, 187 (top), 202,
203, 206-7. All other illustrations
were supplied by the author.

MPC Production Team:
Editor: Tonya Monk
Designer: Jonathan Moss
Cartographer: Alastair Morrison

CONTENTS

Key to Symbols Used in Text Margin and on Maps

♠	Church/Ecclesiastical site	🏃	Recommended walk
♣	Parkland	🏠	Building of interest
π	Archaeological site	🏰	Castle/Fortification
🏞	Beautiful view/Scenery, Natural phenomenon	🦌	Nature reserve/Animal interest
🏛	Museum/Art gallery	⛷	Skiing facilities
☀	Other place of interest	✻	Garden
🐚	Cave	⛵	Watersports

Key to Maps

● 🏘	Town/City	– — - –	National boundary
═════	Motorway	- - - - - -	Provincial boundary
▬▬▬	Main road	⌒⌒	Rivers
▭▭▭	Railway	🗾	Lakes

How To Use This Guide

This MPC Visitor's Guide has been designed to be as easy to use as possible. Each chapter covers a region or itinerary in a natural progression which gives all the background information to help you enjoy your visit. MPC's distinctive margin symbols, the important places printed in bold, and a comprehensive index enable the reader to find the most interesting places to visit with ease.

At the end of each chapter an Additional Information section gives specific details such as addresses and opening times, making this guide a complete sightseeing companion.

At the back of the guide the Fact File, arranged in alphabetical order, gives practical information and useful tips to help you plan your holiday — before you go and while you are there.

The maps of each region show the main towns, villages, roads and places of interest, but are not designed as route maps and motorists should always use a good recommended road atlas.

ABOUT THE AUTHOR

Andrew Beattie was born and brought up near London and was educated at Mansfield College, Oxford University, where he read Geography. His travels in Europe, the Middle East and elsewhere have included the occasional forray behind the old 'iron curtain', many walking trips in the Alps, and a 1,287km (800 mile) journey by bicycle from Venice to the English Channel. An opportunity to write about the city of Prague and on walking in the mountains of Slovakia, as well as an interest in the politics of the new, post-cold war Europe, led him to write about Czechoslovakia.

ACKNOWLEDGEMENTS

The author would like to thank the following for their assistance in the compilation of this book: staff in the offices of Reklama Čedok Ltd, Prague, and at Čedok (London) Ltd; Maria for her meticulous translations from German; and Imogen Bright for her valuable advice.

On a personal note, I would like to thank my parents, who somehow shared my faith in this project and helped me in all sorts of ways; Diana, for being excellent company in Prague and for cooking such a good 'vegetable mush'; and Tim, for putting up with me in Prague and Marienbad.

INTRODUCTION

B efore 1989, few Westerners considering a holiday in continental Europe would have thought of putting Czechoslovakia on their list of possible destinations. Many of the popular conceptions of Czechoslovakia were negative ones, based on half-truths, prejudice and a lack of information about what the country was really like or what it had to offer tourists. It had an alien political and economic system, an obscure language, was a member of the Warsaw Pact, and therefore a potential enemy of the West, and had a seemingly impenetrable border that required waging through mountains of red tape to cross—everything, in fact, conducive to making most people not want to go there. The country had a fair amount of tourists before 1989, but most Western visitors were German or Austrian, and the few English-speaking visitors who did go there would rarely venture far outside Prague.

Then this situation suddenly changed. For a few days in November 1989, Czechoslovakia came under the world's gaze when 10 days of demonstrations in Prague, which were encouraged by the changes that had already occured in Poland and Hungary, led to the fall of the Communist government and its 40-year-long stranglehold on the politics, economy and society of the country, in a chain of events that became known as the 'Velvet Revolution'. Václav Havel, the slightly maverick, ever-smiling playwright-turned-president, seemingly more at home in casual togs rather than formal suit, was catapulted from obscure philosopher to the status of a European leader; within months he was steering Czechoslovakia into the choppy waters of a nascent market economy. The ensuing rapid changes benefitted visitors to Czechoslovakia as well as its citizens: gone, suddenly, was the barbed-wire frontier, the unfriendly political system, the red tape and the misconceptions. Czechoslovakia was suddenly 'one of us' rather than 'one of them', and to prove it, in November 1990 President George Bush became the first serving American president ever to pay an official visit to the country; the British Prime Minister Margaret Thatcher had made her own equally ground-breaking, official visit a few months before.

Very soon, tourists began to follow in the footsteps of Western leaders and in 1990 Czechoslovakia welcomed five times as many tourists than it had in 1989, an astonishing increase in such a short period of time. These tourists found that the variety and breadth of attractions this newly-discovered country has to offer is surprising: there are thousands of historic castles and châteaux, many well-preserved historic towns, rock caves, spectacular natural scenery, and, crowning it all, the beautiful city of Prague, where the demonstrations of 1989 forced the Communists to resign, and put the country on the path to becoming 'Western'. In the 1990s, Czechoslovakia is changing from the position of being a destination of the very few to one of a country now firmly on the itinerary of many tourists.

History

Up until 1918, Czechoslovakia itself did not exist. Its three constituent parts, Bohemia, Moravia and Slovakia, were regarded as territorial prizes for belligerent empire-builders, rather than as countries in their own right. The history of Czechoslovakia, as of most of central Europe, is a complex one of wars, rebellion and external control; the great German chancellor Otto von Bismarck summed it up neatly when he remarked that 'whoever controls Bohemia, controls Europe', and most of the noted figures in the history of Central Europe seem to have taken this piece of advice to heart.

Most of Czechoslovakia never came under Roman rule and little of its known history can be described as 'ancient'. At the time of Christ, a tribe called the Boii lived in parts of present-day Bohemia, and gave the land its name. By the sixth century Slavik tribes were in control of the lands between the Danube and the Elbe, and one of these tribes was the Czechs, who eventually established a power base in central Bohemia; they built a castle on a strategic site on the River Vltava, and the settlement that grew up around it in the ensuing centuries became the city of Prague. One noted ruler at this time was Prince Václav, better known as Wenceslas, an extremely pious man who was murdered by his brother Boleslav in AD929 during a dynastic power struggle. He was immediately canonised and became Bohemia's patron saint, though he is remembered more by English-speakers as the subject of a Christmas carol. He is buried in the church that he founded — St Vitus' Cathederal in Prague.

In 1114 Bohemia became a princedom of the Holy Roman Empire. In 1355 Charles I, the Bohemian king, was crowned Holy Roman Emperor by the Pope, and as Emperor Charles IV he moved the Imperial capital to Prague. The city's most glorious age had begun: Europe's top scholars, architects, sculptors and painters flocked to the city, and some of them helped to build the 'Golden Prague', with which many of today's tourists fall in love. But more difficult times soon followed. John Huss, a Bohemian cleric who mixed desires for religious reform with those of Czech Nationalism, caused dissent and faction within the Czech ranks. Although burned at the stake in 1415 (in Constance), the influence of the Hussite movement which he founded was felt for many centuries. Still revered as a Czech hero, an enormous memorial to him in Prague's Old Town Square celebrates the memory of the country's first Nationalist martyr. Future Nationalists were forever recalling the name of

John Huss, as they spoke out against the four centuries of Habsburg control of the Czech lands, which lasted from 1516 until 1918. The Habsburgs governed their vast Austro-Hungarian empire from Vienna with a cast-iron fist, and one of their most notorious pieces of heavy-handedness was placing a devout Catholic prince, Ferdinand of Styria, on the Bohemian throne in 1617. His attempts at reconverting wayward Bohemian Protestants to Catholicism did not please the small but powerful Protestant aristocracy in Bohemia, a delegation of whom in 1618 marched on Prague Castle and threw two of his deputies out of one of the castle windows. They landed in a fortuitously-placed heap of dung and survived, but the so-called 'defenestration of Prague' was the spark that set Europe alight from 1618 to 1648 — the Thirty Years War, one of the bloodiest in the continent's history.

Meanwhile, different things were going on in lands to the east of Bohemia. Although Moravia was briefly under Hungarian rule in the fifteenth century, it largely shares its early and medieval history with Bohemia. Slovakia, however, has a very disimilar history to either of the two Western lands. Like Bohemia and Moravia, it was occupied by Slavik peoples, but despite a common ethnic ancestry Slovaks often see themselves as having a very different culture to the Czechs who live in the west. Slovakia was never a part of the Holy Roman Empire and it became influenced by Hungarian culture as Bohemia was influenced by German culture. Slovakia never went through the cultural renaissance that Prague experienced in the Middle Ages, and its economy and society remained largely backward and peasant orientated. From 1526 Slovakia was part of the Austro-Hungarian empire, and like Moravia and Bohemia it was ruled from Vienna. After 1867 however, this empire split in two and Slovakia came under Hungarian rule from Budapest which was harsh and oppressive. Social and economic conditions did not improve, and many Slovaks emigrated to the USA during the latter decades of the nineteenth century.

The Habsburgs were defeated in World War I, and their vast lands, which spread through much of central Europe, were broken up. In 1918 two Czech dissidents, Tomaš Masaryk and Edvard Beneš, who had foreseen Austro-Hungary's defeat at the hands of the allies, issued a declaration of Czechoslovakian independence, jointly from Paris and Washington. A new, united and fully independent state of Czechoslovakia was proclaimed in Prague on 18 October 1918. For the next 20 years, the country was run on the lines of a parliamentary democracy, and Czechoslovakia is unique amongst the countries of Eastern Europe for once having operated under such a system. But in the early 1930s, the first cracks began to show: the German-speaking minority in the country became agitated by their financial suffering during the years of the Great Depression and in 1933, Konrad Henlein, a school gym teacher, founded the Sudeten German Party, which soon began to voice support for the Nazi Party in neighbouring Germany. In 1938 Britain and France sold Czechoslovakia short, and by the infamous Munich Agreement they allowed Hitler to invade and occupy Czechoslovakia, thereby expanding the Third Reich to include the Sudeten Germans. Leaders who had run the country during its

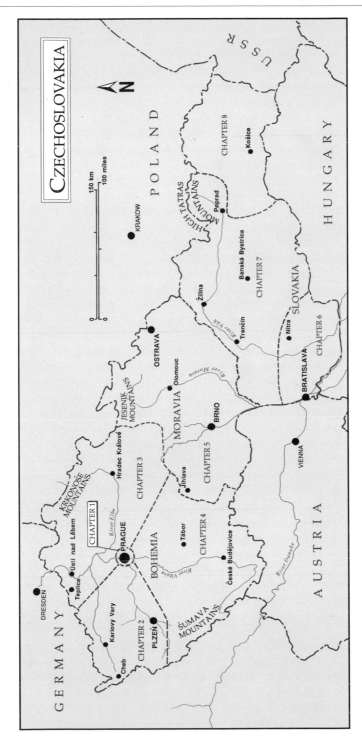

previous period of democracy fled, or were killed; Churchill allowed one of the country's original founders, Edvard Beneš, to set up a Czech government-in-exile in London during the war. However, it was the Soviet Red Army that liberated most of the country from Nazi rule, finally freeing Prague after a popular uprising there in May 1945.

There was a lot of mistrust of the West in Czechoslovakia after the war, partly because of what was seen as the sell-out at Munich. The Czechoslovak Communist Party, which had worked successfully underground during World War II, gained 36 per cent of the votes in a general election in 1946. In 1948, Klement Gottwald, now a figure held in the deepest contempt by most Czechs, became the country's first Communist president. Gottwald took his orders from Stalin, who wielded considerable power in the country after the Soviet armies had liberated it, and Stalin sent advisers to Prague to point Gottwald in the right direction. In 1950, the purging of the Catholic church began, and individuals who held out against the regime were tried and executed or imprisoned, and any political opposition was gradually crushed.

In 1968 Alexander Dubček became president; he promised 'Socialism with a human face', and introduced some of the reforms that Czechs clamoured for — new guidelines to protect civil rights, more freedom of the press, and greater freedom for institutions such as the church and parliament. His reforms became known as the 'Prague Spring'. Brezhnev and his Warsaw Pact allies were not impressed with all this bourgeois liberalism, and on 20 August 1968 combined Eastern Bloc forces invaded Czechoslovakia to end the reforms and to force the country to tow the Soviet line. Six months later, Jan Pallach (a student) set himself on fire in Wenceslas Square in Prague in protest at this infringement of Czech independence; he immediately became a national hero. Forced by the Russian tanks rumbling up and down the streets in Prague, Dubček resigned, and Gustáv Husák took over the presidency, returning the country to Communist rule and purging the old Communist party of reformers.

Under Husák, Czechoslovakia became one of the most brutal and totalitarian of all the Eastern Bloc regimes. His government took an even harder line than those before the Prague Spring. Many journalists, writers and composers, who were seen as being a threat to the regime, found themselves engaged in performing menial, manual jobs instead of following their chosen professions. In 1977 a group of these persecuted intellectuals formed the Charter'77 group, which campaigned against the government and its abuse of human rights and freedoms. Many of the group's protagonists were jailed including Václav Havel one of its founders, but the group's name became a byword for human freedom from repression all over the world.

The causes of the revolutions that made a blazing trail through Eastern Europe in the Autumn of 1989 will be discussed and debated by historians for decades to come. The man who seems to be the key figure in creating the conditions that allowed the revolutions to succeed is the Soviet President Mikhail Gorbachov, whose 'glasnost' and 'perestroika' reforms in the Soviet Union gave impetus to reform movements in Eastern Europe. Crumbling and more or less bankrupt, the Soviet Union was in no position to hold onto its European satellites, whose governments toppled like dominoes, one by one, starting with Poland where the seeds of dissent were sown in the early 1980s when the free trade Union 'Solidarity' was founded. Many had realised that the old Marxist-Leninist ideas on which these countries were run had failed and were moribund, but it was not until 1989 that the situation was right to alter the status quo. On 17 November 1989, after several days of fierce demonstrations in Prague, Brno and Bratislava, the Communist rulers of Czechoslovakia resigned, after realising (finally) that they no longer had the confidence of the people they governed. Václav Havel, intellectual, dissident, and man of the people, became the country's first democratically elected president for 40 years, and ushered in a new era of history for Czechoslovakia that will hopefully bring with it those things that have so often been missing in the past — peace, prosperity, freedom and independence.

Geography

Czechoslovakia lies in central Europe and is bordered by five countries: Germany to the west, Poland to the north, the USSR to the east, and Austria and Hungary to the south. The area of the country is 128,000sq km (49,000sq miles), making it roughly half the size of the United Kingdom. Its population is relatively small, and the population density is fairly low. Prague, the capital, is less than a sixth of the size of London, Paris or New York. The second and third cities are Bratislava and Brno, which also have comparatively small populations. Outside the three biggest cities, there are a number of other large centres of population, composed of clusters of industrial cities that the tourist is unlikely to want to visit. These include the north-east Moravian conurbation centred on Ostrava, and coal-mining towns in north-west Bohemia such as Most and Chomutov.

Apart from the lowland area around the River Danube, east of Bratislava, the scenery in Czechoslovakia is characteristically hilly. The scenic highlight for most is the High Tatras mountain range in northern Slovakia, one of the highest ranges in Europe away from the Alps. The highest peak in Czechoslovakia is Mount Gerlachovka (2,655m, 8,708ft), which is the highest mountain in the whole of the Carpathian range, which stretches in a broad arc from Vienna to Bucharest, and which includes the Tatras. Other important ranges in Slovakia are the Low Tatras and Malá Fatra. Away from Slovakia, other mountains ranges are lower but still have fine scenery: they include the Krkonoše Mountains on the border between Poland and Bohemia, the Šumava Mountains in South Bohemia, and the Jeseník mountains in northern Moravia. All these mountains have chairlifts and skiing facilities, and in the Tatras such facilities are well advanced and allow for good skiing holidays — a far cheaper alternative to more traditional destinations in the Alps. The snow season lasts from November to March in most mountain areas. In summer the mountains are a paradise for walkers. In this book, suggestions for winter skiing activities and for summer walking trips have been given for most mountain areas, though the emphasis is very firmly on the High Tatras. The River Elbe is the most important river in the west of the country. It rises in the Krkonoše Mountains and flows through Bohemian towns such as Mělník and Děčín, before crossing Germany and draining into the North Sea at Hamburg. Although the Czech name of the river is the Labe, its better-known German name is used in this book. The River Vltava, Czechoslovakia's longest and most famous river, is a tributary of the River Elbe, joining the latter at Mělník after flowing through Prague. The Vltava is a recurring theme in Czech works of literature and music. In the south-east of the country, the River Danube flows briefly through Czechoslovakia, where the city of Bratislava is built on its banks. Slovakia's other important river is the Váh, which rises in the Tatras and flows into the Danube at Komárno.

Flora and Fauna

Anyone who travels in Czechoslovakia cannot fail to notice the very high proportion of the land surface which is covered with forest. This reflects, in part, the very low population densities. Forests consist of deciduous trees in the west and evergreens in the east. Unfortunately Czechoslovak forests are some of the most affected by acid rain in Europe. Notwithstanding this, great efforts are often taken to preserve forest and wildlife: there are countless designated nature reserves where oak, mountain spruce, beech and other trees are preserved, and an area of the High Tatras is permanently closed to walkers, climbers and skiers to protect the mountain environment.

Wild animals abound in Czechoslovakia. Deer, stag, roebuck and occasionally wild horses live in most of the forest areas. The wilder areas of the mountains in Slovakia are home to wild bears (about 500 in all at any one time), wolves, lynx, wild cats, the chamois and the marmot. The areas where these animals are found are well off the beaten tourist trail and are protected by State laws. It is possible to go on arranged hunting holidays in Czechoslovakia, organised by Čedok and staying in forest and mountain lodges. For anglers, the rivers and streams of Czechoslovakia offer a wide variety of possibilities, though a fishing licence must be obtained to fish in the country.

Food and Drink

The culinary wealth of Czechoslovakia is not particuarly well noted. Most of the dishes are heavily meat based; Czechoslovakia is not a place for gastronomics, vegetarians, and those on a diet. Those looking for exotic cuisine will probably be disappointed. In part, the food available reflects the

Opposite: Czechoslovakia's changing landscape — from the alpine peaks in the High Tatras to the longest river, the Vltava

country's history: German-influenced in Bohemia and Moravia, while in Slovakia the food is more similar to Hungarian cuisine. Pork is the most popular meat dish, and *the* cold starter is Prague Ham *(Pražká Šunka)*. Other very popular meats are duck and goose, the latter a popular Slovak dish. Dumplings *(knedíky)*, which can be made from bread, sweet fruits (particuarly plums), egg or potato, are served with more or less everything. Unsurprisingly, sea fish does not feature very highly on the menu, but there is a certain amount of freshwater fish (mostly carp), much of which comes from the extensive fish ponds around Třeboň in southern Bohemia. Do not be misled by the food shortages in countries like Romania or the USSR — the situation is much better here, though there are still some rarities, such as tropical fruit and good vegetables (boiled cabbage seems to be the national vegetable). Slovak food is characterised by being more spicy, particuarly making use of red peppers; the goulash found here is similar to that in neighbouring Hungary. As regards eating out, use a good phrase book to navigate around the menu, or ask if there is one available in German (possible) or English (unlikely, except in Prague).

Street stalls sell a wide variety of food, from hot sausage to rich, cream-drenched strudels, and *bramborák* (potato pancakes fried in oil) to the more mundane hamburgers and french fries. Ice cream *(zmrzlina)* is found every-where (even in winter!) and Czechs seem to consume more of it than Italians. A *kavárna* is a café, often with no or only very limited space to sit down, which sells fancy cakes and pastries, either deliciously gooey or ridiculously over-sweet, depending on the individual's point of view. It is normally possible to buy cakes here to take away, as well as to eat on the premises. In fact, Czechoslovaks as a people seem to have a very sweet tooth — there are countless varieties of sweets available everywhere. Chocolate is also a very common snack, and is typically solid and nourishing (a good thing to take on the walks described in this book).

The reputation Czechoslovak food lacks is more than made up for by its famous alcoholic beverages. Czechoslovakia is one of the largest beer produc-ers in the world; the city of Plzeň in West Bohemia is home to the original Pilsner Urquell beer, exported all over the world, while Budvar beer from České Budějovice in South Bohemia is reputed to be the original American Budweiser. Most towns in the country have their own local brewery. Beer is astoundingly cheap and can be drunk in *pivnice*, beer halls. Wine bars are called *vinárna* and often serve wines that are the produce of vineyards in southern Moravia and Slovakia, although there are also some wine-produc-ing areas in Bohemia (particuarly around the town of Mělník, north of Prague). White is *bílé*, red is *červené* . The famous plum brandy Slivovice is a product of Moravia, while Becherovka herb liqueur comes from the spa town of Karlovy Vary. Borovička Spirits are drunk all over Slovakia.

Cultural Life

Czechoslovakia has rich traditions in the arts and music, which flourished under Communism due to the high subsidies the various cultural institutions received from the government although many artists and writers whose work contravened the ideology of the State were banned. Most towns in the country have a theatre, and in some cities one can attend excellent opera or ballet performances, or music concerts, for a fraction of the price usually paid in the West.

Ironically, the country's most famous writer is probably Franz Kafka, who wrote all his works in German. He was born in Prague in 1883, of German-Jewish ethnic stock, and his writing, which is for most people shrouded in intellectual obscurity, focused on the alienation of twentieth-century man, and other esoteric meditations which are definately *not* the stuff of popular fiction. His most famous works were *Metamorphosis* (1912), and *The Trial* and *The Castle*, both of which were published posthumously. He died in 1924, in a sanitorium near Vienna, and is buried in Prague. Both his sisters were executed in Nazi gas chambers in Germany in the 1930s.

Other writers include Karel Čapek, whose play *R.U.R. (Rossum's Universal Robots)* brought the word 'robot' into the English language, and Jaroslav Hašek, famous for his work *The Good Soldier Schweik*, one of the most noted Czech novels of this century. Václav Havel, elected President of Czechoslovakia in 1989, wrote many plays, some of which were also seen in other countries, such as *The Garden Party* (1963). He also wrote many philosophical works which were frowned on by the State. One of the most well-known Czech writers is Milan Kundera, who lived in exile in Paris from the regime he often criticised in his works. His most famous novel is *The Unbearable Lightness of Being* (1984), which received a wide audience abroad and was made into a film. Much of the work is set during the Prague Spring, and both the book and the film were banned in Czechoslovakia.

Czech composers have gained a high reputation outside the country. The greatest composer is undoubtably Antonin Dvořák (1841-1904), although ironically his most famous work, his ninth symphony entitled *From the New World*, is a series of musical impressions inspired by a visit to America. Both he and fellow Czech composer Bedřich Smetana (1824-1904) wrote music based on Czech folk songs and dances. Smetana is also known for his symphonic poem *Má Vlast (My Fatherland)* which includes the movement *Vltava*. The most famous twentieth-century Czech composer is Leos Jánaček. Classical music performances are frequently staged in Brno, Bratislava, Karlovy Vary and other towns, and are the staple diet of Prague's entertainment scene. The tradition of classical music is very strong in Czechoslovakia — the first performance of Mozart's opera *Don Giovanni* was given in Prague, where some of the piece was also written. Mozart also visited and performed in other cities in the country, including Brno.

There is a long tradition of film-making in Czechoslovakia, particulary in animated and puppet films. Czechoslovak films are rarely seen outside the country, however. An international film festival is held in Karlovy Vary every second year. The country's most celebrated film director is probably Miloš Forman, who made many films in Czechoslovakia before moving to Hollywood and winning oscars for his direction of the films *One Flew over the Cuckoo's Nest* (1977) and *Amadeus* (1984), which was filmed in Prague.

Only a few Czech painters are truly well known outside the country; they include Josef Maneš and Alphonse Mucha. Most towns in Czechoslovakia have an art gallery, which exhibits the work of local artists. There are also large art galleries in Brno, Prague, Bratislava and Hluboká Château (amongst other places) which exhibit the works of other European artists. Glass making is probably the most famous Czech art form; many glass designers and sculptors have gained world renown, and one of the world's finest and largest collections of glass can be found in the Museum of Decorative Arts in Prague. Bohemian cut glass and crystal is sold everywhere and is the most popular souvenir foreign tourists buy in the country.

People, Politics and Economy

Czechoslovakia is made up of three historic lands, two nations and one State. Bohemia, Moravia and Slovakia were joined together in 1918 to form the State of Czechoslovakia. Since 1969, the country has been a Federal State consisting of two nations: the Czech Republic (Bohemia and Moravia), with its capital Prague; and the Slovak Republic (Slovakia) with its capital Bratislava. So, Prague is the capital of the old Kingdom of Bohemia, of the Czech Republic, and of the State of Czechoslovakia as a whole. The boundary between the Czech and Slovak Republics is often shown on maps, though it is a 'benign' border with no formalities (like the Anglo-Scottish border, for example). The President of the country, and members of the national and regional parliaments, are elected democratically. A huge variety of political parties has grown up since the Velvet Revolution.

The Czechs of Bohemia and Moravia, and the Slovaks of Slovakia, are both closely-related Slavik peoples; the languages they speak, Czech and Slovak, are also very similar. There is a small number of minority peoples: most of the German population was expelled from the country after the war, though a few still remain; there are also Hungarian and Polish speakers living near the country's borders. Eastern Slovakia has a large Ukranian-speaking minority, and also a large number of gypsies, many of whom have settled in the town of Košice. Those visiting industrial cities (such as Ústí nad Lábem or Děčín in northern Bohemia) will notice many Vietnamese, who were invited into the country by the Communist government as guest workers to help alleviate the labour shortage. Many Czechoslovaks are Roman Catholic and church attendance rates are high. The church was viewed with great distrust by the Communist Party. There are also a few practicing Jews and Russian Orthodox Christians in the country.

In January 1991, President Václav Havel said of the Czechoslovak economy

Bohemian crystal is one of the most popular souvenirs to buy in Czechoslovakia

Colourful Bohemian folk costumes

that 'what originally seemed to be a neglected house is, in fact, a ruin'. Under Communism, inefficiency, overmanning, out-of-date working practices and gross neglect were the hallmarks of Czechoslovak industry. The transition from a Marxist to a market-led economy is not an easy one. Many State enterprises have been privatised; those that proved to be too inefficient have closed, bringing unemployment, which never existed before — everyone used to be guaranteed work. Very little care was taken of the physical envrionment, and many towns (such as the steel-making city of Ostrava) still suffer badly from pollution. Rivers and forests have also been badly damaged, though the problems are slowly being cleared up. Czechoslovakia was always the second strongest East European economy, after East Germany, producing cars, steel (there is abundant coal), machinery, chemicals, glass, railway equipment and so on. Now East Germany has gone, and the country's future economic prospects are reckoned by many to be far better than those of Poland, Romania or Hungary, though the country may be many decades off achieving the standards of living that exist in West European countries such as France or Germany. Some economic analysts have predicted that the country may be ready to join the European Community around the year 2000.

Czechoslovakia's Attractions

The city of Prague is the most important destination for most visitors to Czechoslovakia; a considerable proportion of any amount of time in the country is likely to be spent seeing this incredibly beautiful and, until recently, comparatively undiscovered city. Prague is now awash with tourists who jam its narrow medieval lanes and admire its elegant, wide squares at all times of year. However, the rest of the country is less well known, and although this book has a lengthy chapter devoted to Prague, the chapters that follow it allow the visitor to escape the city crowds and head for the beautiful scenery, castles and historic towns in other parts of the country.

Great efforts were made by the previous Communist administration to preserve the country's historical monuments. So much so that the medieval core of a town can look sparkling and well cared-for, while the residential districts a short distance away can boast some of the ugliest and most ill-maintained housing areas one is ever likely to see. Such contrasts are both an indictment and a measure of praise for the previous regime, and may be one of the most endearing impressions Western visitors have of Czechoslovakia. Throughout the post-war years in a process that is still continuing, many towns have been restored and have been designated 'historic town reserves', with stringent protection orders governing the maintainance of the old parts of these towns. These reserves now number about fifty towns, found in virtually all areas of the country. They normally have an interesting history, and their monuments may include churches, town buildings, medieval forti-fications, and sometimes town castles, palaces or châteaux with their own gardens. Sometimes the 'historic town reserves' form the core of a tiny, country town, such at Telč in western Moravia; or, in the case of Olomouc, Brno or Bratislava, the preserved core is surrounded by a thriving industrial metropolis. Notable among these preserved towns are the three famous spa towns in western Bohemia, Karlovy Vary, Mariánské Lázně and Františkovy Lázně. Out in the countryside there are about 2,500 castles, châteux and country houses in Czechoslovakia. Many of them date from the rich leagacy of the Austrian Habsburg family and its various branches, who governed Bohemia, Moravia and Slovakia for many centuries. Bohemia is particuarly rich in castles. Many of the castles are not open to the public, and this book does not pretend to include descriptions of all the rest that are — inevitably, only the most well-known have been included. Inside such buildings there are often well-organised collections of period furniture, hunting equipment and trophies, paintings and other aristocratic paraphernalia. Visitors usually see the castles in guided tours which are conducted in Czech, Slovak or German — an English text is normally available to buy or borrow.

Many of the châteaux also have adjoining parks and gardens which visitors are free to wander round. The most famous medieval castle in Czechoslovakia is probably Karlštejn Castle, near Prague, but other notable examples exist in many places, though not so much in Slovakia. Regarding châteaux, as opposed to castles, the most visited are probably Hluboká Château in southern Bohemia, and Lednice Château in south-east Moravia, which is set in a beautiful park. The same thorough restoration work has been carried out on castles as in the historic towns — always check that the castle you intend visiting is not in the process of being restored, otherwise there is a possibility of arriving at the place and finding it covered with scaffolding, and the door locked. There are also many hundreds of ruined castles, often set in isolated positions which one must walk to, such as Dívčí Kámen Castle in South Bohemia, or Vinné Castle in eastern Slovakia; the ruins of Spiš Castle, also in eastern Slovakia, are some of the biggest in Europe.

Whereas the spread of castles and historic towns is fairly even, the areas visitors should head for if they are looking for scenery are more specific. For serious hill and mountain walkers, the High Tatra Mountains in Slovakia are a highlight; experienced and qualified climbers will also find much to interest them here. The Tatras, however, do get rather crowded, and there are many other areas of the country where interesting scenery may be found — the Šumava Mountains in southern Bohemia, the Krkonoše Mountains in northern Bohemia, or the other mountain areas in Slovakia. A tenth of the country is protected by nature reserves, which prevent damage being caused to the natural environment. The most important natural areas are also protected as National Parks. Forty thousand kilometres (25,000 miles) of marked paths and tracks lead walkers around such areas; the paths are colour-coded on maps and by markers along their length, with distance indictor posts at intervals and at the junctions of paths. The members of local sports clubs are responsible for keeping these paths maintained and properly marked. Sometimes, these paths lead walkers to specific points of interest that are not accessible by road

— ruined castles, gorges, viewpoints, hill summits, waterfalls, or interesting rock formations, such as those in the Elbe Sandstone region, near Děčín in northern Bohemia; or sometimes, just on casual strolls through pleasant scenery, which may be anything from low, forested hills (such as in the Šumava Mountains) or spectacular Alpine scenery (in the High Tatras). This book points out many walking tours but it is easy, with good maps and a little imagination, for individuals to plan their own walking trips in whatever area they are visiting. Many walking tracks are marked as starting from the centre of a town or village and then heading off into the open countryside from there.

For those wanting even more outdoor persuits, mountain and hill areas in Czechoslovakia provide many good opportunities for skiing. For most foreign visitors, skiing means the High Tatras, where there are a number of ski resorts with the usual facilities which include lifts, cableways, ski hiring facilities and so on. The standards are not up to those in the Alps, but nor are the prices. Another very important ski resort is Jasná, in the Low Tatras. Away from Slovakia, the most important destination for skiers is the Krkonoše Mountain range in northern Bohemia, which has a skiing season lasting 6 months. Cross-country skiing is very popular in many areas. Other activites outdoors need more specialist preparation; as well as climbing in the mountains, there are opportunities for hunting, canoeing, fishing, or more advanced walking in mountain areas, making use of experienced mountain guides and staying in isolated mountain chalets or huts.

Other attractions in the country include numerous folklore festivals — the most famous being those held in Domažlice (Bohemia), Strážnice (Moravia), and Vychodá (Slovakia), and some more unusual attractions — tours of famous breweries, boat trips on underground rivers in limestone caves, sailing or boating on various lakes, or tasting mineral waters at source in famous spas. The great variety and endless number of things to do and see in Czechoslovakia is likely to astound many visitors, and will hopefully make them want to visit this consistently surprising and interesting country again.

1

PRAGUE

The visionary words 'I see a big city whose beauty touches the stars...', were probably never spoken in reality, but the city of Prague effortlessly lives up to them. The cleric and historian Cosmas, working in the twelfth century, attributed them to Princess Libuše, who was supposed to have founded Prague more than two centuries before. The legend of the city's foundation is that she sent two of her loyal henchmen into the forest, telling them to establish a town at the spot where they saw a ploughman *(přemysl)* constructing the threshold *(prah)* of a house, thus naming both her Royal dynasty (the Přemyslids, who ruled Bohemia for 400 years) and the city, Praha, known to English speakers as Prague. The last kings of the Přemyslid dynasty died out in the fourteenth century, but their capital city lived on, and the beauty of 'Golden Prague' became as legendary as that of the story of its foundation. One hundred and fifty years ago, the Moravian writer Charles Sealsfield wrote that 'Prague is one of the finest and most picturesque cities on the continent...it would be a foolish enterprise to write a history of the world without previously visiting this ancient capital.' Franz Kafka, an inhabitant of the city rather than a visitor, summed up the effect many tourists will find that Prague has on them: 'Prague does not let go, either of you or of me. This little mother has claws. There is nothing for it but to give in...' Prague's beauty has survived intact all those things that have denigrated other European cities — revolutions, wars, poverty and the seemingly never ending quest of architects to modernise and change whatever their predecessors have built before them. The spires of the Old Town and the Lesser Quarter have defiantly protected the extraordinary wealth of medieval history, picturesque charm and graceful character that has existed beneath their gaze for centuries. Prague has many travel guide writers reaching for superlatives by the basketful, so perhaps to avoid falling into the trap of using unnecessary hyperbole, it is safest to use only one: Prague is the most beautiful city in Europe.

Take Prague slowly; there is a grave risk of trying to see it all, and then remembering nothing. There is enough in this city to keep the dedicated sight-seer or museum-goer busy for weeks. Almost at every turn there is a new piece of history, a famed building or another medieval square. Books thicker than this one have been written on just a certain aspect of Prague, and it can take several volumes to do full justice to the city. Keep looking upwards as there is always something new to see amongst the gabled roofs, such as elegant window frames of medieval houses, or some new spire protruding from the rooftop which merely forms another blip on the staccato skyline of central Prague. Walk in the lanes and squares to capture the full flavour of the city. There is no need to drive in order to see Prague. Unlike other cities, such as Paris or London, where the important sights are liberally sprinkled over a wide area, Prague's most interesting monuments and museums are all confined within a small, central core where almost every other building has a new and interesting history to it. Many of the streets in the Old Town and Lesser Quarter are, in any case, closed to traffic. Those that are open must be navigated according to a complex system of one-way streets. The tours below are walking tours of the five ancient districts of Prague, which were joined together in the fourteenth century to form a city whose modern, growing suburbs now spread out in all directions from its historic core. The five districts have indefinable boundaries and merge into one another, but together they make up the central area of the city. On the east (right) bank of the River Vltava, which cuts through the centre of the city in a path shaped like a giant question mark, is the Old Town and the New Town, with the Jewish Quarter forming a tiny part of the former; on the opposite bank is the Lesser Quarter, with the magnificent sight of Prague Castle, which forms the city's most dominant landmark, rising above it on Hradčany Hill. The Lesser Quarter and the Old Town are linked by what many consider to be the city's finest monument, the Charles Bridge, whose medieval arches span the River Vltava.

It is all to easy, when describing Prague, or any city like it, for a guide book to bury the reader beneath huge chunks of medieval history, under the pretext that an understanding of such background material is necessary for a full appreciation of the multitude of sights that are described. This book places the major sights within their historical context, but aims to do no more. Prague's tourist machine is now well in gear, and any further information the visitor wants can easily be obtained at most of the places of interest listed here. Like all cities, it is not so much the memories of the sights themselves which visitors will take home with them; still less, the intricate detail of their histories. What is more important is what is seen and done away from the confines of a guide book: people-watching in the Old Town Square; wandering the embankments on the east side of the Vltava with the floodlit Charles Bridge and Prague Castle reflected in the still water; finding a medieval tavern which provides a filling Czech meal washed down with a glass of cold Bohemian beer, or catching the performance of an impromptu street entertainer in the serene surroundings of a medieval square. It is these pursuits, even more than admiring a Renaissance façade or the Baroque detailing in a church, that lie at the heart of enjoying a visit to Prague.

The New Town (Nové Město)

The New Town is only so called because it is newer than all the other parts of central Prague. It was founded by Charles IV (whose name crops up again and again in Prague's history) in 1348, to relieve the overcrowding that existed in the other districts of the city. Now virtually all the ancient buildings have gone, and the area again lives up to its original name. Many of the hotels, restaurants, shops, museums, theatres and offices of central Prague are here, thus continuing a tradition that dates back to the fourteenth century, when the area was colonised by artisans and traders and became the mercantile district of the city. Although there are some reminders of the medieval times, they are lost in the throng of nonetheless elegant nineteenth- and early twentieth-century buildings which characterise most of this part of Prague. Much of the area, including the main shopping streets, is pedestrianised, and it is here one finds the bustle of commuters, shoppers, tourists and hamburger bars that is usually associated with any large city.

Wenceslas Square

The heart of the New Town — and to some extent Prague itself — is Wenceslas Square (Václavské Náměstí), which is not really a square at all but a long, elegant boulevarde, over 60m (197ft) wide and 700m (2,297ft) long, the sides of which are lined with some of Prague's plushest hotels and restaurants. Despite the fact that no building in Wenceslas Square dates from before 1900, it has a long history. It was laid out as a horse market in the time of Charles IV. Some people may feel they recognise this square — many of the famous black-and-white newsreel shots of the Prague Spring show Russian tanks rumbling up and down it. The square's appearance has altered much since this time; in the 1980s the whole of the roadway was dug up and metro lines laid underneath, and when it was all reconstructed the central part of the square was laid out as a pedestrian plaza, which stretches its whole length. Two metro stations serve the square, Mustek at the bottom end, and Muzeum at the top which is the more interesting end.

The square is gently sloping, and forming a dominant dark-coloured silhouette at the top (south-east) end of it is the impressive building of the **National Museum** (Národní Muzeum), built in the 1890s (a description of the contents is in the Museums section later on in this chapter). The entrance to Múzeum metro-station is just below this building. Although it has the look of a palace or parliament building, it was designed to house the collections of the museum, which itself was founded some decades before. A constant stream of traffic screaches past the steps up to the front door. To one side of the museum is the modern building of the **Federal Assembly** — the country's parliament, and, before the Communists took over, a stock exchange. The building was enlarged in the 1960s by constructing another deck on top of the older building, and holding this up with stilts. Beyond it, it is just possible to see the grandiose arched roof of the main railway station (Hlavní Nádraží).

Below the museum is the statue that gives the square its name — the
Wenceslas Statue (1913) with Wenceslas, the patron Saint of Bohemia, riding
a horse, with four other saints surrounding the base of the statue. So beguiling
is the legend of St Wenceslas to many Czechs, that it was Wenceslas Square,
especially the top end near the statue, that became the gathering point for
crowds during the revolutions in 1968 (the Prague Spring) and 1989 (the
Velvet Revolution). The latter event saw the greatest demonstrations here,
when, every night for 10 days from 17 November to 27 November, over

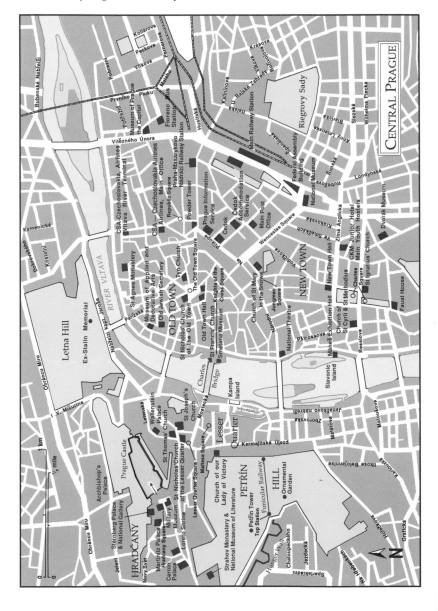

250,000 people thronged the square, calling for the overthrow of the Communist government, which finally came the day after a general strike had been organised by the opposition (now government) movement called Civic Forum. Twenty years before, during the Prague Spring, the square had witnessed another, though very different, show of opposition, when a student named Jan Pallach set fire to himself to protest against the Soviet invasion of Czechoslovakia that crushed the reform movement of Alexander Dubček. On the site of the place where he died, next to the Wenceslas Statue, is the sombre **Jan Pallach Memorial** which commemorates the event in the form of a   ❋ poignant circle of red flowers surrounded by a ring of melted candlewax, which has resulted from the continuous burning of candles on this site. Heads of state visiting Czechoslovakia are often brought to see this memorial, which has only been in existance since the departure of the Communists in 1989. Before this date, the memory of the Prague Spring and of Jan Pallach was rigorously suppressed by the government. In the evenings, however, any association Wenceslas Square has with these events is almost forgotten amidst the modern bustle of nightclubs, cinemas, expensive restaurants and hotels. The whole square — art nouveau buildings, with their gushing architectural embellishments, and cheek-by-jowl modern, concrete-box affairs — is lit up by neon signs and advertisements, and comes alive to the sounds of modern Western rock music emanating from the nightclubs along its length.

Na Příkopě, Národní Třída and Charles Square

At the bottom (north-west) end of Wenceslas Square is the junction of roads called Mustek, in the heart of the commercial district of modern Prague.

Sightseeing in style using traditional transport

Entrances to Mustek metro station are to be found here. A street called **Na Příkopě** leads off to the right; this pedestrianised street is also home to cafés, shops, hotels, offices and restaurants, and is one of the busiest streets in Prague. Its name means 'on the moat', which originates from the time a moat stood here, separating the Old Town from the New Town. The moat was filled in to form the street in 1760. One of the most interesting buildings along this street is the **Sylva-Taroucca Palace**, on the right hand side. It was built in the 1740s and houses a rather plush restaurant. In summer, tables are set up outside in one of the courtyards. At the end of this street is the Powder Tower.

Also leading from Mustek, running off to the left, is another pedestrianised street, called 28 Října Street. After a short distance this road leads into **Jungman Square** (Jungmannovo Náměstí), a small, but busy square. From here an entrance leads into the **Church of St Mary in the Snows**, an ancient building forming an island in a sea of modern constructions. This church was founded by Charles IV in 1347, and the original grandiose conception was that its nave was to be 100m (328ft) in length; these plans were never fulfilled, however, which is why the church seems so high for its short length, giving it a rather awkward, lopsided appearance. A mosaic on the outside wall above the main doorway shows the Virgin and Child. Inside, there is more Baroque decoration including an altar of 1724. A monastery used to occupy the buildings next to the church. In the cellars of the old monastery there is a wine bar, accessible from the pleasant gardens behind the church, which were laid out in 1950 as a haven of peace amidst the commercial bustle of the New Town.

Back in Jungman Square, **Národní Třída** (National Avenue) continues in a westerly direction, with more shops and commercial institutions lining its sides. A street on the left, called Spálená, leads to **Charles Square** (Karlovo Náměstí). Charles Square, served by Karlovo Náměstí metro station, is in fact a spacious park, a more restful place than Wenceslas Square with none of the dashing traffic of the latter. Statues of Czech writers and intellectuals pop up between the trees, adding to the quiet serenity of the place. The square was founded and is named after Charles IV; the city's cattle and vegetable markets used to be held here. The **New Town Hall** (Novoměstská Radnice) is the building that is probably encased in several layers of scaffolding on the left hand side of the square as one enters from Spálená Street. It is one of the many old buildings in Prague which is undergoing an extensive period of renovation. When it re-opens, probably in the mid-1990s, it will be possible to go up the tower. It was constructed in 1347 as the town hall for the recently-founded New Town, and since losing this function in the eighteenth century it has been used as a prison, and for various administrative offices. The New Town Hall was the site of the first, and less famous, of the two 'defenestrations of Prague'. The Church of St Mary in the Snows, nearby was one of the main rallying points of the Hussite movement, founded by the revolutionary Bohemian preacher John Huss in the fifteenth century. One Hussite priest who preached in this church was Jan Želivsky, who led a march from the church to the New Town Hall in 1419, when the Hussite mob threw some of the city councillors out of the window of the building.

On the left (east) side of the square is the Baroque Jesuit **St Ignatius' Church** (Kostel Svatého Ignáce), dating from the seventeenth century. It is sumptuously decorated, with seemingly every corner covered in some adornment, sculpture or painting. On the south side of the church is the eighteenth-century mansion called the **Faust House** (Faustuv Dum). There are many legends attached to this building, which tell of it once being used by alchemists (medieval scientists who tried to turn base metal into gold) and that a hapless young Czech unwittingly sold his soul to the Devil here, giving the building its name. Considering the number of similar late Baroque mansions that there are in Prague, this building is in fact pretty ordinary, and is closed to the public (part of it now contains a modern pharmacy, hopefully not upholding the traditions of nefarious medieval potion mixing that once went on here).

The Vltava's East Bank

A road called Resslova Street leads off Charles Square (from opposite the Jesuit Church) and runs west. On the right is the **Church of St Cyril and St Methodius** (Kostel Svatého Cyrila a Metodĕje), dedicated to the ninth-century monks who brought Christianity to the Slavs, and who invented the Cyrilic alphabet. In 1942, Czech freedom fighters parachuted into the country from England and hid in this church after assassinating Reinhard Heydrich, the Nazi ruler of Czechoslovakia. The German SS caught up with them and killed them in this church — look at the bullet holes in the wall around the crypt which also contains a small exhibition. A reprisal by the Nazis for the death of Heydrich was the destruction of the village of Lidice (see Chapter 2 on Western Bohemia).

Resslova Street continues to the River Vltava. Turn right along the elegant embankment, from where there are fine views over towards Prague Castle on Hradčany Hill above the opposite bank. The tower by the river is called the **Šitek Tower**. It was built in 1495 and used to supply fountains in the city with water. Next to it is the interesting modern building of the **Mánes Exhibition Hall** (1930) which houses temporary modern art exhibition and beyond this there is a way across to **Slavonic Island** (Slovansky Ostrov) with its pleasant parks. In the middle of the island is a large nineteenth-century restaurant building, where balls, dinners and concerts are often given. In the past, this was a gathering place for Prague's most important citizens, and where honoured visitors to the city were entertained. Continuing along the embankment, on the right hand side opposite the northern tip of the island is the **National Theatre** (Národní Divadlo). The first building on this site was constructed in 1881, and burned down soon after it was completed. The rebuilt structure is now the country's most important opera house, comprising an ornate nineteenth century façade which elegantly overlooks the Vltava. Next to it is the New Stage, a modern structure built of glass and steel and dating from the 1970s.

The Old Town (Staré Město)

❋ The Old Town was originally founded in the tenth century, after the original settlements in the Lesser Quarter, on the other side of the river, became too crowded. By the eleventh century, the Old Town was a sizeable settlement in its own right, which developed separately to the castle and the Lesser Quarter.

Old Town Square (Staroměstské Náměstí)

The Old Town Square has been the heart of the Old Town, and of Prague, for nine centuries. This vast, irregular, beautiful square is surrounded by houses and buildings of all colours and architectural styles, and overlooked by the distinctive twin spires of the Tyn Church (in the north) and the Gothic tower of the Old Town Hall (in the south). It has also been the scene of many events which have shaped the history of Prague and of Czechoslovakia. In 1422 and then in 1621, it witnessed the mass executions of, consecutively, a group of

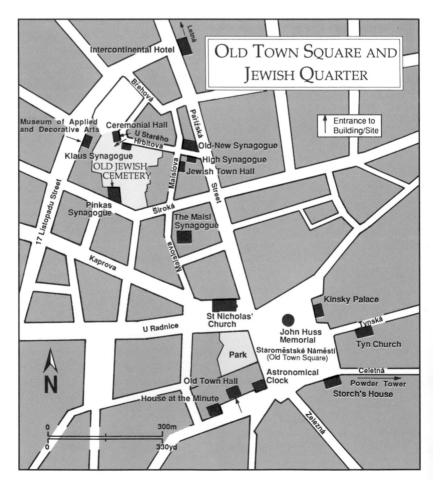

OLD TOWN SQUARE AND JEWISH QUARTER

Intercontinental Hotel

Brehová

Museum of Applied and Decorative Arts

Ceremonial Hall

Pařížská

U Starého Hřbitova

Old-New Synagogue

Klaus Synagogue

OLD JEWISH CEMETERY

High Synagogue

Jewish Town Hall

Entrance to Building/Site

Maislova

Pinkas Synagogue

Siroká

Street

The Maisl Synagogue

17 Listopadu Street

Kaprova

Mal_ová

Kinsky Palace

St Nicholas' Church

John Huss Memorial

Tynská

U Radnice

Park

Staroměstské Náměstí (Old Town Square)

Tyn Church

Astronomical Clock

Celetná

Old Town Hall

Powder Tower

Storch's House

House at the Minute

Železná

N

0   300m

0   330yd

The Old Town Square

The spires of Tyn Church have overlooked the Old Town for nearly 500 years

Hussite and then Protestant rebels. In 1918, the people of Prague celebrated the foundation of the new state of Czechoslovakia in the square. In 1948, they applauded Klement Gottwald, the first Communist President of the country, and celebrated the beginning of a Socialist state. When it ended in 1989, they celebrated here again, probably more audibly.

In the centre of the square is a huge memorial to John Huss, the founder of the Hussite movement, and one of the first Czech Nationalists. It was erected in 1915, on the 400th aniversary of his martyrdom. During the Prague Spring, students draped the memorial in black, in deference to the violation of Czech independence (which Huss had called for and had, in part, died for), caused by the Russian tanks which rolled along Prague's streets to crush the reformist movements of Alexander Dubcek. The inscription reads Pravada Vitezí (Truth Prevails), the rallying call of many a Czech revolutionary. There are seats all round the stark monument, which somehow compliments rather than detracts from the much older buildings that line the square. It is a popular meeting place, and a good place from which to watch Prague (or, more correctly, Prague's tourists) go by.

In the north-west corner of the square is the glorious Baroque façade of **St Nicholas' Church of the Old Town** (Kostel Svatého Mikuláše), the oldest church in the Old Town, founded soon after merchants began to settle on the right bank of the River Vltava. The original building was demolished in 1732 and replaced with the present church. Inside, its most distinctive features are a huge chandelier, made in the nineteenth century from Bohemian crystal, and many beautiful wall and ceiling paintings. The church is now the principal place of worship for the Hussite movement in Prague which is why the interior, although florid, is less rich and effusive than the exterior, originally built for a Catholic church, might lead one to expect. Franz Kafka was born in one of the houses next to the church.

Another distinctive eighteenth-century building on the square is the **Kinsky Palace**, complete with effusive stucco decorations which adorn the top ledges of its tall windows. It is named after its first owner, Prince Rudolph Kinsky. In 1948, Klement Gottwald, who had just become the country's first communist president, addressed a huge crowd in the square from the first floor balcony. The building now houses temporary collections of the National Gallery, as well as a permanent exhibitions of drawings. This side of the square is overlooked by the multi-turreted spires of the **Tyn Church**, set back a little from the square itself, and open rather limited and eccentric hours while it is undergoing an extensive period of restoration. Parts of the church, including the Gothic vaulting inside, date from the 1380s, and the spires (said to represent Adam and Eve) were completed in 1511. Those who do manage to see inside will find a gloomy, rather dour church, still undergoing repair, and although there are the usual Baroque decorations the only real point of interest is the marble tomb of the Danish scientist Tycho Brahe, who died in 1601. For 2 years he was the court astronomer to the Emperor Rudolph II, but he asserted that the sun went round the earth, rejecting the then heretical theories of Copernicus.

More distinctive buildings, now restaurants and expensive shops, line the eastern side of the square. All the buildings are very colourful, but the most noteworthy among them is one called **Storch's House**, with a huge picture of St Wenceslas on horseback on its façade, which was painted at the beginning of this century. Another noted façade, though older, is that of the **House at the Minute** (Dum u Minuty), on the other part of the square, whose designs show classical and biblical scenes, and date from the early seventeenth century. The building is now part of the **Old Town Hall** (Staroměstská Radnice), which is next to it. This latter building has grown and expanded from its original humble beginnings in 1338, when the citizens of this newly-founded part of Prague purchased the Gothic house that stood here and adapted the building for the purposes of administering the Old Town of the city. The distinctive square tower of the Old Town Hall, which forms one of Prague's landmarks, dates from 1364.

Underneath the tower is one of Prague's most original sights, the **Astronomical Clock**. This marvellously entertaining piece of medieval machinery was built in 1410. The upper disk shows the course of the sun and moon through the sky (the sun going round the earth, of course), and the lower part shows the month and days of the year. The clock was unfortunately damaged rather badly by the Nazis — one of the few things in Prague that was — and the allegorical figures around it, and the lower part of the clock showing the date, are copies. Every hour, on the hour, the clock entertains Prague's tourists, who gather beneath it for a free show, and watch several startling things happen in succession. Firstly, the figure of the skeleton (representing death) pulls a cord, which rings a small bell. He nods his head, and looks at his hourglass, reminding the assembled onlookers of the inevitablitily of death. Nearby a Turk shakes his head, rejecting the warnings of the skeleton. Other figures around the clock include a vain man looking in his mirror, and a miser with a sack of money. The doors above the clock fly open, and a procession of Christ and the twelve appostles appear at the windows, looking down on the crowd below. Then, above the noise of the endless shutter clicking of cameras, the cock crows, the crowd gasps (and sometimes even applauds), and the main bell in the tower chimes the hour. The same thing has been happenening, bar sometimes lengthy periods of disrepair and renovation, for over 500 years. The man who rebuilt the clock in 1490 was blinded by the town's council, so he could never create something as beautiful again.

Around the corner from the clock the date 21.6.1621 is built into the ground of the square in white cobblestones. They mark the spot where twenty-seven representatives of the anti-Habsburg alliance were executed. Here one can also see the break in the stonework of the Town Hall. The building used to extend back from here, over the spot now occupied by a small area of grass, but this part was wrecked and demolished by the Nazis, and has a modern but unobtrusive façade. A casket set into the wall, with the word 'Dukla' written on it, contains earth from the Dukla Pass in eastern Slovakia, which was the scene of some of the fiercest fighting of World War II as the Soviet Red Army began the liberation of Czechoslovakia.

After the chiming of the clock one can go round the interior of the Town Hall on a guided tour. The finely decorated rooms, with their medieval ceilings and Renaissance wall paintings, are still often used for city functions, and weddings are reguarly held in the Wedding Hall. Bride and groom are taken away from the building in elegant carriages pulled by well-manicured horses. The entrance door to the Old Town Hall also affords access to the steps and (for the elderly and disabled) a lift up to the outside viewing gallery at the top of the Tower, from where there is one of the best views of Prague's Old Town and beyond.

(Opposite) A close-up of the Astronomical Clock

The Old Town Hall

Other Old Town Monuments

Nothing else in the Old Town quite matches the Old Town Square, and a fair amount of this district, which used to comprise many slums, was pulled down in the nineteenth century to make way for more modern buildings. Neverthe-

less, there are a few other important places of interest.

A street called Celetná, lined with old mansions that now contain Prague's most fashionable shops, leads east from the Old Town Square, and after a spot of idle window shopping this brings one to the **Powder Tower** (Prašná Brána), the only remaining part of the medieval fortifications of the Old Town. It was begun in 1475, but fell into disuse when the Royal palace that used to stand next to it was abandoned in 1484, and Prague Castle once again became the royal residence. In the eighteenth century it was used to store gunpowder, hence its name. It was restored in 1875, when its distinctive roof was added. One can go up the stairs inside for another good view over Prague. Next to the tower is the **Municipal House** (Obecní Dum), built on the site of the afor-mentioned palace. The current building, its façade adorned with intriguing sculptures, statues and mosaics, is art-nouveau in style and dates from 1912. The building houses the Smetana Concert Hall and a restaurant and wine bar.

The Powder Tower used to be reached by crossing a moat, which sur-rounded the Old Town. Na Příkopě Street, which means 'on the moat', leads south from the Powder Tower. This is a pedestrian-only street, lined with shops, banks and offices. On the left hand side of the road, one passes the Prague Information Service, and the main Čedok office in the capital, before turning right down Havirska Street which brings one to the **Tyl Theatre** (Tylovo Divadlo), the oldest in Prague. When it was first built, the theatre was called the Nostitz Theatre, and it is famous for staging the world premiere of Mozart's opera, *Don Giovanni* in 1787, 4 years after the completion of the theatre. Mozart was a frequent visitor to Prague; in 1787, *The Marriage of Figaro* was greeted with a raptous reception in the city, while a year before, it had opened in Vienna but had closed after only nine performances. Encouraged by the success of *The Marriage of Figaro*, rich city sponsors commissioned Mozart to write a new opera to be staged in Prague. The work was *Don Giovanni*, his darkest and blackest opera. The tragedy of the opera was partly influenced by the death of his father, which occured during the period of its composition. A famous tale is that he did not complete the composition of the opera's overture until the evening before the opening performance, handing the music to the unforturnate orchestra musicians with the ink barely dry, to be played without rehersal before a first night crowd. Prague opera goers did not seem to mind, however, and greeted *Don Giovanni* with the same delight as they had *The Marriage of Figaro* the previous year.

Behind the Tyl Theatre is the **Karolinium**, the Charles University. When it was established by Charles IV in 1348 it was the first university in central Europe, founded only 100 years after Oxford University. John Huss was rector here from 1409 to 1412. The most notable part of the building is a stately oriel window (1383), which overhangs the street Ovocny Trh, at the back. The rest of the building dates from the eighteenth century.

Not part of the Old Town, but conveniently accessible from it, is **Letná Hill**, a fine park and gardens which overlook the Old Town. From the Old Town Square, walk down Pařízská Street, past the Jewish Quarter (discussed later), and the Intercontinental Hotel, and then cross over Svatopluk Czech Bridge

(Most Svatopluka Čecha), which dates from 1908 and has some nice sculptures on its piers. At the other end of the bridge, a flight of steps lead up the hill to the park, and an enormous plinth, on which there was once an huge 30m (100ft) high bust of Stalin, which sat glaring out over Prague until it was removed in 1962 when the cult of Stalinism was discredited. The plinth, liberally decorated with graffiti, now stands as a useless memorial to a best forgotten age, but it provides for a good view back over the Old Town, and Prague's bridges. The National Museum of Technology is nearby.

The Jewish Quarter (Josefov)

The Jewish Quarter occupies a tiny part of the old town, to the left (west) of the elegant boulevarde called Pařížká (Paris Avenue) which leads from the Old Town Square to Svatopluk Czech bridge (Most Svatopluka Čecha). Despite its small size, a good few hours at least should be set aside for seeing the area, and some of the sights.

The Jewish community of Prague dates back at least to the year AD950. It was originally located in the Lesser Quarter, on the other side of the river. In 1179 a Papal Decree forced city governments in Europe to separate the living quarters of Jews from those of the Christians, and the present Jewish Quarter was settled by Jews from about the thirteenth century onwards. By 1500 the area was a ghetto, consisting of a warren-like network of lanes lined with grossly overcrowded ramshackle houses, and rudimentary sanitary conditions and drainage. Years of institutionalised persecution of the Jews, which had forced them to live in these ever more cramped conditions, came suddenly to an end in 1780, when Joseph II ended their enforced isolation and allowed them greater freedoms and the right to live in other parts of the city. The Jewish Quarter was then renamed 'Josefov' after him. From 1893 the slums that had developed over the centuries were demolished and replaced with nineteenth-century buildings, including those along Pařížká, and the building of the Museum of Applied and Decorative Arts, which backs onto the Old Jewish Cemetery. However, the most historic buildings were left standing, and now lie somewhat incongruously amidst more modern constructions. Many of the city's Jews were German speakers, and the community included writers such as Kafka and Max Brod, who contributed much to the intellectual life of Prague.

The buildings that are left are all in the care of the **State Jewish Museum** of Prague, though not all of them actually house museums in the conventional sense. The synagogues and the cemetery are also part of the museum. One ticket allows the visitor to gain entry into all the sites of interest described below. By a bitter twist of irony, the founder of the State Jewish Museum was Adolf Hitler, who wanted to gather all the 'memorials to an extinct race' into one place. Synagogues in Bohemia and Moravia were plundered and their treasures brought to Prague, where they remain today on show to visitors. The museum therefore not only charts the history of the Jewish settlements in

Prague, but also serves as a memorial to the 77,200 Jews who were killed by the Nazis while Czechoslovakia was under their control, and of the systematic destruction by the Nazis of Jewish life, faith and traditions between 1938 and 1945.

U Starého Hřbitova Street

The ticket office for all the parts of the museum is at the abrupt bend in this street, which is to the left of Pařízka Street as one approaches from the Old Town Square.

To the left of the ticket office is the door into the **Klaus Synagogue**, a Baroque synagogue (1694) containing an exhibition of the works of Jewish religious scholars, including Hebraic manuscripts, and old prints.

To the right of the ticket office is a gate leading to the **Old Jewish Cemetery** (Stary Židovsky Hřbitov), one of the most unusual and fascinating sites in Prague. This was the principal burial place for members of Prague's Jewish community between 1439 and 1787. Squeezed into an incredibly small area are over 12,000 gravestones, overlooked by thickly branching elder trees. When Josefov was a ghetto, the burial area could not expand outwards, so it expanded in the only other direction — downwards. In some places there are nine layers of burials below one's feet, hence the chaotic confusion of the gravestones which almost lie on top of each other. The wording on the gravestone is in hebrew, but the reliefs on the stones are pictorial representations of the names and occupation of the deceased; for example, a pair of scissors denotes a tailor, scientific instruments a doctor. The oldest gravestones are made of sandstone, the newer ones of marble. The most richly decorated tomb is that of Rabbi Jehuda Löw, who died in 1609 and is meant to have created a *golem*, or artificial man. His tomb is decorated with carved figures of lions.

From one end of the cemetery entry is gained to the **Pinkas Synagogue**, in which there is a memorial listing the names of all 77,297 Jews in Czechoslovakia killed by the Nazis. The synagogue was originally a private place of worship housed in the residence of the Horrowitz family, the most prominent members of the Jewish community. It is likely to remain closed for many years, while extensive restoration work is carried out.

To the right of the entrance into the cemetery is the **Ceremonial Hall** (Byualá Obřadní Síň). It houses a harrowing but fascinating gallery of the pictures drawn by children interred at the concentration camp at Terezín (also known by its German name of Theresianstadt), near Litoměřice, in northern Bohemia. .

Maislova Street

Maislova Street is a hundred metres or so back from the ticket office. Back along Maislova Street, towards the Old Town Square, is **The Maisl Synagogue** (Maislova Synagoga), named after its founder, Mordechai Maisel, a sixteenth-century Mayor of Josefov who also served as the Minister of Finance under Rudolph II. Inside is an excellent exhibition of Jewish silver ornaments dating from between the seventeenth and nineteenth centuries, and plundered by the Nazis from over 150 synagogues and private houses in Bohemia. The collection includes cups, goblets, candlesticks, and various ornaments for Torah scrolls.

The **Jewish Town Hall** (Židovská Radnice), a pink Baroque building on the same side of the road, is the headquarters of the Jewish community of both Prague and Czechoslovakia. It was built in 1586 but reconstructed in the eighteenth century. There are two clocks on top of this building; the lower one, which dates from 1763, is marked with Hebrew numbers, and since Hebrew is read from right to left, its hands turn anti-clockwise. The building itself is not open to the public.

Just around the corner from the town hall, on Červená Street, is the entrance to the rather plain **High Synagogue**. Built in 1586, it was originally part of the adjacent town hall. In the original Renaissance halls inside is an exhibition of ritual Jewish textiles, the oldest dating back to 1592, which include Torah mantles, bride's dresses, and other religious vestments.

Across the street, on the corner of Červená and Maislova Street, is the **Old-New Synagogue** (Staronová Synagóga) the oldest synagogue in Europe that is still in use for religious purposes. It has been given its rather strange name because it is the oldest of all the 'new' synagogues that were set up in the Jewish Quarter after it was moved to here. Its interior is definitely worth seeing. It has a high ribbed vaulted ceiling which covers the twin naves in a structure which has been preserved intact from the thirteenth century. The galleries are reserved for women — only men may worship in the central part of the synagogue. There are two, equally elderly banners in here: one is part of the municipal standard that Charles IV allowed the Jews to fly, and the other was presented to the Jewish community by the Emperor Franz Ferdinand in 1648 to acknowledge their help in driving the Swedes from the city during the Thirty Years War. Unfortunately the building is often closed, even when the rest of the museum buildings are open. In the tiny garden attached to the synagogue is a nineteenth-century bust of Moses.

The Lesser Quarter (Malá Strana)

The Lesser Quarter lies below Prague Castle, at the foot of Hradčany Hill and squeezed in between it and the River Vltava. It is one of the oldest parts of Prague. It grew up in the ninth and tenth centuries, in the defensive shadow of the castle, but most of its monuments date from after the sixteenth century, when a series of fires destroyed much of the area. Now, the Lesser Quarter is awash with the Baroque and Renaissance mini-palaces that the Habsburg nobility built here, which do their best to reflect the glory of the castle that rises above these narrow streets. Most of these buildings are now used by government departments or foreign embassies, but wandering around the attractive streets and squares, crammed with ostantatious black cars marked with diplomatic or official number plates, makes for an interesting few hours. Relaxation away from the sights can be sought in the formally laid out Baroque gardens of the aforementioned palaces, or in the expansive parkland on Petřín Hill.

Knights Of The Cross Square

The Lesser Quarter lies on the west bank of the river. There are more than a dozen bridges across the River Vltava in Prague, the grandest and most beautiful of them all being the Charles Bridge, which links the Old Town with the heart of the Lesser Quarter. Knights of the Cross Square (Křižovnické Náměstí) is part of the Old Town, but its position at the eastern end of the Charles Bridge means that it is conveniently seen just before crossing over to the Lesser Quarter.

In the middle of this tiny, attractive square there is a cast-iron monument to Charles IV (1848), and behind it, on the north side of the square, is **St Francis' Church** (Kostel Svatého Františka Serafinského), a small but fabulously ornate Baroque church built in the 1680s. Among many Baroque decorations inside is a frescoe of 'the Last Judgement' on the inside of the dome. On the east side of the square, across the road, **St Saviour's Church** (Kostel Svatého Salvátora) is a late sixteenth-century building topped by eighteenth-century towers, which was originally a Jesuit church that served the **Clementium**, which can be entered from a door next to it. Ecclesiastical buildings have stood here for about 900 years. The first monastery on the site of what is now the Clementium was built by the Dominicans in 1232. In 1556, the Jesuit Order, a radical Catholic movement founded by the Pope to spearhead the Counter Reformation, was introduced to Prague and members of this order bought the monastery for their own purposes. They gradually aquired all the surrounding houses and built a vast complex of buildings which included churches, libraries and a huge monastery, the construction of which was begun in 1653. In 1773 the Jesuit order was abolished and the buildings of the Clementium were given over to Prague University. Today they are used for university functions and also house the State Library of Czechoslovakia. Visitors can walk through the Baroque courtyards; exhibitions are sometimes held in its rooms. Round the corner from the Knights of the Cross Square is the Smetana Museum (Muzeum Bedricha Smetany).

❋ The Charles Bridge (Karluv Most)

The Charles Bridge is the oldest bridge in Prague. Its construction began in 1357 and completed about 30 years later, under the supervision of a 23-year-old architect (and genius) named Peter Parler. It was built to replace a previous construction, the Judith Bridge, which was built in 1160 (itself replacing an older wooden bridge), and which fell down in 1342. Charles IV ordered Parler to build the present one so that it was solid enough to withstand the floods that had destroyed the previous two bridges. Parler did his job properly, and the bridge has stood here, very nearly undamaged, for over six centuries. The ability of this bridge to withstand the Vltava floods that brought down the previous two led to the growth of many legends surrounding its construction. It was said that the builders added eggs and wine to the mortar, to bond the bricks together harder. When they had used all the eggs in Prague, they sent for some from villages outside the city. Some villagers sent in their eggs hard boiled, believing this would improve the consistancy of the mortar. Other 'useful' things to go in the mortar mix were sent, such as milk and cheese. Parler used some of the old parts of the Judith Bridge in the construction of his masterpiece, which is why the bridge is not quite straight.

Though wide enough for modern-day motorised transport, the bridge is only open to pedestrians. Tourists linger on it to admire the wonderful views of Prague Castle or the other bridges on the Vltava, and to look at the thirty Baroque statues which are built along it its length; but there are distractions on hand to divert people's attention away from even these sights: character artists draw characatures or pictures of volunteer subjects; everything from cut glass to Bohemian jewellery to paintings is sold on the bridge and tourists can simply watch the buskers, street musicians and entertainers, all of whom are almost as permanent a feature of the bridge as the ancient statues for which it is more famous. Nowhere in Prague is beautiful architecture and modern, colourful life so wonderfully blended into such an absorbing cocktail.

From Knights of the Cross Square, the bridge is entered by walking under a high medieval tower, built in the late fourteenth century for fortification purposes. On the Old Town side of the tower, above the archway, are the carvings of a number of figures. There are two saints (uppermost) and lower down, Charles IV and Wenceslas IV (both seated) with St Vitus, the patron saint of the bridge, situated between them, standing on a relief of the bridge itself. The dozen or so heraldic arms are those of the kingdoms ruled by Charles IV at the time it was constructed.

Along each side of the bridge itself, placed at regular intervals and stretching its whole length, are fifteen statues, most of which were added between 1683 and 1714. Four of the statues are eighteenth- and nineteenth-century copies of the Baroque originals, which have been built to replace damaged or badly weathered statues (most are built of sandstone, which is extremely susceptable to the elements). Most of the statues are of saints, each one has its own history, and some tell their own little story. The third statue on the right is the oldest, a crucifix constructed in 1659. In the middle of the bridge, also on the right, is the only bronze figure — that of St John of Nepomouk (made in 1683), which shows the saint holding a small cross with the crucified Christ, and above whose head is a halo. This marks the spot where the saint in question was thrown into the Vltava to his death in 1393, on the orders of the king, with whom St John had had a religious dispute. One of the finest statues is reckoned to be that of St Luitgard, the fourth from the other end, on the left, which portrays her kissing the wounds of the crucified Christ. One of the finest views of the bridge is from the top of the tower at the Lesser Quarter end, which is open daily in summer. This tower is similar to the one at the Old Town end, but was built 100 years later. The squat tower next to it is the only remaining part of the old Judith Bridge.

Mostecká Street runs up from the tower at the Lesser Quarter Square end of the bridge, but alternatively there is a short diversion one can make from here which leads through some of the most charming parts of the Lesser Quarter.

✳ Kampa Island

It is not immediately obvious that when one crosses the Charles Bridge into the Lesser Quarter one arrives first at an island in the Vltava, rather than the city's left bank proper. This island is called Kampa Island and is reached by descending a flight of stone steps which lead off from the left hand side of the Charles Bridge just before the Lesser Quarter gate of the bridge is reached. These steps descend into Na Kampě Square, which used to be the scene of pottery markets. Continuing on south, away from the Charles Bridge, one reaches the parkland that covers the entire southern part of Kampa Island, from where there are good views over the Vltava, the Old Town and the

A winter's afternoon in the Lesser Quarter

Charles Bridge. The parks here were created by amalgamating the former gardens of the small royal palaces on the island.

The main bridge linking Kampa Island and the Lesser Quarter leads one into Maltese Square (Maltézské Náměstí), another of the Lesser Quarter's tiny but charming squares. The striking Baroque building on the left is the **Nostitz** **Palace**, which houses the Dutch Embassy. Other elegant buildings line the square, including one used by the Japanese Embassy. Crossing to the other

Posing for the artist on Charles Bridge

end of the square, one should turn right into Lazenska Street, and then left along Mostecka which leads up to the Lesser Quarter Square, the hub of this part of the city.

Lesser Quarter Square (Malostranské Náměstí)

After being spoilt by the grandeur of the Old Town Square, or the elegance of Wenceslas Square, Lesser Quarter Square with its tramlines and haphazardly parked cars comes as a sad disappointment. The centre of the Lesser Quarter, it is actually divided into two, an Upper and Lower Square, with the massive bulk of St Nicholas' Church separating the two. On the east side of the lower, busier part of the square, amidst the chaos of the trams and cars, is the seventeenth-century **Lesser Quarter Town Hall**, with its distinctive arcade; it is now used for public functions. Just beyond this, there are two cosy Baroque churches, **St Thomas'** (Kostel Svatého Tomáše), on the corner of Letenská Street and Tomášská Street, and **St Joseph's** on Josefská Street. But it is the imposing dome of St Nicholas', one of the landmarks of Prague's skyline, that dominates everything, and walking along the roads either side of the church brings one round to its entrance, on the Upper Square.

St Nicholas' Church of the Lesser Quarter (Chrám Svatého Mikuláše) is the most beautiful Baroque church in Prague, constructed between 1704 and 1755. Its architects were the Bavarian father and son team of Christoph and Kilian Dientzenhofer, who designed the building as a showpiece of the Jesuit church. Inside, the ceiling frescoe alone covers nearly a third of an acre, depicting scenes from the life of St Nicholas. Although the architects were German, the artist, Jan Lukáš Kracker, was Czech, and the effect of this panoramic canvas merely makes one look continually upwards and appreciate the vast scale of the whole church itself. On all the other walls and marble pillars of the church are rich Baroque reliefs, frescoes and sculpture. There are no stained glass windows, however, and the interior of the church is brighter than most when the sun is shining.

Roads and steps lead up from the Lesser Quarter Square to Hradčany Square and Prague Castle, but a longer way round is via Petřín Hill and the places of interest on Hradčany Hill, described below.

Gardens In The Lesser Quarter

From the Lower Lesser Quarter Square, Tomášska Street leads to the north, and into Valdštejnské Náměstí and the entrance to **Wallenstein Palace** (Valdštejnsky Palác, also called Waldstein Palace), the largest and oldest of all the nobleman's residences built in the Lesser Quarter. Its building was commissioned by General Albrecht of Wallenstein, the Supreme General of the Imperial (German) army in the Thirty Years War, who met a sticky end at Cheb in western Bohemia in 1634 when he was assassinated on the orders of the Emperor, who mistrusted the ambitious character of his faithful commander. Now used by the Ministry of Education, the interior of this palace is inaccessible, but the seventeenth-century **Wallenstein Palace Gardens** (Zahrada Valdštejnského Paláce) which are attached to it are the most beautiful formal gardens in the city. These gardens are yet another of Prague's historical monuments that are undergoing an extensive facelift; open only in summer, the entrance should be from the palace itself in Valdštejnské Náměstí, through one of its Baroque courtyards, but if not, then the old entrance from Letenská Street, which leads off from Lesser Quarter Square, may still be in use. Laid out in Italian Baroque style, a pond, a sala terana (with frescoed ceilings depicting scenes from the Trojan War), arched colonnades and a 'grotto' with artifical stalagtite and stalagmite caves, nestle beneath the spires of the cathedral on the hill above. The statues in the gardens are copies of the originals that were carted off by the Swedish army as war booty in 1648. They still remain in Drootningholm Castle, Stockholm.

Most visitors to Prague will by now have noticed a curious structure on one of its hills that looks remarkably similar to the Eiffel Tower. This tower is on the top of Petřín Hill, situated amidst Prague's nicest and most peaceful area of parkland, the wooded and more private parts of which appear to be a favourite romantic meeting place.

Petřín Hill (often just referred to as Petřín on maps) is best reached by returning from the Wallenstein Gardens to the Lesser Quarter Square (Lower Square) and taking Karmelitská Street which runs south, from the opposite side of the square. This street passes the **Church of St Mary the Victory** (Kostel Panny Marie Vítězné), the oldest Baroque church in Prague. The architecture inside is not particuarly inspiring. Most people come to this church to see the famed *Holy Infant of Prague*, hanging up on the right-hand wall of the nave. The wax figure was made in Spain in the sixteenth-century; in 1628 it was given by a princess to the members of the Carmelite Monastery that stood here, and it is still very much revered. Beyond the church, Karmeltiská Street becomes Ujezd Street. After a short stroll, signs direct one to the Lanovká or funicular railway which runs up the side of Petřín Hill. The lower station is on the right hand side of this road, set back a little from the street. The funicular is part of Prague's municipal transport system, and operates from 5am to midnight every day. Use the same tickets as for the metro and trams, or buy a ticket at the bottom station.

From the top station of the funicular, there are a number of options; Petřin Park (Petřinské Sady) stretches in all directions. Turning left, and walking past the observatory, one reaches a beautiful walled **ornamental garden**, one of the most peaceful spots in Prague. Turning right from the top station leads one through the gardens towards four monuments all located next to each other, shrouded in trees. Unfortunately, all four monuments have been shut for some time, undergoing restoration, though all, apart from the Petřín Tower, should re-open after this work has been carried out. The **Petřín Tower**, now looking decidedly shabby, is 60m (200ft) high, and was built in 1891 for the Prague Industrial Exhibition as a copy of the Eiffel Tower. Obviously, there is a good view from the top, but the closed sign on the door has been there for years and the view is unlikely to be enjoyed again by visitors for some time to come. The small, domed **St Lawrence's Church** (Kostel Svatého Vavřince) is an eighteenth-century reconstruction of a church that was founded here in the twelfth century. Buildings near by house the **Mirror Maze** (Bludiště), whose oddly-shaped mirrors will provide ample entertainment for children, and a pavilion containing a diorama of the battle between Prague's students and the Swedish army, fought in 1648 at the end of the Thirty Years War.

Near this group of monuments runs the **Hunger Wall** (Hladová Zed) which surrounds Petřín Hill. It was built in the time of Charles IV, and is so-named because its building was commissioned to provide the citizens of Prague with employment during times of hunger. The road that runs beside it leads to the Strahov Monastery, but a much more pleasant route round to the monastery is to head down from the tower and around the natural bowl in Petřín Hill towards the monastery which sits opposite on Hradčany Hill; this latter path provides for excellent views over the Lesser Quarter, and enticing glimpses of Prague Castle. Those who walk round to the monastery this way will enter one of its courtyards through a back door. The tour of the Hradčany District, described below, commences from Strahov Monastery.

Hradčany

With Petřín, Hradčany is one of the two hills that rises above the west bank of the River Vltava. Its main feature is Prague Castle, but there are a number of other interesting sights here. The Loreto Shrine and the Library of the Strahov Monastery rank amongst the most important things to see in Prague.

Strahov Monastery (Strahovsky Kláster)

The first monastery founded on this site, south-west of the castle on the boundary between Petřín and Hradčany Hill, and at the highest point above sea level within the city boundaries, was constructed in 1140; subsequently subject to many further rebuildings, the current appearance of this structure dates from Baroque times. The monastery ceased to function in 1948, when the Communists closed down all religious houses. It can be entered by a path leading from Petřín Hill, or from the street Strahovské Nádroví or 8, Pohořelec Street.

There are two Baroque churches in the complex. One has been converted into an exhibition hall, the other, the Church of the Assumption, is the principal monastery church, replete with the usual Baroque adornments. Mozart played the organ in this church on one of his visits to Prague. However, the monastery is primarily known for its library which is divided into two huge halls, the Theology Room and the Philosophy Room. Together they contain 500,000 books, many of which are priceless old volumes. The oldest book in the library's possession is the so-called *Strahov Gospel Book*, dating from the tenth century and displayed in a case in the corridor which runs between the Theology and Philosophy rooms. Although one cannot wander round the rooms themselves (they are only visible from a small patch of carpet by the entrance doors) this library should be seen for its magnificent frescoed ceilings, lavishly decorated ornaments and Gothic vaulting, as well as for its rows and rows of ancient books. The Theology Room dates from the 1720s, and the frescoes here were painted by one of the monks of the abbey. The Philisophy Room (dating from the 1780s) was built slightly larger in order to house ornately-carved book shelves from a monastery in South Moravia; the frescoes here depict scenes showing mankind's quest for wisdom. Both rooms are part of the National Museum of Literature. The rest of the monastery buildings contain possibly more mundane exhibition rooms of this museum (see section on museums later on in this chapter).

Loretánské Náměstí

A short distance away from the Strahov Monastery, walking along Loretánská Street in the direction of the castle, one reaches the square Loretánské Náměstí, with two Baroque buildings occupying its west and east sides. The pile on the west side is the **Černín Palace**, built by an aristocrat in the seventeenth century and now housing the country's Ministry of Foreign Affairs. It is the building opposite the Černín Palace that commands most attention. This is the **Loreto Shrine**, simply 'Loreto' in Czech which is the best known of over fifty such Loreto Shrines in Bohemia, which was founded to re-Catholicise ordinary people of Bohemia during the days of the counter-reformation. The Loreto is named after the town of Loreto on the east coast of Italy. In the thirteenth century, angels were meant to have carried the Virgin

The Archbishop's Palace, Hradčany Square

Mary's house from Nazareth to this Italian town, thereby causing the first and original Loreto Shrine to be built, an event which gradually led to the building of hundreds of similar Loreto Shrines all over the world. The Loreto's impressive eighteenth-century façade is another creation of the Dientzenenhofer father and son team, who were responsible for many of Prague's Baroque buildings including St Nicholas' Church of the Lesser Quarter. Soaring above this façade is an elegant clock tower, which dates from an earlier time than the rest of the façade. Installed in the bell tower is a carillon, which plays a Marian hymn on the hour, every hour, on 27 bells which were cast in Amsterdam in 1694. The bells are operated by means of a keyboard, rather then being rung independently.

The central part of the complex is a grassy courtyard surrounded by a two-storeyed cloister, in the middle of which is the **Santa Casa**, one of the holiest sites in Bohemia. This tiny building, dating from 1626, is a representation of the house in Nazareth in which the Virgin Mary was born. A similar building lies at the heart of the Italian Loreto, and some of the bricks incorporated into this building are said to have come from the original Italian shrine, over 725km (450 miles) away. Both the outside walls and the interior of this chapel are beautifully decorated; inside there is a silver altar and a carved wooden figure of the Madonna, and on the walls there are pictures of scenes from the life of the Virgin. On the east side of the cloister is another small chapel, the Church of the Nativity, which post-dates the Santa Casa by 100 years.

A door from the upstairs cloister leads into the Loreto's treasury, which contains valuable monstrances from the seventeenth and eighteenth century. The pride of this priceless collection is the incredible Diamond Monstrance, made in Vienna in 1699 and encrusted with 6,500 diamonds.

From here to the Černín Palace, a street called Černínská runs downhill towards the tiny district of Hradčany known as the New World (Novy Svět), situated on the side of the hill just below the Loreto. This used to be the area where the poor of the city lived, and there are still a number of small, interesting cottages and houses along the street called Novy Svět, which is a right turning off Černínská Street.

❋ Hradčany Square (Hradčanské Náměstí)

Walking up Novy Svět street and then Kanovnická Street brings one into Hradčany Square, the centre of this district. This is a long, wide square, with a few trees and grassland in its centre, and it is lined with palaces, some of which now house museums. Also in the middle of the square is a Plague Column, erected by the survivors of one of the many epidemics of the eighteenth century. The square slopes down towards the entrance gates of the grandest palace of them all, Prague Castle.

The most interesting buildings lining the square are as follows: on the left (north) side, as one enters the square from Kanovnická Street, is the **Martinitz Palace** (Mart Incky Palác), distinctive because of the *sgraffito* designs on the walls facing the square. This palace was built in the sixteenth century and was once owned by one of the two city govenors who were defenestrated from the window of Prague Castle (see below). The *sgraffito* designs (ie designs etched into the stonework) date from the 1630s and depict Biblical scenes. Some of this *sgraffito* work was only discovered in 1971, when the designs were uncovered during restoration work. The interior of this building is closed to the public.

Diagonally opposite is the **Schwarzenberg Palace** (Schwarzenbersky Palác), whose present appearance dates from the early years of the nineteenth century. Look at the outside walls of this palace — the apparently faceted masonary is an architectural joke, called *Trome L'oeil*, cleverly produced by etching different designs into the stonework to conjure up the illusion of light and shadow. The Military Museum is installed in this palace (see section on museums later on in this chapter).

Opposite this palace is the **Archbishop's Palace** (Arcibiskupsky Palác), the most graceful architectural flourish on this square, a striking building which several bouts of reconstruction work (the last being carried out in the 1760s) have turned into a Baroque palace, with a sumptuous façade of white marble. The interior is just as grandiose, but it can only be enjoyed by those visitors who are in Prague on the one day of the year that it is open (Maundy Thursday). A short passageway to the left of this palace leads to the Sternberg Palace, behind it, whose rooms now form the principal exhibition area of the Czech National Gallery (see section on museums later on in this chapter). Next to the Archbishop's Palace is the main entrance to Prague Castle.

Prague Castle (Pražsky Hrad)

Situated on Hradčany Hill, and forming Prague's most distinctive and most beautiful skyline, is the magnificent complex of buildings that make up Prague Castle. It is quite easy to spend a day wandering round the castle area and looking in all the museums and galleries. Visitors should note that, despite the castle being one of the most important things to see in the whole of Czechoslovakia, it is closed every Monday, even in summer.

Unlike most other castles in Czechoslovakia, Prague Castle, including the interiors of the Old Royal Palace, does not necessarily have to be seen with a guide. One is free to see all the sights mentioned below at one's own pace. It is possible to hire guides for the castle area at the castle's tourist office behind the cathedral (see map). It is also possible to surreptitiously attach oneself to one of the many guided tours of the castle that are conducted in English. Orientation in the castle is fairly easy, and visitors who want to see the castle at their own leisure will find a full description of it in the following pages. The tour assumes that visitors will enter the castle through the main gateway on Hradčany Square, though there are a number of other entrances.

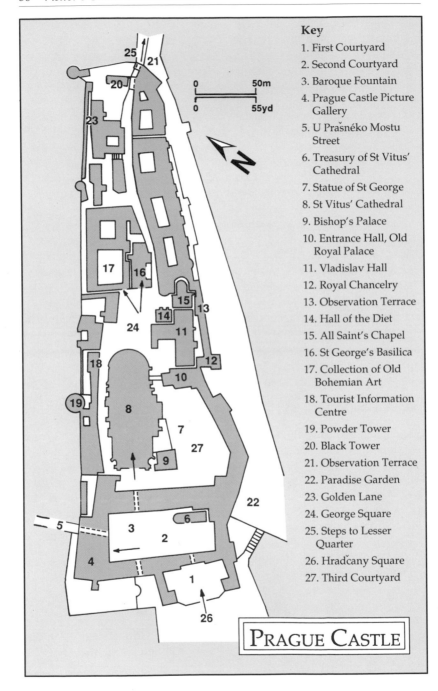

Key

1. First Courtyard
2. Second Courtyard
3. Baroque Fountain
4. Prague Castle Picture Gallery
5. U Prašnéko Mostu Street
6. Treasury of St Vitus' Cathedral
7. Statue of St George
8. St Vitus' Cathedral
9. Bishop's Palace
10. Entrance Hall, Old Royal Palace
11. Vladislav Hall
12. Royal Chancelry
13. Observation Terrace
14. Hall of the Diet
15. All Saint's Chapel
16. St George's Basilica
17. Collection of Old Bohemian Art
18. Tourist Information Centre
19. Powder Tower
20. Black Tower
21. Observation Terrace
22. Paradise Garden
23. Golden Lane
24. George Square
25. Steps to Lesser Quarter
26. Hradčany Square
27. Third Courtyard

PRAGUE CASTLE

A Brief History

For over 1,000 years Prague Castle has been the seat of the government of the Czechs, from tribal princes and glorious kings to Communist dictators and democratic presidents.

The founder of the castle was Prince Bořivoj, who as leader of the Czech tribes moved their capital from further north along the Vltava Valley to the present-day site of Prague Castle in the late ninth century. Bořivoj was the first Christian ruler of the Czechs and founded a church and fortified administration centre of the Přemyslid dynasty on the present site of the castle. In the eleventh century stone fortifications replaced earthen ramparts, and the present-day ground plan of the castle was gradually set out. In 1158, the first Czech king, Vladislav I, ruled over his subjects from the castle, and 200 years later Charles IV governed the whole of the Holy Roman Empire from here. Over the course of the sixteenth and seventeenth centuries the castle was rebuilt as a Renaissance palace to replace the previous medieval fortress. More reconstruction took place between 1753 and 1775, when the castle gained much of its present appearance.

After the Thirty Years War, the Czechs were ruled from Vienna by the Habsburgs, and Prague Castle took on a secondary role and its importance declined. In 1918, however, four centuries of Habsburg rule ended and the first President of the newly-created united State of Czechoslovakia, Tomas Masaryk, took up residence in the castle. Various organs of Czechoslovak government were also set up in the castle buildings. The last bout of rebuilding work came in the 1920s, to suit the new purpose of the castle as the seat of the government and administration of Czechoslovakia, and as the living quarters of the President. Václav Havel was the first Czechoslovakian President not to actually take up residence in the castle, saying that the place was still too readily identifyable with the previous Communist regime. The castle is still however used for State ceremonial and administrative functions.

Castle Gardens

The castle has extensive gardens. The nicest are the Royal Gardens (see below). A ramp from Hradčany Square (next to the castle's main entrance) leads down to the Paradise Garden (Rajská Zahrada, twentieth century) and beyond it the garden on the ramparts (Zahrada na Valech, nineteenth century), both of which were closed at the time of research (winter 1990) for a period of about 3 years while reconstruction work is carried out. These gardens, when open, are probably best seen after a tour of the castle has been made.

The First Two Courtyards

The main gates of the castle lead from Hradčany Square into the first courtyard. They are guarded by two mythological statues above the gates, who ward off their enemies with a dagger and a bludgeon, and by two sentries, whose new (post-1989) uniforms are designed by Theodor Pistek, Milos̆ Forman's film designer, who won an oscar for designing all the *Amadeus* costumes. Passing under their watchful gaze leads one into the first and smallest courtyard, which dates from the eighteenth-century reconstruction of the castle at the behest of the Empress Maria Theresa. The passage from here to the second courtyard passes under the Matthias Gateway, a triumphal arch built in 1614 but incorporated into the eighteenth-century structures that surround it. The coat of arms of the Emperor Matthias, and his name (part of the Latin inscription), can be seen in the gable above the gateway. On either side of the gateway are two enormous flag poles, made out of the trunks of Czech fir trees and added in 1920. On the right as one passes into the second courtyard is a grandiose staircase leading up to state reception and function rooms (closed to the public).

The second courtyard is larger than the first and predates it by 200 years, though renovation has given it all a unified Baroque appearance. There is a Baroque fountain in the centre of the courtyard, and next to it is a well of the seventeenth century.

Opposite the passage under the Matthias Gateway is the eighteenth century Chapel of the Holy Cross, now housing the **Treasury of St Vitus' Cathederal**. This treasury was founded by Charles IV and houses a collection of valuable religious works of art dating from between the eighth and nineteenth century, including St Wenceslas's coat of mail, a sword made over 1,000 years ago purportedly belonging to St Stephen, and a fourteenth-century silver bust of St Ludmilla. In the left-hand part of the courtyard are the old stables which house the **Prague Castle Picture Gallery** which includes works of art by Tintoretto, Rubens and other European and Czech masters. This was also the site of the first church of Prague Castle, built in the ninth century and dedicated to Our Lady, though little remains of it now except foundations.

A passageway leads from the left of the second courtyard out of the castle, across a bridge over the old moat to U Prašného Mostu street. On the left are the buildings of the Riding School, built in the seventeenth century and now housing a gallery of modern art. There are extensive parks and gardens attached. Opposite the riding school are the **Royal Gardens** (Královská Zahrada), the most pleasant gardens of Prague Castle, which are only open in summer. They were founded in 1534. At the bottom of the gardens is the **Royal Summer Palace** (Královsky Letohrádek), also known as the Belvedere Palace, a beautiful summer palace built in Italian Renaissance style in the sixteenth century, which was unfortunately damaged by a disastrous fire in 1989 and will be closed for many years while it is renovated.

St Vitus' Cathedral (Chrám Svatého Víta)

Returning to the second courtyard, one must pass through the passageway that links the second courtyard to the third; here one is almost assaulted by the sheer size and beauty of the west wing of St Vitus' Cathedral, by far the most stunning Gothic building in central Europe and one of the continent's most beautiful cathedrals. The main door of the west wing usually acts as the entrance to the cathederal for tourists, taking one under the soaring western spires into the well-lit and airy interior.

The original St Vitus' Cathedral was founded in AD926 by St Wenceslas and since AD973 it has been the main cathedral church of Prague. In 1344 Prague was raised to an archbishopric and in connection with this new status, the Czech King and Emperor Charles IV decided to order the building of a new cathedral. The first architect engaged on the project was a Frenchman named Matthias of Arras, but he was succeeded by the cathedral's principal architect, Peter Parler, also responsible for the Charles Bridge. Like all cathedrals, St Vitus' has been enlarged, embellished and altered through the centuries, and though the foundation stone was laid in 1344 its construction was not actually completed until 1929 — 1,003 years after St Wenceslas first dedicated a church to St Vitus on this spot. The vaulting of the main nave, and the façade on the western walls, date from this century. The main steeple was completed in 1560. The oldest parts of the cathedral, built in the fourteenth century, are in the eastern part (furthest from the entrance door).

The following is merely a sketch of the main points of interest in St Vitus' Cathedral; hours could be spent in this cathedral, simply letting one's gaze wander amongst the incredible beauty of nearly 600 years of art, sculpture and architecture. A plan of the cathedral and information about it in English, can be purchased at the entrance. The roof of the cathedral is supported by 28 piers; around its side walls, there are 21 small chapels, each one dedicated to a particular saint. The organ, in the gallery on the left (north) side of the nave, contains 6,500 pipes and was built in 1757. There are many fine stained glass windows in the cathedral, most of which date from the early decades of the twentieth century. One of the most important windows is above the western doorway; entitled *The Creation of the World*, it was built in 1928. On the right hand wall of the cathedral, off the central part of the nave, is the most important chapel in St Vitus'. The Chapel of St Wenceslas was built in the fourteenth century above the tomb of the saint, with wall paintings from this time depicting the Crucifixion scene (lower paintings) and the *Legend of St Wenceslas* (upper tier). The walls are also encrusted with over 1,300 semi-precious Bohemian stones. Preserved here is the lions-head door-ring onto which St Wenceslas clung when he was murdered by his brother Boleslav in either AD929 or AD935 (historical sources vary). A staircase leads up from here to the rooms where the Bohemian crown jewels are kept; they are put on show to the public only on very rare occasions.

In the eastern (far) part of the cathedral is the high altar built in the nineteenth century, with the Bishop's throne, and next to it is the magnificent silver tomb of St John of Nepomouk, made in Vienna in the 1730s. St John actually died in 1393, when he was thrown off the Charles Bridge in Prague after a dispute with the king (see under 'Charles Bridge', above). Behind the altar is the tomb of St Vitus. In the centre of the cathedral is the Royal Mausoleum, made in Innsbruck in the sixteenth century, out of white marble. Below this (there are stairs near by; one must pay to go in) is the Royal Crypt, containing the sarcophagi of Charles IV and other Czech monarchs and their children, and some of the remains of the original tenth-century church of St Vitus.

The Third Courtyard

Coming out of the cathedral and turning left brings one into the third courtyard. Turning the corner into the courtyard one passes the **Bishop's Palace**, built in 1662 and not particularly beautiful, and a peculiar granite plinth which is not decorated with any writing or designs of any kind, and is in fact a memorial to the victims of World War I. In the courtyard itself, one can admire the impressive south wing of the cathedral, including the mosaic called the

One of the many fine stained glass windows in St Vitus' Cathedral

Golden Portal above the south doorway, built by Peter Parler in 1367 though much restored. The picture shows the Last Judgement. Further up and to the left is an interesting gold-filigreed grille set into a Gothic window. Above this are two clocks; the top, and more obvious face, has only one hand, which shows the hour; the quarter-hour is indicated by the clock below it. Through a grille next to the south wall of the cathedral one can see more archaeological remains of the original church and fortifications that stood on this site. In the middle of the courtyard is an equestrian statue of St George. Around the other side of the third courtyard are the various buildings housing state and administration rooms, which are not open to the public.

The entrance to the **Old Royal Palace** (Královsky Palác) is on the far side of the third courtyard. The origins of the Old Royal Palace date back to 1135, but much of its present appearance dates from the fourteenth and fifteenth centuries. The Palace was the royal residence of Czech kings and the seat of the most important government institutions, but these functions declined at the end of the sixteenth century. Now, as most of the old rooms are used only for very special occasions, they have been opened to the public.

The most imposing part of the palace is **Vladislav Hall** (Vladislavsky Sál), built in the 1490s. It is the first room one enters from the ticket office, a vast medieval hall which is 13m (43ft) high, still with its original and much-admired medieval vaulting. It was used for coronation banquets, tournaments, meetings of the diet (parliament) and in more modern times the President of Czechoslovakia has been elected in this hall. To the right of the hall is the door to the small **Royal Chancelry** (Česká Kancelář). In 1618 three of the city's Catholic royal governors were thrown out of the window of the far room by members of the rebelling Protestant nobility — the so-called 'defenestration of Prague'. They landed on a dung heap fortuitously positioned outside the window; Catholics claimed their survival was a miracle. The defenestration of Prague was the event that sparked off the Thirty Years War which tore central Europe apart between 1618 and 1648. Opposite the entrance door of Vladislav Hall, at the far end of the hall, is the entrance to **All Saint's Chapel**, a beautiful church founded by Charles IV, yet another design of the architect Peter Parler, though rebuilding work in the 1570s after a fire means that little of Parler's original conception is left. The remains of St Procopius lie in the centre of the chapel. Off the left side of Vladislav Hall is the **Hall of the Diet** (Stará Sněmovna), built in 1563, where the Czech monarch presided over meetings of his parliament. The royal throne in the room is nineteenth century, and paintings of Habsburg kings adorn the walls. It is now used for ceremonial purposes — newly-elected Presidents sign the constitutional oath here. Opposite the entrance to the Hall of the Diet is an observation terrace, affording good views over the city and the river.

Next to the Hall of the Diet are two flights of stairs, one leading up to rooms with sixteenth-century furniture housing the Royal Archives and New Land Rolls, and open to the public, and one leading back outside. The latter staircase is very wide, to allow knights to ride up the stairs on horseback for the equestrian tournaments that were held in the hall.

East Wing

The exit from the Old Royal Palace, down the wide staircase, leads into George Square (Jiřské Náměstí), a less impressive part of the castle area. In one corner is the door leading to the convent of St George (Jiřsky Kláster), founded in AD937 and dissolved in 1782, the present buildings of which date from 1680 and house part of the National Gallery — the **Collection of Old Bohemian Art.** This building houses some of the most important art-historical collections and treasures in the city; ecclesiastical sculptures and paintings from churches all over Bohemia, and other parts of Europe, are on display here. The most important exhibit is the set of fourteenth-century icons which used to be in Karlstejn Castle (see Chapter 2).

Also on the square is the entrance to **St George's Basilica** (Barzilika Svatého Jiří). Unprepossessing from the outside, this small church is one of the oldest in Bohemia, founded in AD912, though much of its present appearance dates from the seventeenth century after previous buildings were damaged by fires. It is now used as a concert hall. In the main nave, which is suitably gloomy for such an old church, and one that contains the remains of so many dead saints in such a small space, are the medieval arcades and a number of tombs, including a wooden tomb of the fifteenth century containing the remains of Vratislav I, the founder of the church who died in AD925. Off the nave is the Chapel of St Ludmilla, designed by Peter Parler in the fourteenth century to contain the bodily remains of another of Bohemia's saints who was murdered in AD921. Her grandson, Prince Wenceslas, was murdered only a few years later. One can also see the remains of ceiling paintings (entitled *Heavenly Jerusalem*) from the thirteenth century — the oldest in Prague. Various other saints and ecclesiastical dignitaries are buried here, and in the 1950s archaeologists found that the earliest Czech monarchs — those of the Přemyslid Dynasty of the tenth and eleventh centuries — had been buried in the previous churches that once stood on this site.

Just up from George Square, along the lane that leads behind the cathedral, is the **Powder Tower**, next to the tourist information centre. This tower was part of the medieval defences of the castle. It houses a small and seemingly rather neglected museum, which includes an exhibition of Renaissance science and technology.

In the other direction, Jirska Street runs down from George Square; on the left is **Golden Lane**, a short, picturesque dead-end street one side of which is lined with tiny medieval houses which have brightly coloured façades actually built in and under the castle's defensive walls. It originated in the sixteenth century, when goldsmiths and alchemists settled here, giving the street its name. After the tradesmen left, artists and writers lived in the houses, including Franz Kafka who lived in house number 22 for a short while in 1917. Most of the houses are now souvenir shops and snack bars.

Returning from Golden Lane to Jirska Street, one should continue on down the street towards the **Black Tower**, the original gate of Prague Castle which was built in the twelfth century. It was used as a debtors prison, but walled up in the thirteenth century when it was superceeded by new defences. Beyond the tower is an **Observation Terrace** which used to be an artillery bastion. From here there are steps down to the Lesser Quarter.

Museums and Galleries

Museums associated with Prague Castle and the Jewish Quarter are dealt with in those sections. The full addresses and opening times of the following museums can be found in the Additional Information section at the end of this chapter.

Dvořák Museum (Villa Amerika)
This museum, housed in a Baroque mansion that was once a summer house, and set in an extensive garden, honours the most famous Czech composer, Antonín Dvořák, (1841-1904). Exhibits include scores, letters, documents, personal belongings and photographs relating to the composer, whose most famous work was his symphony *From the New World* (1894). This museum, on Ke Karlovu Street, in the southern part of the New Town (near I.P Pavlova metro station), will re-open in the early 1990s after restoration work has been carried out.

Military Museum (Vojenské Muzeum)
Schwarzenberg Palace, on Hradčany Square, is home to this museum, which documents the history of warfare from prehistoric days to modern times. The most important collections are those of old arms and uniforms. There are also many plans and maps of famous battles (not all of them Czech).

Mozart Museum (Bertramka)
Mozart was a frequent visitor to Prague and the city has many connections with him and other composers, which live on in the many classical concerts and operas which are staged every night in the capital's concert halls, theatres and churches. *Don Giovanni* was given its world premiere here in 1787, in the Tyl Theatre (see entry under 'Old Town'). Part of the opera was written in the picturesque villa called Bertramka, where Mozart frequently stayed as a guest of the Dušek family that owned it. The Bertramka, unfortunately situated a little way from the centre of Prague, in the south-west corner of the Lesser Quarter, now houses an excellent museum devoted to the composer's life and works, which includes the clavier on which he composed *Don Giovanni*, other musical instruments, and letters, cuttings and photographs.

Museum of Applied and Decorative Arts (Umělecko-Prumyslové Muzeum)
The collections of this museum are housed in a nineteenth-century building which backs onto the Old Jewish Cemetery. They comprise Czech, and some European, porcelain, crystal, furniture, textiles and books, dating from 1500 to 1900. Most famous is the collection of cut glass and crystal, the largest of its kind in the world, with pieces from Venice, Holland, Silesia, and Germany as well as Bohemia.

Museum of Musical Instruments (Muzeum Hudebních Nástroju)
A collection of old musical instruments from the eighteenth and nineteenth centuries, housed in a Baroque palace on Velkopřevorské Náměstí (Grand Priory Square) in the Lesser Quarter. Concerts are often given in summer, in the gardens of the palace.

Museum of Prague the Capital (Muzeum Hlavního Města Prahy)
An excellent documentation of the history of Prague, from the prehistoric age to modern times. Exhibits include the original face of the astronomical clock, painted

by Josef Mánes in 1865 and an excellent model of Prague, built in the early nineteenth century, showing the city as it looked.

National Gallery (Národní Galerie)
The Czech National Gallery is housed in the Sternberg Palace (1707), situated behind the Archbishop's Palace on Hradčany Square, very close to the entrance to the castle. The worthy collections here feature paintings by European (i.e. non-Bohemian) artists from 1400 to 1800, including Crannach, Holbein, Tintoretto, Canaletto, Rubens, Van Dyck, Frans Hals, and Rembrandt. Pride of place goes to the German artist Dürer's work *Festival of the Rosary* (1506), and also (surprisingly) to a large collection of nineteenth- and twentieth-century French art, which includes paintings by Monet, Cézanne, Renoir, Gaugan, Toulouse-Lautrec, Matisse, Chagall and Picasso. Other collections include medieval religious icons from Russia and Germany, and sculptures by Degas and Rodin, which are in the French art section.

National Museum (Národní Muzeum)
Despite its name, and its palatial setting in the huge neo-Renaissance building at the top end of Wenceslas Square, this museum is not so interesting as the others listed in this section. It is the country's oldest museum, founded in 1818. Collections include botany, geoglogy and zoology specimens, and archaeological exhibits which include a 5,000-year-old skeleton. There are busts of famous Czechs in the grand entrance hall.

National Museum of Literature
Housed in Strahov Monastery, this museum shows the development of Czech literature.

National Technical Museum (Národní Technické Muzeum)
An uninspiring pre-war pavilion, inconveniently situated behind Letná Gardens, houses one of Prague's best museums. In the main hall there are many old cars, trains, railway carriages, motorbikes and engines, while ancient aeroplanes 'fly' overhead, suspended from the ceiling. The side halls should not be overlooked. They document the evolution of astronomy, time-keeping devices (including working models of the astronomical clocks in Prague and Olomouc, and of Big Ben), of cinematography and photography, including many Victorian 'magic Lanterns', and of electronics, including Hi-Fi, engineering and scientific instruments.

Smetana Museum (Muzeum Bedřicha Smetany)
This museum, overlooking the Old Town side of the Charles Bridge, was established in 1928 to celebrate the life and work of Bedřich Smetana (1824-1884) who, despite the number of concert halls named after him in Prague, is still only the second most famous Czech composer, after Dvořák. Exhibits in this small museum include original scores, letters, cuttings, reviews, programmes, and some of Smetana's personal belongings. Outside the museum is a statue of Smetana (1984), and a nice place to sit and watch the Vltava flowing under the Charles Bridge. The *sgraffito* (ie etched designs) on the walls of the building shows the defeat of the Swedish army in Prague, in 1648, at the end of the Thirty Years War.

Other Art Galleries
The Kinsky Palace on the Old Town Square has exhibitions of drawings and other temporary exhibtions. The Mánes Exhibition Hall on the eastern embankment of the Vltava holds temporary exhibitions, mainly of modern art or sculpture. In the Gothic buildings of St Agnes' Monastery (Kláster Anežsky), there are exhibitions of nineteenth-century Czech paintings, and a certain number of porcelain and crystal objects on display.

Prague's Suburbs

Vyšehrad ❋

The first royal seat at Vyšehrad was established 1,000 years ago. From this time the palaces here competed, to a large extent unsuccessfully, with Prague Castle as the main royal residence of the Czech kings. Vratislav I (1061-1092) chose to rule from Vyšehrad rather than Prague Castle, but by medieval times the latter was firmly established as their seat of power, and Vyšehrad was neglected or developed half-heartedly, according to the whims of successive monarchs. Charles IV patronised the place and from his time Vyšehrad marked the start of the coronation route which wound its way down from here through the Old Town and then across the Charles Bridge and up to Prague Castle. Some of the old walls that Charles IV built still remain, but there is little left of the old palace which once stood here. Instead, there are half a dozen monuments dating from various times, which are situated on the top of a high, flat hill above the Vltava, south of the centre of Prague. One can reach Vyšehrad by taking any of the trams that run along the eastern embankment of the Vltava, getting out at the stop immediately before the old steel railway bridge, then walking under the railway bridge and up the long flight of steps on the left hand side of the road. Note that the attractions here are much less easily approached from Vyšehrad metro station, despite its name.

The first monument in Vyšehrad one is likely to come across, and the area's landmark, is the twin-spired **Church of St Peter and St Paul**. A church has ⧆ stood here since the year 1070, but the current church is neo-Gothic and is less than a hundred years old. Only a few of the decorations and ornaments inside are medieval or Baroque, and they date from the previous churches that stood here. Various eleventh-century rulers of the Přemyslid Dynasty, who ruled Bohemia from Vyšehrad rather than Prague Castle, are buried in the crypt in the church. Archaeological excavations underneath the church means that its interior will be closed for some time.

Next to the church is a beautiful cemetery surrounded by elegant nine-teenth-century arcades, where the ornate and well-tended graves of leading Czech citizens are shaded by trees. Dvořak and Smetana are buried here, as well as many other writers, musicians, painters, artists and performers. The cemetery is one of the most peaceful spots in Prague.

The rest of the Vyšehrad area comprises mainly parks, from where there are views over the Vltava and the southern part of Prague. Behind the church and cemetery is an inconspicuous round building, **St Martin's Rotunda**, which dates from the time King Vratislav held court at Vyšehrad, though it been rebuilt a number of times and at one time was used to store gunpowder. Nearby is the Leopold Gate (1670), part of the old fortifications of Vyšehrad, and in the other direction, a tiny Baroque chapel dedicated to St Mary the Virgin. Beyond this group of buildings are more parks, and views from the ramparts here are over the Nusle Valley, which is crossed by an enormous road bridge. At one end of this distinctly unelegant structure is the tall Forum Hotel, and next to it the Palace of Culture, built in 1981 to hold Communist Party conferences (amongst other things), which is now a concert hall and conference centre.

✳ **Troja**

The suburb of Troja is a fair distance north of the centre of Prague. One can drive there, but the most convenient way of reaching the attractions here is to take bus 112 from outside Holešovice railway staion (Metro: Holešovice) which terminates outside the entrance to the zoo and Troja Château.

Troja Château was re-opened to the public in June 1989 after being closed for a 10-year period of restoration. It was built in the late seventeenth century for Count Václav Vojtěch Šternberg and its most noteworthy features are the effusive Baroque ceiling paintings which adorn dozens of the halls and rooms in the château, the mythological and religious scenes now beautifully clear after being thoroughly cleaned and restored. There are few furnishings, but some of the rooms house exhibitions of Czech paintings, sculpture, cut glass and porcelain. The château is set in large ornamental gardens.

Opposite the château is the entrance to Prague's expansive **zoo** (Zoologická Zahrada), which has achieved notable fame for its breeding of Przewalski horses, now extinct in the wild.

After The Sightseeing

After seeing Prague on foot, a different impression of the city can be gained from a cruise boat on the River Vltava. Boats operate from about May to September. The landing stages and ticket and information office are on the Old Town side of the Vltava, between the bridges Palackého Most and Jiráskuv Most. There are boats to Roztoky, in the northern part of Prague, where there is a castle to Slapy Lake (see Chapter 4), and boats which just chug up and down the Vltava for a short distance. They may not operate if the water level is too low. Some boat trips (especially out to Slapy) are very popular and it may not be very easy to get a ticket. There are several places along the Vltava in central Prague where small rowing boats can be hired.

As regards eating, Prague has hundreds of restaurants, but, as indicated in the introduction, Czech food is not so very special. To escape the endless heavy meat dishes, head for the Indian restaurant, Prague's only ethnic eating place, on Štěpánská Street, just off Wenceslas Square. The waiters here speak English. It is normally necessary to book in advance to eat here. In fact, booking is advisable in many of the restaurants in central Prague, which are full even in the early evening. Another idea is to break up the sightseeing by having lunch in the middle of the day, thereby avoiding the evening which is by far the busiest time. Those that have not booked a table are more likely to find a place at one of the restaurants around Náměstí Míru (Metro: Náměstí

Míru), rather than in the very centre of Prague. Many 'fast food' places are opening, particuarly around the New Town. Do not overlook the possibilities for eating and drinking over the bridge, in the Lesser Quarter, where there are many taverns, *vinarna* (wine bars) and *pivnice* (beer halls). 'Kosher' food is available in the Jewish quarter. There is one tavern which is also a tourist attraction: U Kalicha at 12, Na Bojišti Street is featured in the novel *The Good Soldier Schweik* and is often full of busloads of tourists. In summer, many restaurants set up tables outside in the street, allowing one to while away a summer evening people-watching amidst beautiful surroundings, perhaps over a few glasses of Czech wine or beer.

After dark, many parts of Prague are floodlit, including the castle and Charles Bridge, which take on a haunting beauty at night and assume a very different character to that in the daytime. The busking and the street entertaining continue until late into the evening, and many places are still very lively and crowded with people after dusk. But there is ample entertainment to be found inside, as well: Prague is one of the music capitals of Europe, and every day there are concerts in the city's concert halls, theatres and churches. There are many leaflets full of listings of concerts, plays, operas and other forms of entertainment, for example the English language booklet *The Month in Prague*, which is published monthly and available in bookshops, hotel reception desks, tourist offices etc. Many useful addresses of other institutions that tourists may need while in Prague (anything from restaurants to lost property offices) are included in some of these booklets. However, it is often quite difficult to get tickets for concerts and plays, as many are booked well in advance; the Prague Informtion Service normally has information on what there is to see, what seats are still available and may even sell visitors a theatre or concert ticket. Failing this, try Čedok offices and hotels, as well as the theatres themselves. The music scene is busy all year round, but the pace picks up particularly from mid-May to early June, during the famous and well-established spring music festival. It begins on 12 May, Smetana's birthday, and the opening concert is normally a performance of his work *Ma Vlast (My Fatherland)* in the Obecní Dum. Concerts are given by Czech and international performers, and often palace gardens and medieval courtyards are used as venues. In 1991 Čedok offices abroad had leaflets detailing how tickets for events in this festival could be booked well in advance by visitors in their home countries, and then picked up once they arrive in Prague — definitely a wise line of enquiry for those who are coming to Prague especially for its musical life. For other sorts of music, many Western Jazz and rock groups visit and perform in Prague, though the modern music scene definitely has a long way to go before it reaches the fame of the classical music concerts here.

The many theatres in Prague are also well-patronised. It is probably pointless seeing something in Czech, but many excellent operas are staged in the capital's theatres and opera houses. Touring theatre companies from the USA and the UK (often very well-known, with good actors in their casts) are increasingly making Prague a stop on their European tours, so look out for any posters that are put up to catch the eyes of English-speaking tourists. The most famous theatrical show in Prague is the Magic Lantern Theatre *Laterna Magika* at 40, Národní Street, which innovatively blends live-acting with mime, cinema, dance, humour and music. This is also normally booked out; there are often ticket touts selling tickets on the street outside, before the performance. There are cinemas all over the New Town; some English-language films are shown in their original versions, with Czech subtitles. Many hotels have nightclubs, discos, cabarets and casinos. Alternatively, catching a mime or other performance in the street is as good an option as any.

Excursions from Prague

There are many places near Prague that are viable destinations for day-excursions from the city. These places are covered in the next three chapters. The most obvious excursion from Prague is to Karlštejn Castle, Bohemia's finest medieval castle, which is only 23km (14 miles) away (Chapter 2). Other places near Prague include Křivoklat Castle, the Koněprusy Caves (part of the Bohemian Karst) and Lidice (Chapter 2); the wine-making town of Mělník, and the medieval cathedral town of Kutná Hora (Chapter 3) Konopiště and Česky Šternberk Castles, and Slapy Lake (Chapter 4). Many places described in the next three chapters can be seen in a day trip from Prague (by those with a car, at any rate), depending, of course, on how far one wants to travel in a day. Some people make day excursions to Hluboká Castle (Chapter 4), Karlovy Vary (Chapter 2), or the Krkonoše Mountains (Chapter 3), all of which are

Prague Castle is spectacularly floodlit at night

about 113 to 129km (70 to 80 miles) from the capital. Čedok in Prague offer many day-excursions by coach to places all over Bohemia (see Fact File at the end of this book).

Additional Information

Much practical information relating to Prague, including many useful addresses, can be found in the 'Fact File' section at the end of this book.

The nearest metro station is given for most places. Most places are also accessible by tram, but as tram routes are constantly changing, tram numbers are not given. Tram routes and numbers are shown on current city maps.

Places of Interest

Jewish Quarter (Josefov)
All monuments are in the care of the **State Jewish Museum**. Includes Klaus Synagogue, Old Jewish Cemetery, Ceremonial Hall (U Starého Hřbitova Street); Pinkas Synagogue (entrance from Old Jewish Cemetery); Maisl Synagogue, High Synagogue, Old-New Synagogue (Maislova Street). Metro: Staromestska.
Open: daily except Saturday, 9am-5pm (4.30pm in winter).

Loreto Shrine
Loretánské Náměstí
Prague-1
Open: daily except Monday, 9am-1pm, 1.30pm-4.30pm.

Old Town Hall
(Staroměstská Radnice)
Staromestske Namesti
(Old Town Square)
Prague-1
Metro: Staromestska. Open: daily, 8am-6pm (5pm in winter).

Powder Tower (Prašná Brána)
Náměstí Republiky
Metro: Náměstí Republiky.
Open: April to October only, daily 10am-6pm (5pm in April and October).

Prague Castle (Pražsky Hrad)
and Hradčany Palace
Including: Prague Castle Picture Gallery, Treasury of St Vitus' Cathedral, St Vitus' Cathedral, Powder Tower, Old Royal Palace, St George's Basilica,
Collection of Old Bohemian Art of the National Gallery. Front entrance on Hradčanske Náměstí.
Metro: none convenient.
Open: daily except Monday, 9am-5pm (4.30pm in winter).

Prague Zoo
(Zoologická Zahrada)
Troja Suburb
Opens: at 7am every day. Closes: April, 5pm; May, 6pm; June to September, 7pm; October to March, 4pm.

Strahov Monastery
(Strahovsky Kláster) Including the National Museum of Literature
8 Pohořelec street
Prague-1
Metro: none convenient. Open: daily except Monday, 9am-5pm.

St Nicholas' Church of the Lesser Quarter
(Chrám Svatého Mikuláše)
Malostranské Náměstí
(Lesser Quarter Square)
Metro: Malostranská. Open: daily, 9am-4pm (September to January), 5pm (February, March, August) 6pm (April to July).

Wallenstein Gardens
(also Waldstein Gardens, Zahrada Valdštejnského Paláce)
Metro: Malostranská. Open: May to September only, daily 9am-7pm.

Museums and Galleries

Military Museum
(Vojenské Muzeum)
Schwarzenberg Palace
Hradčany Square, Prague-1
Metro: none convenient.
Open: May to October only, daily except
Monday, 9.30am-4.30pm.

Mozart Museum (Bertramka)
2 Mozartova Street
Prague-5
Metro: none convenient. Open: daily
except Tuesday, 10am-5pm.

**Museum of Applied
and Decorative Arts**
(Umělecko-Prumyslové Muzeum)
2, 17 Listopadu Street
Prague-1
Metro: Staroměstská. Open: daily except
Monday, 10am-6pm.

Museum of Musical Instruments
(Muzeum Hudebních Nástroju)
Velkopřevorské Náměstí
Prague-1
Metro: Malostranská.
Open: April to October only, daily
except Monday, 10am-5pm.

Museum of Prague the Capital
(Muzeum Hlavního Města Prahy)
Sady Jana Švermy
Prague-1
Metro: Florenc. Open: daily except
Monday, 9am-12noon, 1pm-5pm.

National Gallery (Národní Galerie)
15 Hradčanské Náměstí
Prague-1
Metro: none convenient.
Open: daily except Monday, 10am-6pm.

National Museum of Literature
See Strahov Monastery.

National Museum
(Národní Muzeum)
Top end of Wenceslas Square
Prague-1
Metro: Muzeum. Open: daily except
Tuesday, 9am-5pm (4pm on Monday
and Friday).

National Technical Museum
(Národní Technické Muzeum)
Kostelni Street
Prague-7
Metro: none convenient. Open: daily
except Monday, 9am-5pm.

Smetana Museum
(Muzeum Bedřicha Smetany)
1, Novotného Lávka
Prague-1
Metro: Staroměstská. Open: daily except
Tuesday, 10am-5pm.

St Agnes Monastery
(Kláster Anežsky)
Art Gallery
Anežská Street
Prague-1
Metro: none convenient. Open: daily
except Monday, 10am-6pm.

2

WESTERN BOHEMIA
AND THE SPA TOWNS

W estern Bohemia covers a very small area of Czechoslovakia, but it is a region full of things to do and see and is probably the most visited part of the country outside Prague. Many visitors travelling overland from Britain or other parts of Western Europe to Prague will probably pass through this region. It is also possible to see many of the places described here on a day's excursion from the capital. For those who only want a glimpse of what Czechoslovakia has to offer apart from Prague, a visit to this region is ideal, for it boasts all of Czechoslovakia's attractions — castles, caves, historic towns, cultural festivals, pleasant scenery and the three famous spas — in a small area where travelling is easy and distances between places are short.

Excursions West Of Prague

There are a number of places of interest to visit in the area immediately to the west and south-west of Prague. Some may choose to see one or more of these attractions en route between Prague and Plzeň or Karlovy Vary, but they are most conveniently seen as day or half-day excursions from the capital. Karlštejn and Křivoklát Castles, and the Koněprusy Caves, are all fairly close to the soap-making town of Beroun, which is on rail routes between Prague and Plzeň, while Lidice is a fair distance to the north of this cluster of attractions. Those who have their own car could easily visit two, or perhaps even three, of the following places on a full day's excursion from Prague. All four places are accessible by public transport, though visitors will find that it is easier to journey between Prague and the places of interest by train or bus, than to travel by public transport between the attractions themselves. Čedok in Prague operates excursions from the capital to all four places. The map entitled *Okolí Praha*, available from bookshops in the capital, shows the countryside to the west and south-west of Prague, and shows clearly the locations of the four places of interest describes below.

Lidice   ✳

Twenty-two kilometres (14 miles) north-west of Prague, a short distance east of the coal mining town of Kladno, is the village of Lidice, which has come to symbolise the worst excesses of Nazi atrocities that were committed in Europe during World War II, and which for many Czechs has become a virtual pilgrimage centre where the suffering of their countrymen during that time is most profoundly evoked.

Bohemia and Moravia were occupied by Nazi Germany between 1938 and 1939 after the Munich agreement that Hitler signed with Britain and France.

Opposite: Karlštejn Castle

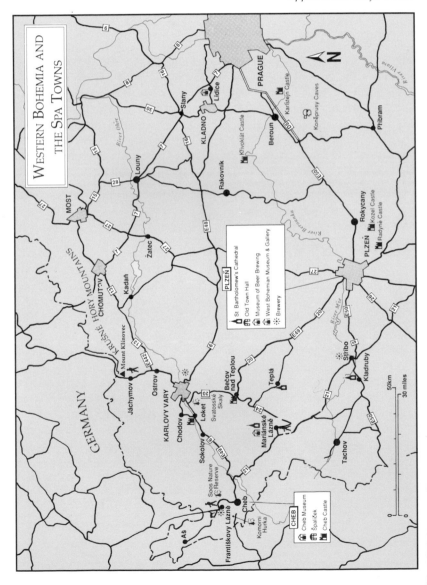

The British Prime Minister Neville Chamberlain announced that it had brought 'peace in our time', but for Czechs it was the beginning of a 6-year-long reign of terror perpetrated by the Nazis over their occupied country. In 1942, Czech underground freedom fighters assassinated Reinhard Heydrich, deputy leader of the SS and the man that Hitler had put in charge of occupied Czechoslovakia. As a reprisal for this, Hitler decided that one Czech village should be liquidated as a lesson to those he ruled over in Czechoslovakia. Lidice was chosen after a very flimsy connection was made between two families in the village and the parachutists who had assassinated Heydrich. On 10 June 1942, 6 days after the death of Heydrich from bomb injuries, the Nazis rounded up all the men of the village, hauled them off to a local farm, and shot them all. The 196 women were sent to concentration camps, where many of them later died. Many of the children, after having been found to be 'racially pure', were deported to Germany to be brought up and re-educated as Germans in German families. Over the next 2 years, Lidice was systematically burned, destroyed, and levelled to the ground.

After the war, the full horrors of the Lidice tragedy, and the fact that it symbolised in one incident the destruction that German fascism had wrought on the peoples of occupied Europe, was gradually recognised. Many villages all over the world were renamed Lidice. Lidice was a mining village and many miners from Britian and the USA formed movements which led to the rebuilding of the new village of Lidice, in a spot adjacent to where the old one had stood.

A rose garden has been planted over the hillside where the village once stood. The mass grave is overlooked by a group of trees. Next to the garden is a small but excellent museum of the Lidice tragedy. Those visiting the museum with a group, or who are visiting the museum when an English-speaking group turns up, may be allowed to see a film about Lidice, which includes actual footage of the destruction of the village which was taken by the Nazis.

The simplest way to reach Lidice from Prague is via road 7 (Prague to Chomutov) and then branching off this road onto the road to Kladno. Lidice is on the Prague to Kladno bus route; buses are frequent and the journey time is about half an hour. The Kladno bus leaves from outside Dejvická metro station in Prague, and stops outside the museum. Some Čedok day excursions from Prague to Karlovy Vary also include a stop at Lidice, as it is also not very far from the Prague-Karlovy Vary road, and could also easily be seen by independent travellers journeying between these two centres.

Karlštejn Castle (Hrad Karlštejn)

By virtue of its pleasing appearance and beautiful position, and the fact that it is only 28km (17miles) from the centre of Prague, Karlštejn Castle is the most visited castle in Czechoslovakia. It is also a favourite (and almost mandatory) excursion into the Bohemian countryside for those visiting Prague who will see very little else of Czechoslovakia outside the capital city.

The castle is situated above the picturesque wine-making village of Karlštejn, due south-west of Prague. Motorists should take take road 4 (Prague to Stakonice). This road is a dual carriageway and Karlštejn is signposted from it 10km (6 miles) from the centre of Prague. There are frequent trains to Karlštejn from Smíchov station in Prague (metro: Smíchovské Nádraží) which take about 40 minutes. Most of these trains are local trains travelling between Prague and Beroun via Karlštejn. It is a 20-minute walk from the station at Karlštejn to the castle. Between Černošice and Karlštejn both road and rail routes take travellers through the scenic valley of the River Berounka, which is a good introduction to the scenery that is characteristic of Bohemia — rolling, forested hills, small villages, and pleasant river valleys.

The castle was founded by the Bohemian King and Holy Roman Emperor Charles IV, the builder of St Vitus' Cathedral and the Charles Bridge in Prague. It was constructed between 1348 and 1357, built as an inpenetrable fortress to house the imperial crown jewels and the relics of various saints. All appearances suggest the unassailability of this mighty fortress: the castle is situated on a steep, rocky hill overlooking the valley of the River Berounka, and its medieval walls are 6m (20ft) thick. However, the castle came under frequent assault throughout its long history, often capitulating to successful attackers. In 1422, it barely withstood a long siege of 7 months by the Hussites, and in 1648 its medieval defences failed to keep out a Swedish army equipped with 'modern' field artillery, who inflicted considerable damage on the castle in the last stages of the Thirty Years War. After this time the importance of the castle declined. As a result of frequent and successful onslaughts on the castle by various medieval marauders, the imperial jewels were removed in 1420, and are now in Vienna, and the Czech coronation jewels were removed in 1619 and are now kept in a locked vault in St Vitus' Cathederal.

Karlštejn still retains the likeness of what many people think of as a medieval castle. Despite its thick walls and colossal towers, it is a strangely beautiful pile, its beauty enhanced by an impressive setting amidst the surrounding scenery of steep, forested bluffs and craggy hills. The castle was renovated and reconstructed in the sixteenth century and then again in the 1890s, the latter reconstruction restoring it from a near-ruin to its original Gothic appearance. It has been a popular excursion from Prague since the beginning of this century.

The castle is seen on guided tours, in Czech, German and sometimes English. There is plenty of information in English available, and a translation of what the guide says. The attractions on the tour include the Imperial Palace of Charles IV, where in the King's Audience Hall one can see the original wood panelling on the walls and ceilings, and in the Luxembourg Hall a tapestry depicting the family tree of the Royal House of Luxembourg, of which Charles was a member. In the small tower is the Church of Our Lady, with a group of Gothic paintings, and next to it is St Catherine's Chapel, the emperor's private place of worship, the walls of which are inlaid with semi-precious stones. The crown jewels and the most important imperial and state documents were kept in the the Chapel of the Holy Rood (Holy Cross Chapel) in the larger of the two towers. Around the walls of this chapel there are copies of 127 fourteenth-century paintings of saints, whose watchful gaze was meant to deter would-be theives (the originals are in the Gallery of Old Bohemian Art in Prague). There are ample opportunities for walks in the hills surrounding Karlštejn, many of which reveal fine views over the castle. On the road that runs down from the castle there is a track marker post. From here, one can take the yellow-marked track, up through the houses to the right and then around to a nice, sloping clearing, the top end of which gives one a very satisfactory vista.

The Koněprusy Caves (Bohemian Karst) are close to Karlštejn. The road from Dobřichovice through Karlštejn continues on to Beroun, where one may join the E50 (road 5) Prague to Plzeň road, or continue on to Křivoklát Castle.

Bohemian Karst

The Bohemian Karst is a region of limestone caves and scenery. Only one of the caves in the area, the **Koněprusy Cave** (Koněpruské Jeskyně) is open to the public. The cave is near the village of the same name, 5km (3 miles) south of the town of Beroun, 9km (6 miles) west of Karlštejn Castle. The entrance to the cave is on the minor road between Koněprusy and Suchomasty. Prehistoric man used to live in the caves and there have been many archaeological finds from Paleolithic (Stone Age) times here, including animal bones. In the fifteenth century the caves were used by the Hussites to house a mint producing counterfeit coins. These caves are the most extensive in Bohemia, but those who will also be travelling in Moravia or Eastern Slovakia will find far more extensive cave systems in these areas and may not want to visit Koněprusy. Much of the scenery around Karlštejn and Koněprusy is typical limestone countryside, with many steep bluffs and valleys. The Koněprusy Caves are difficult to reach by public transport, and are probably not worth visiting by those without a private car. Those still intent on reaching the caves should take one of the infrequent buses from Beroun, on the Prague-Plzeň railway line.

Křivoklát Castle (Hrad Křívoklat)

From Beroun, on the Prague-Plzeň road and railway line, a minor road and a branch line run north-west along the valley of the River Berounka to the village of Křivoklát, with its attendant medieval castle perched precariously on a sharp promontory of rock which rises above the village. Like Karlštejn, Křivoklát Castle is built above the River Berounka, and both castles are closely associated with Charles IV (his first daughter was born here in 1334), but there the similarities end, as Křivoklát is a very different affair to the larger and more famous castle to the south. Křivoklát is less obviously pretty than Karlštejn, with none of the latter's carefully tended flower beds and brightly-cleaned stonework and false battlements; yet there is a much greater sense of the medieval Gothic here, despite the fact that the castle is a product of over eight centuries of building, rebuilding and extending. The first records of a castle on this spot date from 1110; by 1240, it was used as a hunting lodge by the Czech aristocracy who probably had great fun hunting in the thick forests surrounding the castle, which are now part of an important UNESCO nature reserve called Křivoklátsko. Disastrous fires wrecked the castle in 1643 and 1826, and during the last century the buildings were modified to house a school, brewery and offices. Now the castle is fully restored, and visitors can see its large medieval hall, with its Gothic ribbed vaulting, and the beautiful castle chapel; the origins of both date back to the thirteenth century.

Plzeň and Central West Bohemia

Plzeň

Plzeň is the sixth largest city in Czechoslovakia, and is famous for its two products: Škoda cars, and Pilsner beer, the latter exported all round the world as Pilsner Urquell beer (Pilsen is the old German name for the city). Being a large industrial city, many visitors will probably want to bypass Plzeň, or at the most only afford it a cursory visit. However, for beer fans, this is pilgrim-

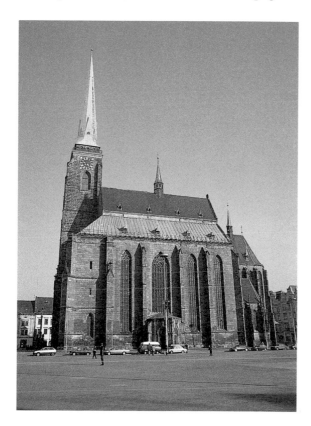

St Bartholomew's Cathedral, Plzeň

age country, and beer lovers head for Plzeň just as wine lovers head for Burgundy or Bordeaux.

Plzeň is 88km (55 miles) by road from Prague. The first part of this distance, the 18km (12 miles) between Prague and Beroun, is covered by a motorway (D5) which is now being extended beyond Beroun — consult an up-to-date map. There are five trains a day each way between Prague and Plzeň, which take about 2 hours. Whether arriving by car or train, it is easy to orientate oneself towards the centre — the high tower of St Bartholomew's Cathedral, on the main square, is an obvious feature of Plzeň's skyline, which is otherwise dominated by grimy factory chimneys. As a busy commercial and industrial city, as well as a tourist destination, Plzeň has a number of hotels, ranging from the very plush to the very cheap, and a few in between.

Plzeň has been the cultural, religious, administrative and commercial capital of West Bohemia since AD900. The original site of the town was 8km (5 miles) away from the present city centre. This was the site of an extensive tenth-century castle, most of which has now vanished. In 1295 the town was refounded on its present site and soon after this time a cathedral was dedicated to St Bartholomew. In the Middle Ages it prospered due to its advantagous position on the trade route between Prague and Nürnberg, and in 1468, the oldest printed Czech book, the *Trojan Chronicle*, was published here. The nineteenth century saw the development of heavy industry and rapid expansion of the town to include modern suburbs. Along with a new brewery, an engineering works was founded in 1859 which was bought by Emil Škoda 10 years later and re-named the Škoda engineering works. These works are now the major production centre for the famous Czechoslovakian car, the Škoda (pronounced 'Shkodder' in Czech). The town was subject to heavy bombing by the allies in the closing months of World War II, largely because the Škoda works had by then been commandeered by the Nazis to produce weaponry and ammunition. Since the end of the war, the factory has also been producing Nuclear Power reactors for Czechoslovakia and other Eastern Bloc countries, as well as cars, agricultural machinery, railway locomotives and rolling stock and other items of heavy machinery, in the process throwing a lot of dirt and smoke into the atmosphere which has resulted in a thick layer of grime adhering to most of Plzeň's buildings. The development of the city since 1945 has seen the growth of industrial and residential areas.

❋   The tradition of beer brewing in Plzeň dates back to the year 1295, when the town was given the right to brew beer by King Vaclav II. The modern **brewery** was built in 1842 financed by a German banker named Bleichröder. It is very close to the centre of town. It is only possible for groups to tour the brewery. The main Čedok office in Plzeň will arrange for individual travellers to join an English-speaking group that is touring the brewery, though it may be a couple of days wait before such a group turns up. It is always possible to see the outside of the brewery, and the famous gate (Braná Pívovaru Praždroj) at the entrance, a picture of which appears on every bottle of Pilsner beer. Next to the gate is one of the city's most stylish restaurants. Needless to say, the brewery's product can be consumed in large, cheap quantities in *pivnice* in the town.

There are a few other interesting monuments in the town worth seeing (perhaps between glasses of beer!). The main square, Náměstí Republiky, is very large and there is parking space in it. The dominating feature of the square is the formidable **St Bartholomew's Cathedral**, built between 1320 and 1470. The tower of the church is 103m (338ft) high, and is the highest in Czechoslovakia. It is possible to climb the stairs to the observation tower at the top (closed in winter). Inside the church there is much Gothic decoration, including the Plzeň Madonna on the High Altar. On the northern (cathedral) side of the square is the much-admired **Old Town Hall**, designed by the Italian architect Giovanni de Statio and built between 1554 and 1559. The graffito decorations on the front of the town hall were added between 1908 and 1912. The building is still used for its original purpose, and also for weddings and degree ceremonies for students of Plzeň's Engineering University. Opposite the town hall is a Plague Column of 1681. There are other interesting old buildings all round the square. A couple of blocks away from the square, on Perlová Street, is the entrance to a network of **Underground Passages** (Plzeňská Historické Podzemí), under the town, which were used for the storage of food, wine and beer. These are open to the public. Other places worth seeing include the **Church of the Assumption of the Virgin Mary**, the church of the Franciscans, on Františkánská, just down from the square. Organ recitals are often given here.

There are a number of museums in Plzen. Even non-beer buffs will find the **Museum of Beer Brewing** (Pivovarské Muzeum) quite interesting. It is on Veleslavínova 6, just up from the entrance to the Underground Passages. During the summer one must be taken round the museum with a guide, though during the winter and less busy times it is possible to wander round the museum at one's own pace. There is an English translation available of what the guide says. The museum itself is housed in a fifteenth-century malt house, and it is possible to see the old cellars where the beer was stored and fermented. Round the corner on Pražká Street are a group of old tripple-naved butcher's shops, reconstructed in 1971 and now housing an **Art Gallery** (Masné Krámy) with temporary exhibitions (mainly modern art). Opposite this building is the Old Water Tower, built in 1530, which supplied fountains in the main square with water until the beginning of this century. Nearer the Franciscan church, and towards the railway station, are the **West Bohemian Museum and Gallery** which were closed at the time of research.

As regards travelling on from Plzeň, there are a number of choices: Karlovy Vary, the most important of the three spa towns, is 83km (51 miles) along road 20 (E49); one could head south, to Domažlice or the northern part of the Šumava Mountains (see Chapter 4). The itinerary suggested below takes the traveller to the spa town of Mariánské Lázně via Stříbo.

Excursions From Plzeň

Travellers who want to get away from Plzeň's grime for a few hours will find that the countryside nearby is an excellent retreat. Near the village of Stáhlavy,

11km (7 miles) to the south-east of Plzeň, just off road number 20 (E49), there are two very different castles. **Kozel Castle** (Hrad Kozel) is a picturesque manor house set in a nice park, on top of a low hill in the broad valley of the Uslava, a short distance from Stáhlavy, from where it is signposted. In the opposite direction from Stáhlavy the angular shape of **Radyně Castle** (Hrad Raydyně), poking out of the tops of the trees, interrupts the rolling landscape. The castle was built in the fourteenth century and is now in ruins. Radyně is reached by means of a turning off the road between Stáhlavy and Losiná (this road is not marked on larger scale road atlases).

Made in Plzeň: Pilsner Urquell Beer

In a roll of honour of the top beer-producing countries of the world, virtually all beer connoisseurs would place Czechoslovakia in one of the top two or three positions. Pilsner beer, from Plzeň, and Budvar (Budweiss, or the original Budweiser), from the city of České Budějovice in Southern Bohemia, are the products of the country's two most famous breweries, but there are over a hundred breweries in Czechoslovakia and many large towns produce their own local beer. Bohemian beer is generally accredited as being better and more famous than beer from Moravia or Slovakia; the latter two areas are more famous as wine producing areas, though the occasional field of hops does provide a variation on the endless carpets of vineyards which are prevalent in some parts of Moravia and Slovakia.

Records show that hops have been cultivated in Bohemia since the year AD448. By the tenth century these hops were exported, and 200 years later Bohemian hops were shipped down the Elbe to the famous Hamburg hop market. During the thirteenth century, a large number of new towns were established in Bohemia by royal edict, which were autonomous and self-governing, and which allowed their citizens the right to grow hops and ferment beer. One of these was Plzeň, re-founded in 1295, and by 1300, the Bohemian towns of Prague, Plzeň, and České Budějovice all had breweries.

The Bohemian tavern is a product of the seventeenth century. These taverns had a particuar set of unofficial rules attached to them, called 'Franta's Rules' named after a tap-room in Plzeň. These included the notions that there was no limit to the consumption of food and drink, and that people should live well and die young; and that Sunday should be spent in bed, sleeping off the excesses of the night before when all the week's wages were to be spent in the pleasurable consumption of the local beer. Many *pivnice* today seem to be populated by the clientel who still take these rules to heart!

In the eighteenth and nineteenth centuries there were great technical advances made in beer brewing techniques. These new techniques were the reason for the founding of the new, present brewery in Plzeň in 1842. Beer making increased, and more and more areas of the Bohemian countryside were covered by the wood-and-wire frames on which the hops grow. The fame of Pilsner beer grew and from 1856 beer from the new brewery in Plzeň was exported abroad. In 1859, Pilsner beer was patented and given a trade mark. A hundred years later, in 1959, the beer making museum in Plzeň was opened, to celebrate this event. Today it is possible to buy Pilsner Urquell beer in over a hundred countries in the world. Many other breweries outside Czechoslovakia recognised the fame of beer from Plzeň and began to make their own beer which they called 'Pilsner'. To combat this, all genuine Pilsner beer is called Prazdroj or more familiarly the German word *urquell*, both of which mean 'original source'.

Stříbo

Visitors travelling between Plzeň and the spa towns who have time on their hands may want to stop off at Stříbo and at Kladruby abbey, nearby.

Thirty-two kilometres (20 miles) beyond Plzeň, along road 5 (E50), the town of Stříbo is set on a promontory overlooking the valley of the River Mže. The town is linked to Plzeň, Prague and Mariánské Lázně by rail. Like Plzeň, it grew through its position as a settlement on the trading route between Prague and Bavaria. However, there was an additional reason for its growth — the mining of silver; *stříbo* is the Czech word for silver. In the central square is the Renaissance Town Hall, richly decorated with graffiti wall paintings from the nineteenth century, and many Renaissance burgher's houses. The Town Hall houses a museum of the town and of silver mining. Spanning the River Mže is a Gothic bridge, which has a sixteenth-century gateway that is also adorned with graffiti.

Four kilometres (2¹/₂ miles) south of Stříbo, along a minor road, is the village of **Kladruby** with its attached former Benedictine monastery. This monastery was founded in 1115 and the abbey church is a beautiful example of Czech Baroque art; its original Romanesque appearance was reconstructed by the Baroque architect Giovanni Santini in the years 1712 to 1729. Concerts of the 'Stříbo Musical Summer' festival are held in the beautiful interior of this church.

From Kladruby one must return to Stříbo. The distance from Stříbo to Mariánské Lázně is 39km (24 miles) by road 21. Karlovy Vary is reached by turning onto road 24 just before Mariánské Lázně, and is 47km (29 miles) on from this junction.

The Spa Towns

In the very westernmost part of Czechoslovakia, at the apex of the 'triangle' that Bohemia forms as it juts out into Germany, is one of the country's greatest concentration of things to do and see. Of prime importance are the famous spa towns, Karlovy Vary (Carlsbad), Mariánské Lázně (Marienbad) and Františkovy Lázně (Franzensbad), three handsome, elegant towns all of which exude a nostalgic air of faded grandeur. Near Františkovy Lázně is the equally interesting and very different medieval town of Cheb, and in the northern part of this area are the Krušné Hory Mountains. Add to these a couple of castles and a twelfth-century monastery, and a good few days can be spent touring and sight-seeing in this area.

Any one of the four towns mentioned above can be used as a base for touring this small area. As a rough guide, the three spa towns have a number of very good resort hotels, ranging from average to international standard. Karlovy Vary in particular has some very plush hotels — one of the biggest concentrations of top-class hotels in Czechoslovakia outside of Prague. Visitors who are seeking cheaper accommodation should stay in Cheb.

Public transport links in the area are good, whether the traveller is using train or bus. As well as good connections existing between the main settlements themselves, all four towns have international rail connections with Germany and beyond.

✳ Karlovy Vary

Karlovy Vary (Carlsbad), lying 122km (75 miles) due west of Prague, is one of the most famous spa towns not only in Czechoslovakia but also the world. According to legend, the founder of this town was Charles IV, the builder of Karlštejn Castle and St Vitus' Cathedral, who is supposed to have discovered the hot springs in the town while out stag hunting. Whether or not this is true, the king certainly had a hunting lodge built very close to the present Yuri Gagarin Colonnade, in the centre of the present-day town, and he stayed there on several occasions. Apart from a few scant remains this building has long since vanished, but the ceremony that opens the spa season each year is performed in the tower that stands over the site, in memory of the king who founded the spa and after whom it is named (incidentally, the word *vary* in Czech means boiling). Despite having medieval roots, most of the buildings in the spa date from the eighteenth and particuarly the nineteenth century, when the town grew through the patronage of various visiting VIPs, including Goethe, Beethoven, Schiller, J.S.Bach, Wagner, Brahms, Chopin, Peter the Great and Karl Marx. Although the very rich and famous would no longer consider coming here just to be seen, Karlovy Vary still attracts a varied international cliental, which includes Germans, Americans, Arabs and Russians. The Polyglot conversations one overhears in the street and the price and variety of luxury goods available in the shops attest to the fact that this is no ordinary Czech provincial town, but one, especially considering its size, of the most cosmopolitan places in the country. In summer, the combined numbers of tourists and spa patients doubles the population of the town.

Many people intent on exploring the spa towns will want to make Karlovy Vary their base, as access to all the other places mentioned in this section is fairly easy. There are a large number of excellent hotels in the town, though accommodation for those travelling on cheaper budgets is more limited. The few hotels in the modern, industrial part of the town (north of the River Ohře) will cater for those who want more average-priced accommodation. Visitors are advised to book accommodation well in advance if they are visiting the town in spring, summer or New Year.

The distance between Karlovy Vary and Prague is covered by road 6 (E48). This road does not pass through Plzeň, Stříbo or other towns mentioned previously. The road from Prague enters the town running alongside the River Ohře. After the bridge over the Teplá tributary, visitors will find the spa area on their left, beyond the modern day town centre. Motorists should note that most of the streets in the spa area are closed to traffic.

By far the most sensible means of public transport between Prague and Karlovy Vary is by the frequent express buses, which take about 2 hours (those intending to make this trip should reserve seats in advance). The bus station is in the modern town centre. There are two railway stations in Karlovy Vary, Horní Nádraží, the main station (for services to Prague and Cheb) and, nearer the centre, Dolní Nádráží (for services to Mariánské Lázně, Bečov nad Teplou and Teplá). There are daily services to Vienna and Berlin, which leave from the former station.

Karlovy Vary is a large town and an industrial centre. The largest part of the town, north of the railway line and the River Ohře, is uninteresting. Visitors should head for the spa area *(lázně)*, a thin sliver of settlement in the southern area of the town that occupies land on both sides of the River Teplá, rising up the sides of its steeply-wooded valley. The spa area of the town is small and easy to walk in.

The modern centre of the town is centred on the streets Č.S. Armády and Jugoslávská. Walking south from the modern centre of the town the first spa building one comes across is the rather ugly **Thermal Hotel**, a sixteen-storey hotel block built in 1976 that houses spa patients. It is surrounded by a pleasant pedestrian area, and is the location for many of the town's cultural events, including the bi-annual film festival. A couple of minutes walk from this building, up the hillside on the left (follow the signs to 'Bázen') is a large open-air swimming pool that is heated by the water of thermal springs. There is a restaurant complex here as well, and the terraces of the swimming pool afford fine views over the town.

Continuing from the Thermal Sanitorium up the main valley of the River Teplá, one enters the spa area proper. The best road to be on is Jednotnych odboru on the west (right-hand) side of the valley. The valley swings round to the left. On the right is the complex of **Baths III**, with an attractive colonnade and a small park. A little further on, on the same side, is Pramen Svobody (Freedom Spring), and then the **Colonnade of Czechoslovak-Soviet Friend-ship** (which is also known as the Mühlbrunnen Colonnade in Pernan). It is a nice stone structure consisting of Classical and corinthian columns built in the 1870s which houses three springs and which is fronted by a pleasant plaza. The road on the other side of the river is lined by a number of stylish hotels and restaurants.

Continuing on along the road, one enters Karlovy Vary's main shopping area. On the right are the Castle Tower of 1608, the only surviving part of the castle that Charles IV founded (now housing a *vinárna* — wine bar), the Château Springs Colonnade, and the **Market Colonnade**, the latter a wooden structure decorated with carvings. The valley of the River Teplá then swings round to the right. Across the other side of the river is one of Karlovy Vary's few more ancient buildings, the Baroque **Church of St Mary Magdalene** (built in the 1730s), the interior of which is worth seeing. Its architect was Kilian Dientzenhofer, who also designed many of Prague's Baroque churches.

The **Yuri Gagarin Colonnade** houses the most important collection of springs in the town. It was constructed between 1961 and 1966 and is built of steel, glass and marble. In contrast to the earlier attempts at modern spa architecture in the north of the town, this is a very pleasant and well-designed building. It is named after the first cosmonaut and there is a memorial to Gagarin outside the building. Inside the colonnade the Vřídlo Spring (also known as the Sprudel Spring in German) shoots out of the ground in the form of a fountain. It is the hottest natural geyser in continental Europe (outside

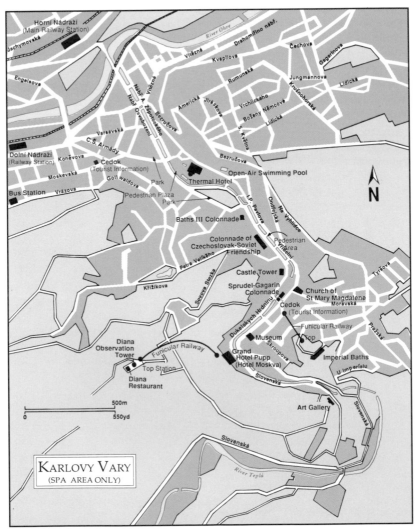

Iceland) and the water comes out of the ground at a temperature of 72°C (159° F). The water coming out of the fountain is actually surface water, which by virtue of the unique geology of the area is able to penetrate 2,000m (6,560ft) down into the earth's crust, where it is enriched by minerals and heated by the natural heat of the earth's crust. It is drawn to the surface again by natural

This swimming pool at Karlovy Vary is heated by water from thermal springs

A view of Karlovy Vary

pressure — there are no man-made pumps. In the neighbouring room it is possible to taste the water from this spring and a number of others, which are a variety of different temperatures and all of which have different supposed curative powers.

Beyond this colonnade is one of Karlovy Vary's nicest areas, a continuation of streets on both sides of the River Teplá. Here there are street cafés in summer, from where one can soak in the atmosphere of the spa and watch some of the rich clientel that forms its long-term visitors. On the left, opposite the Vítězslav-Nezval Theatre, on Divadelní Street, is the entrance to a short **funicular railway** which runs up to the Imperial Baths, the dominating landmark of Karlovy Vary. This sanitorium was completed in 1912, though it is not possible to see round it. At the next bend in the River Teplá is the **Grand Hotel Moskva** (also known by its former name, the Hotel Pupp) — a sight in itself, one of the plushest and most expensive hotels in Czechoslovakia. In 1914, the Austrian traitor and Russian spy, Colonel Redl, met his Russian contacts in the this hotel, in order to give them the plans for the intended Austrian order of battle for the opening stages of World War I. Next to the Moskva is the slightly less grand Park Hotel.

Like all spas, one of the principal activities in Karlovy Vary is walking. There are few laid-out parks as such (apart from the park due east of the Art Gallery) but there are many opportunities for walks that can be made in the wooded valley in which the town is situated. An excellent town map from Čedok should be consulted for a detailed indication of the possibilities. Any walkers in these woods will come across various obelisks, memorial plaques and small chapels hidden in the trees. One of the best, and shortest options, is to take the funicular from just behind the Grand Hotel Moskva to the top of the hill called **Vyšina Přátelství** (Friendship Hill), where there is the Diana Observation Tower (closed) and small restaurant, and then take any of the walks which lead back down to the bottom of the town. Another option is to take a walk up to the Goethe Observation Tower, east of the main spa centre (walk up from Pražká Street). Other observation towers are marked on the map — check with Čedok before walking to them as many are closed on occasions for renovation.

The town's main **museum** is on the street Rosenbergovych. It contains displays relating the the region's history, flora and fauna, and also an excellent model of nearby Loket Castle. Beyond the Grand Hotel Moskva, on Puškinova Stezka, on the right hand side, is an **Art Gallery** (Galérie Umění) housing exhibitions of twentieth century Czech art. Well away from the spa area, in the industrial suburb of Dvory in the northern part of the town, is the **Moser Glass Factory and Museum**. The glass and crystal still made in this factory is some of the most noted in Czechoslovakia.

The town has a symphony orchestra and there are frequent concerts. There is a casino, numerous discoes and night clubs (mainly in the top hotels) and restaurants to provide for evening entertainment. The local Becherovka herb liquor, made in the town since 1805 from 123 different plants and often called the 'thirteenth curative spring', makes a good souvenir from Karlovy Vary.

Excursions From Karlovy Vary

Loket and Svatošské Skaly

Ten kilometres (6 miles) West of Karlovy Vary is the village and castle of **Loket**. Loket must be approached by taking the main road to Cheb (6/E48 and 20/E49) and then a turning off to the left just after the village of Hory. The village is set on a promontory overlooking the steep valley of the River Ohře. In its main square is a Baroque town hall of the late seventeenth century and also a Plague Column of 1718. Above the town, and approachable on foot from the main square, is the commanding feature of Loket Castle, the earliest parts of which were built in the early thirteenth century (the square tower and the walls). In 1815 a porcelain factory was opened in the village, and the castle contains an exhibition of porcelain. The castle has been closed for restoration since 1987, but is due to re-open in 1992. Intending visitors should consult Čedok in Karlovy Vary for further information.

Five kilometres (3 miles) east of Loket above the deep valley of the River Ohře is the granite rock formation called **Svatošské Skaly** (also called Jan Svatoš), which is meant to represent a fossilised wedding procession. This can be seen on the marked tracks leading between Loket and Karlovy Vary. For those who only wish to walk one way between the towns, Loket is linked to Karlovy Vary by train and bus. The nearest road access is from just beyond Doubí, a village to the west of Karlovy Vary (marked on the town map).

Jáchymov and the Krušné Hory Mountains

The **Krušné Hory Mountains** (also called the Ore Mountains) are a low range of mountains that lie to the North of Karlovy Vary and straddle the border with Germany. Unfortunately these mountains are some of the worst affected by acid rain in Europe, and many of the pine forests are almost dead. Beyond the small industrial town of Ostrov a road leads up through the hills to the spa of **Jáchymov**, 14km (9 miles north-east of Karlovy Vary), which grew through silver mining in the sixteenth century. One of the coins minted here was called the 'Joachimsthaler', later the 'Tolar' which gave the English-speaking world the word 'dollar'. Silver mining had stopped by 1600, but in the 1840s uranium was found here, and in the 1950s Jáchymov was the third biggest producer of uranium in the world. In 1903 Marie Curie isolated radium from the ore found here. There is no longer any mining carried out here and the town is now important as a spa. There are a number of nice churches in the town, and some modern spa buildings. When coming from Ostrov, the road into Jáchymov curves round to the left; if one takes the right-hand turning here (immediately after the bend) and continues for a couple of kilometres one reaches the bottom station of a chairlift up **Mount Klínovec** (1,028m, 3,372ft), the highest point of the Krušné Hory. There is an observation tower (built in 1884) and a hotel at the top. There is also a marked walking track from Jáchymov to Klínovec (yellow markers). One can also drive to the top through Jáchymov and Boží Dar, taking a right-turning immediately after Boží Dar just before reaching the German border. A number of ski-lifts (snow-season only) run from the top of the mountain.

Karlovy Vary to Mariánské Lázně

It is 47km (29 miles) from Karlovy Vary to Czechoslovakia's second spa town, Mariánské Lázně (Marienbad), which lies to the south. The road is signposted as road 20 (E49) and for the first half of the distance this road is also the main route between Plzeň and Karlovy Vary.

After 22km (14 miles) the road passes through a pleasant gorge of the River Teplá and the small village of **Bečov nad Teplou**. Above this village is a Gothic castle, built in the fourteenth century, with a Baroque château below it. At the time of research this castle had been closed for some years for restoration, but it should reopen in the early 1990s. Consult Čedok in Karlovy Vary or Mariánské Lázně for further information. Whether it is open or not, the castle is quite an impressive sight, perched on a promontary overlooking a narrow, steep-sided valley. There are excellent views of it from the road itself.

At Bečov nad Teplou the road to Mariánské Lázně parts company with the E49 and one must turn right onto road 20. Very soon after the village of Mnichov one must turn left on a more minor road which leads to the village of **Teplá** and its associated monastery *(kláštery)*. By the tenth century Teplá was a frontier post along a trade route into Bohemia, and the monastery was founded in 1193 and became one of the richest in Bohemia. The three-naved monastery church constructed between 1197 and 1232 remains. The beautiful interior decoration of the church dates from the early eighteenth century. The monastery buildings themselves were destroyed in a fire in 1659 and rebuilding was carried out in the Baroque style. A tour of the monastery includes a view of the church, and of the ornate neo-Classical monastic library which was built earlier this century and has 82,000 volumes installed in it including numerous rare manuscripts. Organ recitals and chamber concerts are sometimes given in the church in summer.

From Teplá it is possible to return to the Bečov nad Teplou-Mariánské Lázně road (number 24) via a different road, before following the signs down into Mariánské Lázně.

Trains between Mariánské Lázně and Karlovy Vary pass through Bečov nad Teplou and Teplá. It is a short walk from the railway stations in both places to the castle and monastery mentioned above.

❋ Mariánské Lázně

The spa area of Mariánské Lázně (Marienbad) has a beautiful setting in a narrow pine-clad valley. Entering from Karlovy Vary the road goes round a couple of hairpins and deposits the motorist in the centre of the spa area. Coming from Plzeň, one travels first through the southern residential suburbs before reaching the spa area. Coming from Cheb one should turn left at the major T-junction in Mariánské Lázně to reach the spa area.

Opposite: (top) Spa colonnade at Mariánské Lázně;
(below) The Rudolph Colonnade, Mariánské Lázně

It is 162km (100 miles) from Prague to Mariánské Lázně on the E48, coming off this road at Bochov, east of Karlovy Vary. It is a slightly longer distance via Plzeň. From Plzeň to Mariánské Lázně is 74km (46 miles), leaving the E50 at Stříbo for road 21. The station at Mariánské Lázně is in the southern part of the town, about a mile from the centre. There are trains running west to Cheb, Nürnberg, Frankfurt and Paris, and east to Plzeň, Stříbo and Prague. It is often difficult to get accommodation in Mariánské Lázně. Intending visitors should book well in advance.

Unlike Karlovy Vary, Mariánské Lázně has no ancient roots. Although the local springs were known in the sixteenth century, the present area of the spa remained a marshy patch of woodland before the springs came to be utilised at the beginning of the last century. The buildings that originated then, including sanitoria, colonnades and hotels, were surrounded by thoughtfully laid-out parks and gardens, which eventually led into woods on the steeper slopes of the valley. The actual foundation of the spa of Mariánské Lázně is accredited to the abbot of the monastery at Teplá (a certain K. Reitenberger) and a physician named J.J.Nehr. The forty springs in the town, all of them cold, are used in the cure of kidney disorders, skin diseases and diseases of the respiratory tract. Dry carbon dioxide is also exhaled from the ground itself, and visiting spa patients can enjoy gaseous baths.

The usual collection of European notables stayed in the town at sometime or other. They include Kafka, the painter Gogol, Ibsen, Chopin, Rudyard Kipling and Mark Twain. The English King Edward VII used to spend most of the summer months in the town when he was Prince of Wales. Many other government figures from countries all over Europe also took spa holidays in Mariánské Lázně, and in the early decades of this century the subtle whispers of unofficial diplomacy would reverberate around the colonnades between the taking of thermal baths. Goethe visited the town as an old man and fell in love with a 17-year-old girl here, named Ulrica von Lewetzow. His work *Marienbader Elegie* was a result of this failed love affair. After it was over, Goethe left Mariánské Lázně, swearing never to return, and died 3 months later. Richard Wagner composed the operas *Lohengrin* and *Die Meistersinger von Nürnberg* here. The spa is also the inspiration for the story of Alain Resnais' peculiar 1962 film, *The Last Year at Marienbad*. However, today's town could not be more different from Karlovy Vary. Mariánské Lázně can no longer attract the same clientel as its neighbour to the north, but the peeling turn-of-the-century elegance and the gentle, almost proud neglect and decay is a curiously beguiling concoction, as if the town itself nostalgically yearns for the time a hundred years ago when, like Karlovy Vary, the guest lists in its hotels read like a 'Who's who' of the age. Its current appearance, of starkly beautiful orange and white buildings poking up above the tree tops, adds to the slightly timeless and surreal air of this once great spa town.

For some years Mariánské Lázně has been undergoing an extensive face lift and part of the centre is a building site. Nevertheless, there are a variety of places to walk in and see. The nicest part of the town, and the centre of the spa, is around the **Maxim Gorky Colonnade** (Křížovy Pramen), a cast-iron struc-

ture of 1889 which houses springs where one may take the water. At one end
of the colonnade is the colonnade of the **Cross Spring** (Kreuzbrunnen Colonnade in German) and in the other direction, the other side of the fountain, is
the colonnade of the **Rudolph Spring**. The fountain mentioned is an interesting piece of watery entertainment, as befits Mariánské Lázně's function as a
spa. It consists of hundreds of jets which are used in different combinations at
different times, each combination producing a different effect. Every odd
hour, on the hour, music is also played (out of loud speakers, not from a live
orchestra), which is why the fountain is known as the **'Singing Fountain'**. The
fountain is illuminated after dusk. The round-shaped **Church of Our Lady**
near the fountain is worth seeing. Concerts are often held here.

The other spa buildings surround this central area. Mariánské Lázně is a
beautiful place to walk in, and is much more spacious than Karlovy Vary. The
parkland that begins near the fountain area extends far to the south. At its
southern extremity is the **Ferdinand Spring**, set in its own park, and a little
further on another outlet of the **Rudolph Spring** . As in the case of Karlovy
Vary, there are numerous opportunities for longer walks around the wooded
valley in which the town is situated; consult the town map. By far the most
interesting ecclesiastical building in the town is set back a little from the spa
area, on Ruská Street. It is **St Vladimir's Orthodox Church** of 1901, which
houses a unique and beautiful ceramic iconostas, produced at the china works
at Loket. There is an information sheet available at the entrance to the church
which explains to visitors the history and significance of the iconostas. On the
same street is a melancholy sight indeed, a delapidated and deserted red-brick
Anglican church, built for the use of the spa's once plentiful number of English
guests.

Just up from the fountain, at number 11 on the elegant square (previously
the Klement Gottwald Square) is the house where Goethe stayed when he
visited the town. It now houses a **museum** about Mariánské Lázně in general,
and Goethe in particular. One can see the desk at which Goethe wrote when
he stayed in Mariánské Lázně. A film in English on the history of Mariánské
Lázně is shown twice a week (check with the museum for showing times).
Next to the museum is the Kafka Hotel. A German inscription above the door
recalls that it was in this hotel that Edward VII stayed during his frequent
sojourns in the town. Just up from Čedok, on the town's main street (Hlavní
Třida), there is a small Chopin museum, housed in a hotel in which the
composer once stayed.

The cultural life of the town is well noted. There are a number of nightclubs
and casinos, though far fewer than in Karlovy Vary. Sporting opportunities
abound, most notably in golf and tennis. A quick glance at the town map or
at the map posted up on a board next to the Maxim Gorky Colonnade, reveals
many walks that can be taken in the forests and woods around the town. There
is a panoramic view of the spa from the rozhledna (Kaiserturm), south-west
of the spa area. Those with more time could walk over the hills to the tiny
children's spa Lázně Kynžvart, where there is an Empire Château which has
been closed to the public since 1981 but might re-open in the 1990s. Like

Karlovy Vary, the town boasts the production of an edible souvenir, but this time it's in the form of sweet sugar or chocolate wafers *(oplatky)*, which can be bought in shops on the main street.

✳ Cheb

Most people see Cheb and nearby Františkovy Lázne, on a day's excursion from Karlovy Vary or Mariánské Lázně. The town is 27km (17 miles) from Mariánské Lázně, along road 21, and 47km (29 miles) from Karlovy Vary, along road 6 (also the E48). There are rail links between Cheb and both towns. There are also a couple of hotels in Cheb, in the restaurants of which, if necessary, those leaving Czechoslovakia and heading for Germany could spend the last of their crowns.

For centuries Cheb has guarded the historic ethnic boundary between the Czechs and the Germans, and since the foundation of Czechoslovakia this function has lived on; 8km (5 miles) west of the town is the frontier post of Cheb-Schirnding, still one of the most important crossing points on the border between Czechoslovakia and Germany. The E48 and the main Prague-Nürn-berg railway line both cross the border here. Cheb became a town in 1204 and was for a long time known by its German name, Eger. So strong were its German traditions that in the 1930s Cheb became the site of the most vehement pro-Nazi demonstrations by the Sudeten German Party, and Egerland, of which Cheb was the capital, welcomed the incorporation of this part of Bohemia into the Third Reich in 1938. After the war, all of Cheb's German population was expelled, reducing the size of the town to only a quarter of

The town square at Cheb

Attractive snow-covered buildings at Mariánské Lázně

what it was before the war. Many of the old German burgher's houses in the town are now dilapidated, the Czechs who live here prefering the modern estates on the town's industrial outskirts. This means that much of the town outside the small, central core is ugly and depressing (for those who arrive by train, the area by the station is particuarly univiting). However, a couple of hours could be spent here before heading off north to Frantiskovy Lázně. Drivers should head for the centre. Users of the train should come out of the station and keep walking straight ahead for 15 minutes — the road veers slightly to the right. This leads to the main square.

✳   The main town square, called the **Square of King George of Podebrady** (Namestí Krále Jiřího z Poděbrad), is very attractive. It forms the core of the town that grew up in the vicinity of the castle in the thirteenth century. At one end of the square are two rows of little houses built in the sixteenth century and used by Jewish shop keepers. These houses are called Špalíček (meaning 'the block'). The tiny alleyway that runs between them gives an idea of what medieval streets were once like. Around the rest of the square are burgher's houses, most of which were built during the seventeenth and eighteenth century. The fountain by Špalíček has a Baroque statue of Hercules. Just down from Špalíček is the Baroque church of St Nicholas (Svatého Mikulaše), an imposing edifice now used as a concert hall. Opposite the church is an old monastery.

Cheb's **castle**, 300m (984ft) north-west of the main square, is testament to the town's historic role as a frontier settlement. It was built between 1179 and 1188 by the Emperor Frederick Barbarossa, on the site of an ancient Slavonic fortified settlement. The formidable fortifications were later additions of the seventeenth century. Much of this castle is now in ruins, destroyed during a French seige in 1742. However, the Black Tower, a thirteenth century addition to the castle, 21m (69ft) high and built of basalt rock, still survives, and there is an observation point on top of it. The two-storey chapel of St Erhard and St Ursula is one of the few remaining parts of the Romanesque palace.

There are three museums in Cheb. All are housed in buildings which are in themselves interesting. Behind Špalíček is **Cheb Museum**, with displays relating to the history of the town and surrounding area. Its exhibits include illuminated manuscripts and Bohemia's oldest bell (made in 1286). The museum is installed in the house where Albrecht of Wallenstein, the supreme Commander in Chief of imperial forces in the Thirty Years War, was murdered in February 1634, on the orders of Emperor Ferdinand II who thought he was becoming too ambitious. The actual assassin was a minor Irish captain named Walter Devereux. Wallenstein was one of the wealthiest men in Bohemia and the Wallenstein Palace in Prague (with its famous gardens) was built for him. One can see the room in which he was murdered, as part of the museum. The German poet Frederick Schiller stayed in Cheb in 1791 while preparing his trilogy about the Wallenstein tragedy.

On the east side of the square is the ornate Baroque town hall, built in the early eighteenth century which houses the **Art Gallery** (Galérie Umění) of much-admired twentieth-century Czech art.

Two hundred metres (656ft) down from the square, on Kamena Street, close to a bridge over the River Ohře, is St Bartholomew's Church (Svatého Bartolomej), no longer used as a place of worship and housing the **Gallery of Cheb** **Gothic Art**. The interior of the church has fine ribbed vaulting, and the remains of fifteenth-century wall paintings. The Gallery of Gothic Art installed in it contains an exhibition of carved wooden sculptures made in Cheb and elsewhere in the fifteenth and sixteenth centuries.

Františkovy Lázně

Františkovy Lázně (formerly Franzensbad) is the smallest of all the spa towns. It is so close to Cheb that the two places almost form one settlement. There are two buses an hour between Cheb and Františkovy Lázně. The town is on the Cheb-Aš branch line, but there are very few trains. It is much easier to find a hotel room here than in the other two spas.

The spa is 450m (1,476ft) above sea level and one of its prime attractions is that it is has an exceptionally favourable and pure atmosphere. Unlike Mariánské Lázně and Karlovy Vary, it is not surrounded by trees and hills. Nevertheless, the spa is well preserved, untainted by modern development. All the buildings are coloured an imperial yellow known as Kaisergelb which contrasts well with the endless greenery all around. So-called 'Cheb water' was taken here in the twelfth century; the spa was founded in 1793, and was named after the Austrian Emperor Franz I. The spa specialises in the treatment of gynacological diseases (particuarly sterility).

Coming into the town from Cheb one finds oneself on the main street (Národní Třída), which cuts through the square Náměstí Míru. In the centre of Náměstí Míru is a pavillion of 1832 which houses the biggest spring in the town, called **František's Spring** (Francis' Spring). Further to the east (on the right hand side of Národní Třída) is the pavillion of the **Glauber Spring** which gurgles from a depth of over 90m (295ft). The Glauber Spring pavillion is situated in the extensive and delightful parkland which extends over the whole southern part of this small town and which contains many other small spa pavillions and springs. Františkovy Lázně is an excellent town in which to simply stroll around. South of this parkland is the Amerika Lake, on the northern shore of which there is a campsite and a rather stylish restaurant.

Near Františkovy Lázně And Cheb

Komorni Hurka is the youngest extinct volcano in Czechoslovakia, 3km (2 miles) south-west of the town. The Empire portal is the entrance to a tunnel dug into the volcano in 1837 on the instigation of the writer J.W. von Goethe, who was interested in discovering the origins of the volcano, which actually has the appearance of an inconspicuous forested hill. Drivers should follow the signposts from the southern part of Františkovy Lázně, taking a turning off the main Františkovy Lázně to Cheb road. Walkers can follow the tracks from Františkovy Lázně.

✳ The **Soos** nature reserve (commonly refered to as just Soos) is an interesting area of extensive peatbogs where mineral springs and natural carbon dioxide bubble out of the ground. The springs have a high salt content and many of the plants that grow here are normally only found near the sea. The whole area (about 200 ha) is a former lake. Soos is reached from the village of Hájek, 5km (3 miles) north-east of Františkovy Lázně. Hájek is a station on the Cheb-Luby railway line, which does not pass through Františkovy Lázně.

The Spa Tradition In Czechoslovakia

Like no other country in Europe, Czechoslovakia abounds in spas. There are 3,000 mineral springs in the country, and a few of the spas (for example, Karlovy Vary, and Teplice in Northern Bohemia) were founded during the Middle Ages. Many more have been founded since this date. There are comparatively fewer spas in Moravia and Slovakia than in Bohemia. Each spa deals with a different ailment, according to the exact mineral properties of the waters that the spa patients bathe in and drink. The spring waters in spas normally have high contents of salts in solution, and are naturally enriched with carbonates of lime, common salt, iron and sulphur. Gas is also present in spa water (normally carbon dioxide). The word 'spa' actually derives from a place of the same name near Liège in Belgium — the original 'spa'.

Karlovy Vary is the country's largest spa, where there are over 4,000 beds for spa patients. All three spas mentioned above are the country's most important 'international' spas, where people from abroad come to take the waters. Visitors come particuarly from Germany, but also from North America and the rest of Europe. Other spas in the country are less well known, except to Czechoslovakians themselves. These tend to comprise modern grey hotel and sanitorium blocks, rather than elegant Victorian arcades and carefully landscaped parklands.

All the spa towns mentioned in the preceeding section are very much working spas. Most of the people visiting them are not tourists but long-term visitors who are recuperating after accidents or illness. For citizens of Czechoslovakia, treatment in a spa is an integral part of the country's national health service, and is a way of life rather than the inaffordable luxury that many spas in Western Europe have become. Spa patients spend anything from three weeks to several months convalescing in their designated spa, engaged in a curious routine of bathing, drinking and walking around the parks or countryside that spas are invariably set in, and also adhering to a strict diet. This means that many of the people one sees in the spa towns are either very old or very ill or both, and give the towns a dour air, particuarly in the off-season when there are fewer tourists about. Nevertheless, spa towns like Mariánské Lázně and Františkovy Lázně are a step back to the lost elegance of Victorian times, and have a uniquely relaxed air about them which the twentieth century in many ways has seemingly passed by.

Additional Information

Places Of Interest

Cheb

Castle (Hrad Cheb)
Central Cheb, entrance from Jánské
Náměstí
Open: April to October only, daily 9am-
4pm (April, October), 5pm (May,
September), 6pm (June, July, August).

Cheb Museum
Behind Spalicek on main square
Open: Tuesday to Friday, 8am-12noon,
1-4pm; Saturday, Sunday, 9am-12noon,
1-3pm.

Art Gallery
(Galérie Umění)
In Old Town Hall, central square
Open: Tuesday to Sunday, 9am-12noon,
1-5pm.

Gallery of Gothic Art
St Bartholomew's Church, Kamena
Street.
Open: Wednesday to Sunday, 9am-4pm;
closed October to March.

Karlovy Vary

Karlovy Vary Museum
Manzelu Rosenbergovych 1
Open: 9am-12noon, 1-4pm, daily except
Monday.

Art Gallery (Galérie Umění)
Puškinova Stezka 6
Open: 9am-12noon, 1-4pm, daily except
Monday.

Karlštejn

Karlštejn Castle (Hrad Karlštejn)
South-west of Prague
Open: March, April, October, November, December, daily except Monday
9am-12noon, 1-4pm. May to September,
daily except Monday, 8am-12noon, 1-
6pm. Closed January & February.

Koněprusy Caves

(Koněpruské Jeskyně)
(Bohemian Karst)
5km (3 miles) south of Beroun
Open: April to October only, closed
Monday.

Kozel Castle (Hrad Kozel)
Close to village of Stáhlavy, 11km (7
miles) south-east of Plzeň
Open: April to October only. Open daily
except Monday, 9am-3pm (April,
October), 4pm (May, September), 5pm
(June, July, August).

Křívoklát

Křívoklát Castle (Hrad Křívoklát)
21km (13 miles) north-west of Beroun
Open: January, 9am-3pm, daily except
Monday; May to September, daily
except Monday, 9am-12noon, 1-5pm
(4pm in September). Closed February,
March, April, October, November,
December.

Lidice

Museum in village 22km (14 miles)
north-west of Prague
Open: Tuesday to Sunday, 8am-5pm
(4pm in winter).

Mariánské Lázně

Mariánské Lázně Museum
House number 11 on the square above
the Singing Fountain (previously
Náměstí Klementa Gottwald)
Open: 9am-12noon, 1-4pm, daily except
Monday.

Plzeň

Brewery
Due north of railway station.
Visits by appointment.

Underground Passages
(Plzeňské Historické Podzemí)
Perlová Street
Open: Wednesday to Sunday, 9.30am-
5pm. Closed November to March.

Museum of Beer Brewing
(Pivovarske Muzeum)
Veleslavínova Street 6
Open: Tuesday, 1-4.30pm; Wednesday
to Sunday, 9am-4.30pm.

Art Gallery (Galérie Umění)
Pražska Street
Open: Tuesday to Friday, 10am-6pm;
Saturday, 10am-1pm; Sunday, 9am-
5pm.

Radyně Castle
(Hrad Radyně)
On road between Stáhlavy and Losiná,
11km (7 miles) south-east of Plzeň
Open: April, May, June, October,
September, weekends only, 9am-6pm
(5pm April, October); July, August,
daily except Monday 9am-6pm.
Always closed 12noon-1pm.

Soos
Nature Reserve
Access from village of Hájek, north-east
of Františkovy Lázně.
Open: 6am-6pm, daily, April to October
only.

Boating, Sailing, Sports

Františkovy Lázně
Tennis and minigolf at Dvořákovy Sady
Boating, swimming, at Amerika Lake in
south of town.

Karlovy Vary
Thermally heated outdoor swimming
pool, on valley side above Hotel Thermal, Karlovy Vary, 2-10pm weekdays,
9am-10pm weekends, closed the third
Monday of every month.
Tennis: 18, Slovenska Street.

Mariánské Lázně
Hotel Golf in Mariánské Lázně (just
outside the town, on the way to Karlovy
Vary) is home to the largest golf course
in Czechoslovakia
Swimming and rowing boats at Lido
Koupaliště in the south of Mariánské
Lázně.

Others:
Swimming and boating on Skalka and
Jesencie Lakes, near Cheb; Hracholusky
Valley Resevoir Lake, between Plzeň
and Stříbo.

There is a taboggan run above
Mariánksé Lázne. There is limited skiing
at Mount Klínovec (a few short ski
tows).

Events

Karlovy Vary
Film festival in July. Travel and tourist
films in odd years, feature films in even
years.

Dvořák Music Festival in Autumn.

Mariánské Lázně
Chopin music festival, September to
October

Plzeň
Beer festival in October. Festival of folk
songs in July. Puppet theatre (Divaldo
dětí Alfa), corner of Moskevská and
Jungmannover Streets.

Transport

ČSA - Czechoslovak Airlines
Karlovy Vary: Leninovo Náměstí 1
☎ 25760
Flights from Karlovy Vary to Prague
(summer only).

Tourist Information Centres and Accommodation Offices

Čedok tourist offices in the region
(also accommodation offices):

Cheb
31, 1 Máje Street
☎ (0166) 339 51

Františkovy Lázně
5 Národní Street
☎ (0166) 2337

Karlovy Vary
23 Tržiště Street
☎ (017) 27798
This office also organises tours in
summer, eg sightseeing tour of Karlovy
Vary on foot, half-day excursion by
coach to Mariánské Lázně.

Mariánské Lázně
In Hotel Excelsior
Třída Odboráru 48
☎ (0165) 2500 and (0165) 2114
This office also organises tours in
summer, eg sightseeing tour of
Mariánské Lázně on foot, day-long tour
by coach to Cheb, Františkovy Lázně,
Karlovy Vary.

Plzeň
10 Prešovská Street
☎ (019) 37419

3

THE RIVER ELBE REGION AND KRKONOŠE MOUNTAINS

Prague to Děčín

Mělník   ✳

Bohemia is known throughout the world for its beer; less well known are its wines, which even in Czechoslovakia are often overlooked in favour of the more popular vintages from Southern Moravia and Slovakia. Although vines have been grown in the rich soil in the region due north of Prague for over 1,000 years, the wines made here are still virtually unheard of outside Czechoslovakia. The most famous wine making town is Mělník, only 32km (20 miles) due north of Prague, and easily accessible by road 8, then 9 (users of public transport should take one of the frequent buses which leave from the stops outside Holešovice railway station in the north of Prague). Mělník's most famous vintage is a white wine called Ludmila, named after the mother-in-law of Prince Wenceslas's mother, who is reputed to have begun the wine-making tradition of this area. Four centuries later, Charles IV improved on Ludmila's work by introducing imported vines to Mělník from Burgundy.

The historic core of Mělník is situated at the top of a steep, vineyard-covered hill which overlooks the confluence of the River Vltava and the Rive Elbe. To add to the confusion, an important canal also joins the Elbe here, just slightly upstream from the confluence of the Vltava. A castle has stood on this defensive site for centuries, but the present one is a result of Baroque modifications of a Renaissance building, its main feature being a fine arcaded courtyard. Housed in the castle are a small museum of wine production, an art gallery, and a wine restaurant, where one can taste the produce of the local vineyards and look out over the River Elbe, whose waters flow directly beneath the castle. Next to the castle in Mělník is a Gothic church, dedicated to St Peter and St Paul. Inside, thousands of human bones in an ossuary have been painstakingly arranged into bizarre artistic patterns. In summer, small rowing boats can be hired on the Elbe from boathouses situated below the castle.

Those who wish to know or see more about wine making in this region could book themselves a place on one of Čedok's half-day excursions from

Prague, which includes a wine-tasting session in Mělník Castle, a visit to the local vineyards, and an excursion to **Veltrusy Château** (Veltrusy Zámek), situated about 20km (12 miles) to the south-west of Mělník. This château was built by the Count of Chotek in the early eighteenth century in the style of a French country house, and is surrounded by an enormous park that the owners once used (predictably) for hunting.

Litoměřice And Terezín

One can continue north from Mělník to Litoměřice; the road follows the Elbe for much of the way. The towns of Litoměřice and Terezin almost face each other across the wide expanse of the River Elbe. Litoměřice is built on the river's northern banks; Terezín is 2km (1 mile) to the south, though located a short distance away from the river itself. Litoměřice is the larger of the two towns and is 37km (23 miles) from Mělník by road.

The architecture of the small, pleasant town of **Litoměřice** serves as a virtual museum to its chief architect, a man named Octavio Broggio who was born in this town in 1688. During the reformation, Litoměřice had embraced Protestantism, and Broggio was determined to bring the town's inhabitants back into the Catholic fold, by rebuilding and redesigning the town's churches and its cathedral. A number of buildings from the sixteenth and seventeenth centuries line the old cobbled market square. The most noted amongst them is the Old Town Hall, with its distinctive arches, now housing a museum; note the aged and now gently peeling sundial on its wall. Opposite is All Saints Church, with a Gothic tower and Broggio exterior.

A street called Michalská leads off from the opposite side of the square. Along here, in a medieval building on the left, is an art gallery called the Severočeská Galerie, and further on, bearing round to the left, is the complex of buildings set on a low hill which surround St Stephen's Cathedral (Chram Svateho Štěphan). The cathedral fronts one side of the peaceful, grassed square called Dómské Náměstí, and much of it dates from the time of the extensive rebuilding of Litoměřice undertaken by Broggio. The square belfry next to the cathedral is the only modern touch, a work of nineteenth-century architects. Next to the cathedral is a monastery, which is still functioning; diagonally opposite is the Bishop's Palace.

From Litoměřice one can walk along the marked track up the hill Radobyl, from the summit of which there are good views. Vineyards cover its slopes; Litoměřice, like Mělník, is an important wine-making town, and in September, a fruit and flower exhibition is held here, which displays the produce of the rich local agricultural region.

Terezín is reached from Litoměřice by crossing a wide, modern bridge over the Elbe. When the town was founded in 1780 by the Emperor Joseph II, it was known by a German name, Theresianstadt. In the nineteenth century, the brick-built fortress, originally built to protect Bohemia's north-western flank, was turned into a prison. Gavrilo Princip, who assassinated the Emperor Franz Ferdinand at Sarajevo in 1914, thereby igniting the spark that set off

World War I, was interred in the fortress and died here in 1918. In 1942 the fortress was turned into a Nazi prison operated by the Prague gestapo. It became the principal concentration camp in Bohemia; 36,000 people, mainly Jews, died here between the years 1942 and 1945. A visit to the fortress is a chilling reminder of the depravity that man can sink to, even in the twentieth century; open every day of the year, the fortress, along with the village of Lidice in Western Bohemia, is the most poignant reminder in Czechoslovakia

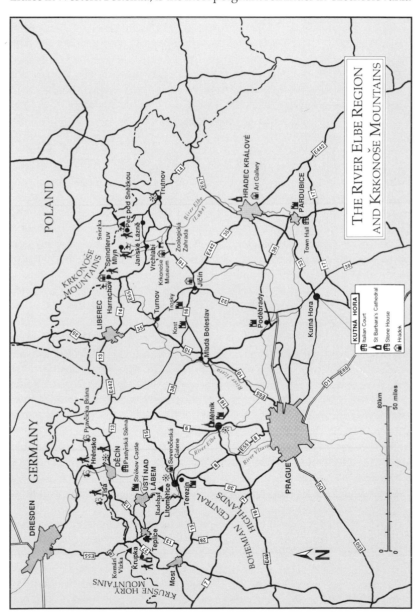

of the terrors inflicted by German Fascism on the peoples of occupied Europe. The fortress can be found just outside Terezín, along the road to Prague. One can purchase a plan of the place from the ticket office, and see the cells in which people were interred, the workhouses and the place of execution. In the former barracks used by the German officers there is a small museum, and one can even see the empty swimming pool which the Germans built for their own personal use. The cinema which the officers used for their own entertainment now sometimes shows films relating to Terezín and the German occupation of Czechoslovakia. Above one of the archways is the German inscription, 'Arbeit Macht Frei' — an instruction to the prisoners of Terezín, which means 'Work Brings Freedom'. The entrance to the fortress leads past a cemetery where nearly 30,000 victims of Nazism are buried. Just a few yards away, the hamburger stall and brightly coloured tour buses in the car park both lend an insensitive touch of twentieth-century commercialism and levity to the place. The town of Terezín itself is as uninviting and gloomy as one would expect of a place that has grown up in close proximity to such a ghastly prison.

Ústí Nad Lábem And Teplice

The next large settlement to the north of Terezín and Litoměřice is the industrial town of Ústí nad Lábem, located 26km (16 miles) from both towns by road. Transport routes between the two towns and Ústí nad Lábem run beside the River Elbe, along the steep sided valley called Porta Bohemica that the river has cut through the main part of the Bohemian Central Highlands. There is a road and a railway on both sides of the river; the more important of the two roads is that on the western banks of the river (road 30) from Terezín, but both roads and railway lines give travellers good views of this picturesque valley, whose sides (when level enough) are planted with vineyards, orchards and fruit farms.

Střekov Castle rises into view on the eastern side of the river just before the road enters Ústí nad Lábem. Those travelling along the main road on the western side of the river must cross over to the other bank by the main bridge in the town. Also known as Schreckenstein, this castle was once one of the most important on the Elbe, and its foundation stretches back about as far as the year AD820. The castle was besieged countless times and there are many legends attached to it. It was finally destroyed in the eighteenth century and is now in ruins. A road leads up to it from the main road along the east bank of the Elbe.

Ústí nad Lábem itself is an industrial town, and one of the biggest centres of the chemicals industry in the country. There are harbours and port facilities along the sides of the River Elbe, which is crossed by a modern steel bridge. Because of its industry, the town was subjected to heavy bombing raids by the allies in 1945; one of the effects of these raids was to jolt the spire of the town's main church almost 2m (7ft) from the vertical. The leaning spire can still be seen today — the church is just up the slight rise from the main railway station, on the west bank of the Elbe. Apart from this minor point of interest, Ústí nad

Lábem is neither very pretty nor very interesting. However, because of its position as a road and rail junction, one of its hotels could provide accommodation for visitors wishing to see Litoměřice, Terezín or any of the places mentioned below. Střekov Castle is accessible on the town's municipal public transport system.

Ústí nad Lábem is a glum, grimy industrial town, but 17km (11 miles) to the west, away from the River Elbe, is the more pleasant town of **Teplice** also ✳ known as Teplice-Šanov, Northern Bohemia's most important spa. Its curative springs were known in Celtic times, and Teplice has attracted the same collection of notable visitors as the more famous West Bohemian spas, such as Wagner, Chopin, Liszt, and Goethe. During the last hundred years or so, both the town's atmosphere and the spring waters themselves have become polluted by the mining activities carried out near the town, and Teplice is now a very pale shadow of its former nineteenth-century glory, when its impressive guest lists once rivalled those of the three West Bohemian spas in terms of the numbers of European notables who stayed here. Ignore the few spa buildings and head for the extensive area of beautiful parkland in the town, which includes two lovely lakes surrounded by trees. Other than this, the town's only other point of interest is its castle, once owned by an aristocratic family, which is now a museum concerned with the many visitors that the town once received.

Five kilometres (3 miles) north of Teplice is the small town of **Krupka**, founded in the fourteenth century near tin and copper mines. In the central part of the town (called Bohosudov) is a magnificent Baroque church of ⌂ pilgrimage. Inside is a unique four-posted altar. Signs from the church lead to the bottom station of a chairlift (*lanovká*) which takes one on a satisfyingly long journey up to the summit of the hill Komáří Vížka, on the eastern limb of the Krušné Hory mountains which stretch from here to Karlovy Vary. From the top there is a fantastic view over frankly uninspiring scenery. In the valleys on 🏰 the other side of the hill one can see the villages of Saxony, only a mile or so away across the German border. A blue-marked walking track, which does not follow the route of the chairlift, links its top and bottom stations.

Děčín And The Elbe Sandstone Area

Returning to the valley of the River Elbe, **Děčín**, like Ústí nad Lábem, is another grimy industrial city, with little to recommend it. Děčín is the nearest thing to a port that exists in landlocked Czechoslovakia, and the banks of the Elbe here are lined with docks and industrial facilities — including, once again, a pronounced emphasis on the chemicals industry. Steeply wooded hills surround the town. Overlooking the town, on a promontory above the east bank of the Elbe, is Děčín's most prominent landmark, a large château complex that has developed from a castle built here in the twelfth century. Until recently it was used by the Soviet army, and it is now looking very shabby. On the other side of the river, opposite, is another, smaller château, 🏯 **Pastýřská Stěna**, with gardens, a restaurant and a good view. To reach it, walk

The River Elbe at Děčín

A chairlift in the Krušně Hory Mountains at Krupka

along the road from the centre of Děčín towards Dresden. After a couple of minutes one reaches a lift (*vytah*) that runs inside the cliff up to the château. If it is not running, continue along the road for a short distance to the bridge over the river, and take the red-marked walking track that leads to the left.

Notwithstanding this, Děčín is really only of interest as a place to stay while visiting the interesting scenery of the Elbe Sandstone Region nearby, with its fascinating rock features, gorges and streams which lie amidst the steep, thickly-forested hills which stretch to the north and west of the town. The landscape features of this area were developed in the Cretaceous Geological period, which began 135 million years ago, and result from the fact that sandstone is a very soft rock, easily eroded by the actions of wind and water, which over hundreds of millennia have moulded the rocks into their present form. The fast-flowing streams and rivers of the area have also carved out steep-sided valleys and gorges, the sides of which are covered with dense forests of spruce and pine trees.

There are two principal areas of interest: that called Jetřichovické Stěny, around the village of Hřensko, to the north of Děčín, and that called Děčínské Stěny, around the village of Tisá, to the west. A map called *Česky Svycarsko*, which shows all the walking tracks and other features described in this section, can be bought from bookshops. Visitors who want to appreciate the full benefit of this region should be prepared for a lot of walking, since most of the places of interest are not accessible by road. The area is known equally well as the Elbe Sandstone Region (Labské Pískovce), the Děčín Rocks (Děčínské Stěny) and Bohemian Switzerland (České Švycarsko), the latter name being attributed to the area because of two Swiss painters who came here in the eighteenth century and never returned to their home country, saying that they had discovered a 'new' Switzerland here.

Hřensko Area (Jetřichovicke Steny Area)
Hřensko is a pretty little village 12km (7 miles) north of Děčín on the main road between Děčín and Dresden. It is from here that one can walk to the main

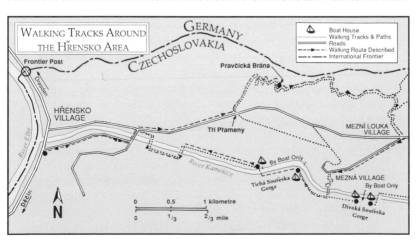

places of interest of the Elbe Sandstone Region, the most important attraction being the fantastic sight of the rock arch Pravčická Brána, the highest natural arch in Europe. Apart from driving to Hřensko from Děčín, through the beautiful gorge of the River Elbe, one can also walk to Hřensko on the marked track, or, probably the best option, take a boat along the Elbe from Děčín to the landing stage at Hřensko. Boats run from mid-April to the end of September. Boats also ply the River Elbe from Děčín to the German city of Dresden — providing a further idea for a day excursion from Děčín. Děčín and Hřensko are also linked by a regular bus service.

This section of the River Elbe has always been an important waterway. In the past, the rich produce of Bohemia (timber, sandstone, wine and fruits) was exported to the lucrative markets of Germany along this route, and today industrial barges travel the same route as their medieval counterparts, also trading with the still lucrative German markets to the north. Hřensko itself was developed as a centre for the production of timber, which was cut in the sawmills that were established in the village, before being sent in boats down the Elbe. The land on the opposite side of the Elbe to Hřensko is in German territory, and just north of Hřensko there is a frontier post on the Czechoslovak-German border. The Elbe seems to have narrowed here from its wide course at Litoměrice, and its gorge is narrow enough to allow one to stand by its banks at Hřensko and read the large sign boards of the railway station on the opposite side of the river, which serves the German village of Schöna. In the nineteenth century, Schöna and Hřensko were linked by a steam powered ferry, but today there are no means at all of crossing the river at this point.

Although it is possible to drive a car a little further on from Hřensko, to Tři Prameny, the lengthy walks in the surrounding countryside are described as if one is taking them from Hřensko. There are a couple of hotels and restaurants in Hřensko, to allow for welcome refreshment after the strenuous but rewarding hike described below, which may take as much as a day. It is a round walking trip which starts and finishes at Hřensko, but it can only be followed in the form presented here between the months of May and August, when boats operate along the gorges Tichá (Dolní) Soutěska and Divoká Soutěska. Those visiting the area outside the summer months must alter their walking itinerary from that presented here. It may be wise, before setting out for Hřensko, to check with Čedok at Děčín that the boats along the gorges are running on the day you intend to visit.

From Hřensko, walk the first 3km (2 miles) along the minor road that leads east, running alongside the River Kamenice. Soon the entrance to the gorges of Tichá Soutěska and Divoká Soutěska (see below) is reached, and there are a couple of restaurants here by the road side. But to reach Pravčická Brána, following the round walking tour presented here, continue on along the road, which now leads away from the River Kamenice, to Tři Prameny, where a track leads off from the road to the left; there is limited parking at Tři Prameny. This is the nearest one can get to Pravčická Brána in a car. The sign post at Tři Prameny gives the distance to **Pravčická Brána** as 2km (1 mile), but it is a quite a stiff walk up to the arch, taking maybe an hour and a half or so, along steep paths which run through thick, unrelenting forest. However, the paths are well-made and used by many walkers. At the top, the bridge itself is a fantastic sight, 30m (98ft) long and 21m (69ft) high; the highest rock arch in Europe, only two other natural arches in the world, both of which are in Utah, supersede Pravčická Brána in length or width.

The wild scenery surrounding Pravčická Brána, of jagged, highly weathered sandstone rocks poking out from thick fir trees, lends a surreal air to the whole area, particuarly if cloud or mist collects in isolated pockets between the rugged cliffs in the area immediately below and surrounding the arch. A restaurant built into the cliff by the arch, which dates from the nineteenth century, provides walkers with much-needed refreshment at the top.

For those who do not head back to Hřensko the same way they came up, and who wish to continue following the circular tour, a marked walking track leads from Pravčicka Brána to the village of Mezní Louka. It takes another couple of hours to cover this distance, through more interesting sandstone scenery, and it's down hill much of the way. There are a couple more restaurants at Mezní Louka, and a hotel, for another break.

An option from Mezní Louka is the more ambitious walk that leads up to a smaller rock arch, called **Malá Pravčická Brána**, about an hour's walk away from the village. However, to complete the round-trip back to Hřensko, walk about 1km ($^1/_2$ mile) down the road from Mezní Louka to the village of Mezná, and then follow a green marked track which leads down from Mezná to the River Kamenice. The track crosses the river via a bridge. Then there are two options: turning left, and walking along the river a short way, brings one to the **Divoká Souteska Gorge**; turning right and walking along the river brings one to the **Tichá Souteska Gorge**. Both gorges are steep-sided, narrow valleys; it is not possible to walk along the sides of the river here, but between May and August small tourist boats carry people along the stretch of river that runs through the gorges, taking the weight off walkers' feet but still allowing them views of fantastic scenery, only now from the comfort of a boat. Boat trips on the River Kamenice have been operating since the year 1890. After the boat ride along Tichá Souteska, a short walk on along by the banks of the River Kamenice bring one back to the road, more restaurants, and then, after a further short walk, back to Hřensko.

Tisá Area (Decinske Steny Area)
Possibly less interesting, though still rewarding, is a visit to the 'rock town' called **Tiské Stêny**, which is $^1/_2$ km up from the village of Tisá, west of Děčín. Reach Tisá by taking road 13 towards Teplice, and turning right at the village of Libouchec, 13km (9 miles) from Děčín. **Tisá** is the first village along this road. A system of well-marked walkways and tracks lead around the rocks. Compared to the Hřensko area, much less energy is required for a visit to Tisá, as the rocks can be reached by road.

Since Tisá is just off the road to Teplice, a visit to the latter town and its close neighbour Krupka could be combined with a visit to Tisá, thereby making a full day's excursion from Děčín. Teplice is 34km (22 miles) from Děčín. Roads also lead north from Děčín to Berlin (through Hřensko) and east to the Krkonoše Mountains (via Liberec and Jablonec).

Towns On The River Elbe East Of Prague

The wide loop that the path of the River Elbe forms as it flows through Northern Bohemia means that for a certain distance, between the towns of Mělník and Pardubice, its direction of flow is from east to west, across flat, intensively farmed countryside, and through many industrial towns. There are a number of interesting towns on this stretch of the River Elbe as well, which could be seen either on their own or on the way to or from another destination, such as Moravia or the Krkonoše Mountains.

✳ **Kutná Hora**

Although it lies some 65km (40 miles) from Prague, Kutná Hora, situated just off road 38, is another favourite excursion from the capital. The town lies in the flat, fertile plains of East Bohemia, always covered with crops rather than forests, on the small River Vrchlice, a few miles to the south of that river's confluence with the Elbe. In the Middle Ages, it was the second largest town in Bohemia and its importance was due to the rich deposits of silver that were found nearby. Silver was mined and minted at Malín, just north of Kutná Hora, from the tenth century onwards, and a Cistercian monastery was founded near here, at Sedlec, in 1142. According to a legend, the first really rich deposits of silver ore in Kutná Hora are supposed to have been discovered by one of the Cistercian monks in the thirteenth century. Between 1300 and 1547, a mint was situated in the town, which struck coins called the Prague Gröschen, the use of which radically reformed Bohemia's coinage system. Kutná Hora (known as Kuttenberg to German speakers) became the place of residence of many Czech kings, and gained many privileges as a royal town. By 1726, however, the mines were worked out, and their closure heralded the start of a long period of decline in the town's fortunes. After 1945 a number of small, light engineering and other industries were established here, but the present comparatively small population shows that economic success in the twentieth century has proved to be more elusive than in the Middle Ages, and now only the town's collection of medieval buildings, and its fabulous Gothic cathedral, point to Kutná Hora's previous period of wealth and importance.

Those who choose to travel by train between Kutná Hora and Prague, using Praha-Masarykova Nádraží or Praha-Hlavní Nádraží stations, should be aware that the town's main railway station, Kutna Horá-Hlavní Nádraží, which lies on many internal and international rail routes, is at Malín, a fair distance from the town centre. Kutná Hora-Město station, on a branch line, serves the centre of town. The main points of interest in Kutná Hora itself are all situated a short distance from one another, and the town's authorities have posted small signs around the centre of Kutná Hora, which point the way to the various sights. The short walking tour described below, which assumes that the visitor will use these useful signs, starts from the town's main square, Palackého Náměstí.

From the square, take the road opposite the Čedok office that leads round to the **Italian Court** (Vlašsky Dvur), the building whose thick, fortified walls ⛩ once housed the Czech royal mint. The name of the building derives from the fact that Wenceslas II, who set up the royal mint, did so with the expert help of minters from Florence, the home of the famous florin. The present appearance of the building is a result of modifications made to it in the 1890s. The actual minting of the coins was carried out in rooms surrounding the main courtyard. The public can see inside the medieval assembly hall, which is decorated with twentieth-century murals, depicting important events in the town's history (such as the election of Vladislav Jagiello as Czech king in 1471). There is also a small art gallery here, exhibiting works of art by Felix Jenewein, who lived in Kutná Hora, during the last century. There is an excellent view over the valley of the Vrchlice, towards the cathedral, from the park just below the court. Just up from the Italian Court is **St James' Church**, founded in 1330, which has rich interior decorations, though it is often locked. Its 83m (272ft) high steeple is a distinctive local landmark.

Follow the signs up from St James' Church, past a magnificent plague column (1715) to **Kamenny Dum**, the 'Stone House', the oldest house in Kutná Hora, built in 1485 and adorned with a beautiful stonework façade and a fine oriel window. Its interiors house a museum; there is a small chapel inside, as well. From here, one can walk round the corner to a large, 12-sided fountain, (Kamenna Kasna), which used to supply water to seven public fountains in the town, via a network of wooden pipes. A short distance from here is **Hrádek**, which dates from 1420 and served as both a Gothic palace and as part of the town's fortifications. Many of the medieval halls and rooms inside, which house the exhibits of a mining and minting museum, have fine Gothic rib-vaulted ceilings, and are decorated with medieval paintings and murals. In the garden one can see a medieval machine which was built to lift silver ore out of the mining pits (the machine was actually used in the mines at Jáchymov, near Karlovy Vary). Entrance into the old silver mines can also be gained from here.

The gardens of Hrádek overlook the steep valley of the Vrchlice, and from Hrádek it is a short walk past the old Jesuit's college (1700), and its interesting avenue of statues of saints outside (1703-1716), to **St Barbara's Cathedral** (Chrám Svatého Barbory), the most important monument in Kutná Hora. This splendid Gothic building, dedicated to the patron saint of miners, and built between 1388 and 1565, is probably the second most beautiful and impressive cathedral in Czechoslovakia, after St Vitus' in Prague. The whole building attests to Kutná Hora's boom-town history, and to the egotism of the town's medieval guildsmen and civic leaders, who had enough pride in their town and enough money to throw around that they thought they would build a cathedral to rival St Vitus' in Prague. Its exterior, whether viewed from the gardens of the Vlašsky Dvur, or from close up, is incredible. The roof of the five-aisle naved central part of the church is supported by a myriad of flying buttresses, and is adorned with pinnacles, towers and spires. Inside, coats of arms of medieval miner's guilds decorate the fine Gothic rib vaulting, and in the Minter's Chapel there are fifteenth-century frescoes showing Florentine minters at work. Paintings elsewhere in the church continue the associated themes of mining, minting and money, on which Kutná Hora's medieval fortunes were built. The oldest object inside the church is the Gothic statue of the Madonna and Child (1380), but a few of the other decorations, including the neo-Gothic altar (1903), date from more recent times.

Other Towns In The Region

An excursion from Prague to Kutná Hora could also include a short visit to the town of **Poděbrady**, 27km (17 miles) by road from Kutná Hora, to the north. Poděbrady lies on the E67 Prague-Warsaw road, and also the road between Prague and the main part of the Krkonoše Mountains. There are fast road and rail connections between Poděbrady and Prague. In fact, motorists can cover much of the 48km (30 miles) between Prague and Poděbrady by motorway. Since 1908 Poděbrady has been an important spa town, its thirteen curative springs aiding the treatment of cardiovascular diseases. Poděbradka mineral water comes from here. As well as being a spa, Poděbrady is also known as being the birthplace of King George of Poděbrady (1420) one of the most famous Czech kings, who ascended the throne in 1458 after one and a half centuries of foreign rule. In the town's main square there is a fine equestrian statue of him. From the square, entrance can be gained to the Castle in which he was born. The original medieval castle was built in the sixteenth century as a Renaissance château, and it was later used as a hunting lodge. Parts of it now house a museum of the history of Poděbrady. Behind the castle, there is a lock and weir on the River Elbe. A walkway, which leads through pleasant parks, and the main area of the spa, links the square with the railway station. Bohemian cut glass and crystal (under the 'Bohemia' trade mark) is made in Poděbrady, and at the end of the walkway, a grey building by the railway station allows visitors to inspect and buy the factory's products.

Pardubice is 41km (25 miles) to the east of Kutná Hora by road, and like Poděbrady it lies on the River Elbe, although the river passes through the suburbs of this industrial town, rather than its centre. Pardubice is famous for the steeplechase that is run here every October. Over 50,000 spectators come to watch the race, which is run over a length of 6.9km (4.2 miles) and whose course includes 39 obstacles. The town also hosts a famous motorcycle race. All this sporting activity overwhelms a distinctly modest past, although in 1340 the Pope ordained Arnošt of Pardubice as the first Archbishop of Prague. The town's main square, Pernštejnské Náměstí, is entered through a Renaissance gateway, Zelená Brána (1507), the upper gallery of which is open to the public in summer, affording a good view. The most distinctive building in the square is the ornate Town Hall (1894), coloured orange, brown and white, and decorated with graffito illustrations; a Baroque group of statues (1680) stands in front of it. From the square, one can walk down Pernštejnské Street, and under an archway, to the town's castle, which is surrounded by a now dry but easily discernible moat, and other fortifications. The present appearance of the castle is a result of modifications to the original medieval building, carried out in the 1520s. The castle houses an art gallery and a small museum of the area.

A short distance to the north of Pardubice is a small village called **Semtín**. This is a rather unlikely site for a vast and until recently highly secretive chemicals works, which was the main production site for one of Czechoslovakia's most notorious exports, the plastic explosive Semtex (named after the village). The small town of **Chrudim**, 12km (7 miles) to the south of Pardubice, is host to Czechoslovakia's principal festival of puppetry every summer. The Puppet Museum (Muzeum Loutkářskych Kultur), in the centre of the town, is all well worth visiting (opening times are available from local Čedok offices).

There is little to detain one in **Hradec Králové**, only 22km (14 miles) to the north of Pardubice, and also on the Elbe. It is the biggest town in East Bohemia, and like Pardubice, its economy is dominated by the food and engineering industries. Much of the evidence of the town's rich history has gone; the Habsburgs built a fortress here to ward off the Prussians, but it was demolished in 1884. Jan Žižka, the one-eyed Hussite general, is buried here. A Baroque plague column stands in the centre of the main square, Žižkovo Náměstí, which is named after him. The brick cathedral of the Holy Ghost, on the square, was founded in 1307, but its present appearance is a result of nineteenth-century rebuilding. Next to it stands a tall belfry (1589), which houses an enormous bell, and behind it there is an interesting row of brightly coloured Renaissance buildings. Other buildings on the square include a preserved red and white Renaissance town house, a Jesuit church with Baroque decoration, and opposite the church, a grey building which houses a gallery of twentieth-century Czech art and sculpture. Hradec Králové is known in German as Königgratz, and in 1866 it was the site of one of the bloodiest battles ever fought in Europe in the nineteenth century — a six-week engagement between the armies of Austria and Prussia which resulted in the wholesale slaughter of the Austrian forces. The Battle of Königgratz marks the beginning of Prussian (German) supremacy over Austria in European political history.

The Krkonoše Mountains

The Krkonoše Mountains (also known as the Giant Mountains), which straddle the border between Czechoslovakia and Poland, offer visitors the finest mountain scenery in Bohemia. The main ridge of the mountains stretches round in a broad arch, from Tanvald to Trutnov, and the main Krkonoše resorts — Pec pod Sněžkou, Spindleruv Mlyn, and Harrachov — nestle in steeply wooded valleys overlooked by the typically rounded but nonetheless impressive bare peaks of the central part of the range. The highest point in the Krkonoše is Mount Sněžka (1,602m, 5,255ft), the highest mountain in Bohemia and Moravia, which is situated on the border. Its rounded, dominant peak overlooks the resort of Pec pod Sněžkou, from where there is a chairlift up to its summit. Another principal resort, Špindlerluv Mlyn, is the first settlement on the River Elbe, whose source lies high up in the central plateau of the Krkonoše. In summer, there are many opportunities for walking in these mountains, for those who can bare the notoriously unpredictable weather, or whose visit fortunately coincides with a dry spell. The snow season is the longest of any Czechoslovak mountains, and there are many facilities for skiers. Owing to their position, less than 161km (100 miles) from Prague, and even closer to large industrial towns such as Liberec and Děčín, the Krkonoše are very popular, especially at weekends; but a dense network of marked walking paths and cross country skiing tracks can take the more adventurous visitor, who is in possession of the detailed winter or summer map of the area, away from the crowds and deep into the mountains.

Like many mountain areas, the Krkonoše have always been sparsely populated. Until medieval times, the only people who ventured into the mountains were hunters, who gained access to the game-rich forests of the lower slopes of the Krkonoše along mountain rivers. A few limited trading routes were

The Town Hall at Pardubice

established over the mountain passes. In the Middle Ages, the natural wealth of the Krkonoše was discovered, and settlers from Bohemia and from many other parts parts of Europe began to prospect for gold and to establish glass and timber works. It was during this period that the legend of the 'Krakonoš' first began to enter the popular culture of the area; Krakonoš was thought to be a giant who lived in the hills and wrought thunderstorms, tempests and snow storms on those who dared to settle and farm in the mountains. The legend was not enough to stop the gradual development of the area, however, and by the seventeenth and eighteenth centuries, miners, wood cutters and herdsmen began to build *boudas* (wooden huts) high up in the mountains. The Krkonoše have been popular with tourists for over two centuries; the first travellers in the area sought accommodation in the local *boudas*, and soon *boudas* were built especially for walkers and tourists. Now a *bouda* in the Krkonoše is anything from a luxury hotel to a timber-built hut, but in the true tradition of mountain huts, they are only accessible on skis or on foot — never by road.

Partly to protect the mountains from overutilisation by walkers and skiers, and also to help counter the increasing damage caused by pollution, the area was proclaimed a National Park (known as KRNAP) in 1963, which has sought to protect the unique natural environment of the mountains, including the conservation of 1,000-year-old peat bogs and of the many alpine plants and animals which are native to the region. Many species have become extinct in the Krkonoše because of the development of the mountains by man; the last bear was shot in 1736, and wolves, lynx, and wild cats all disappeared from the Krkonoše in the nineteenth century. The Krkonoše is one of the areas of Europe most affected by acid rain, which has been gradually killing off many trees and harming water life, thereby destroying in a few decades ecosystems which have been established in these mountains for thousands of years. KRNAP compliments a simliar National Park set up in the Polish side of the Krkonoše in 1959. On the instructions of KRNAP, some of the walking tracks have been closed, and many roads cannot be used by private motorists. Many of the resorts have large car parks to keep their streets relatively free of traffic. However, the limited efforts by KRNAP to attempt to alleviate the damage caused by 40 years of Communist mismanagement of the environment is mostly too little, too late. Protection of the environment is one of the top priorities of the new regime in Czechoslovakia, but many now believe that no amount of money or expense can revitalise the ecology of this once wild and undeveloped area.

Walking And Skiing In The Krkonoše

The Krkonoše Mountains are excellent walking country. Some walks are described below, but those who buy the walking map of the area can easily plan their own. KRNAP regulations require visitors to keep to the marked and obvious paths, the total length of which is 1,000km (620 miles). Routes along ridges are colour coded red, those in valleys as blue, and those along the side of a mountain, running along the contours, are coded green. Shorter yellow marked paths connect these tracks. Western visitors cannot use the 'Path of Czechoslovak-Polish Friendship', which runs along the ridge marking the border, although one can walk up to the border along valleys. Walkers should be aware of the notorious weather in these mountains. It rains or snows one day out of every two. Weather conditions can change very quickly. Many of the mountain peaks are flat, and are very high and exposed, and the walker may find himself suddenly caught out in heavy snow or rain storms, strong winds, or thick fog which can descend very quickly. Walking in these mountains can be rewarding but needs the same care and proper planning as walking in mountain ranges which are much higher.

Most walking tracks in the mountains are closed in winter. There is snow on the ground in the Krkonoše for 6 months of the year; the first snow falls in November, and does not melt completely until April or May. The skiing season lasts from November to March. The snow and skiing season here is the longest of any mountains in Czechoslovakia, but the mountains are popular, there are long queues and the facilities are not of the same standards as they are in Slovakia or Western Europe. The winter map of the area shows the degree of difficulty of the runs, graded by colour coding from black (hardest) through red to blue (easiest). There are also many cross-country skiing tracks, marked with poles, and there are ski jumps at Harrachov. However, few Western visitors come to the Krkonoše to ski.

Principal Centres In The Krkonoše: Vrchlabí And Trutnov

While not resorts in themselves, Vrchlabí and Trutnov are the main towns in the area and most of those visiting the Krkonoše will have reason to at least pass through them, if not to actually find accommodation in them. **Vrchlabí**, on the River Elbe, is the principal gateway to the Krkonoše. The town is 126km (78 miles) from Prague by road. The main route is by motorway D11 from Prague and then through Poděbrady and Jičín. Poděbrady, a spa town on the River Elbe, is described above, and Jičín is one of the starting points for the Bohemian Paradise, and the rock formations Prachovské Skaly lie very close to the town (see below). Trutnov, a less useful centre than Vrchlabí, is 140km (87 miles) by road from Prague, following more or less the same route. A road route via Mladá Boleslav and Turnov takes one to the western part of the Krkonoše and to the lower, separate Jizerské Mountains north of Jablonec and Liberec, which are not described in this book.

The main Čedok office in the Krkonoše, which controls many of the hotels in the mountains is on the main street in Vrchlabí. Further along, the street opens up into a square, lined with Renaissance buildings. On one side of the square is a Renaissance château, with its four towers topped by copper-coloured onion domes. The château houses the main administration offices of the Krkonoše National Park, and its interiors are inaccessible to the public. Behind the château, however, there is a nice park, with a lake, and small zoo, the Zoologická Zahrada. Further along the main street, up from the square, a picturesque wooden building houses both the Krkonoše Museum, and the information office for the Krkonoše, where one can find a certain amout of literature in English, as well as tourist souvenirs. Part of the museum (with exhibits relating to nature conservation in the Krkonoše) is housed in a former Augustinian monastery on the edge of the aforementioned park. There are a number of hotels in Vrchlabí, including a Čedok interhotel, and the town is the main centre for public transport in the Krkonoše.

Trutnov is an industrial town and an important rail and road junction. A ✳ number of Renaissance and Baroque buildings line the town's main square, including a church with a notable 63m (207ft) high tower. In the square are a group of Baroque statues of the Holy Family, and a Column of the Holy Trinity (1704).

Those visiting the Krkonoše by public transport should use the bus service. There are few railway lines in the region. Vrchlabí, Trutnov, Pec pod Sněžkou, Špindleruv Mlyn and Harrachov are all linked to Prague by express bus services which run several times a day.

The main resorts in the Krkonoše lie in the valleys of the Rivers Elbe, Úpa and Jezira, which run parallel to each other in a north-south direction. There is little or no road access between the valleys themselves; only walking paths run over the ridges. Road access between the valleys is normally via the lowland towns of Trutnov or Vrchlabí, to the south.

The Elbe Valley

From Vrchlabí, a road runs north along the Elbe Valley for 14km (9 miles) to the resort of **Špindleruv Mlyn** (850m, 2,788ft), the most important resort in the ✳ Krkonoše. The road along the Elbe is set in the river's deep, steep-sided valley that is typical of the Krkonoše. Just before entering the town, the road passes by a small dam and lake on the river. Špindleruv Mlyn itself is very pleasant, set in a sharp bend of the River Elbe, where a smaller river, the Dlouchy, joins it. The town is named after one of the first settlers in the mountains, a man named Špindler who constructed a mill *(mlyn)* on the River Dlouchy near the present day settlement. Tourism began after the completion of the road up from Vrchlabí in 1871. Modern accommodation buildings built up the sides of both river valleys blend in well with the smaller wooden hotels, many of which were built in the last century. Two chairlifts run from near the town. One kilometre ($^1/_2$ mile) away, up the Dlouchy Valley, is a chairlift up to the summit of Mount Plan (1,196m, 3,923ft), while in the other direction, a short way along the Elbe Valley, there is a chairlift up to Mount Medvêdín (1,235m, 4,051ft). There are also many ski lifts and tows in and around Špindleruv Mlyn and on the slopes of Mount Plan and Mount Medvêdín.

Špindleruv Mlyn is the first settlement on the River Elbe, which here is little more than a mountain stream flowing in a rocky, boulder-strewn bed. A popular walk in the Krkonoše is to follow the river from Špindleruv Mlyn all the way up to its source, at Pramen Labe, 9km (6 miles) away along a blue-marked track called the Harrach Path, which was built in 1879 by Count

The River Elbe at Špindleruv Mlyn, in the Krkonoše Mountains

The resort of Pec pod Sněžkou, overlooked by the snow-capped Mount Sněžka

Harrach who also established the first nature conservation area near here in 1904. The walk follows the Elbe all the way. From Špindleruv Mlyn it runs along the Labsky Dul Valley, getting gradually steeper and steeper, until after about 8km (5 miles) it winds its way steeply up past waterfalls, including the Labská Waterfall, which is 45m (148ft) high, to Labská Bouda, an isolated mountain hotel (the road up to the hotel from Horní Mísečky, shown on maps, is closed). From here it is a 1km ($^1/_2$ mile) walk across a broad, high plateau to the source itself, at Pramen Labe (1,384m, 4,540ft). A plaque nearby displays the coats of arms of all the towns along the River Elbe. The spot is set in the middle of a flat, marshy bog, and is the somewhat un-exciting destination of an otherwise pleasurable walk. From Pramen Labe one can return to Špindleruv Mlyn back the way one came, or via Horní Mísečky and Mount Medvědín, taking the chairlift down from Medvědín to Špindleruv Mlyn. Whichever route you take, this expedition is an all day affair. The area offers numerous other opportunities for walks; for instance, from Labská Bouda one could walk a short distance along the red-marked track towards Horní Mísečky to see another high waterfall on the River Pančava. Those who prefer to see their scenery from the road could continue up along the road from Špindleruv Mlyn to Špindlerova Bouda (1,198m, 3,929ft), set at the summit of a mountain pass into Poland, and reached by a number of twisty hairpin bends. This road is only open to buses in winter (but the services run very frequently).

The Úpa Valley

The Úpa Valley runs parallel with the Elbe Valley, to the east of it. The only access by road between the two valleys is at the southern end, via Janské Lázně and Vrchlabí.

Another scenic road in the Krkonoše runs from a junction on the Vrchlabí-Trutnov road at Čistá through the village of Černy Dul and then to the small spa town of **Janské Lázně**, which is tucked away at the bottom of a deep valley. ✳ The main road along the valley here bypasses the town and runs above it, rather than through it. Janské Lázně is a charming place, with a park and a notable art-nouveau colonnade (1893). The warm mineral springs of the area were discovered in the fifteenth century, and Janské Lázně was founded in 1677. Many people still come here to seek out the curative effects of the spring waters, and the spa is noted for its treatment of children's diseases. A cable car runs up from the town to the summit of Černá Hora (1,299m, 4,261ft). The first cableway up to Černá Hora was built in 1928, making it the oldest lift in Czechoslovakia, but this original lift was dismantled in 1980 when the present one was installed. There is a lookout tower at the top of the mountain, and a red-marked path takes walkers back down the valley sides to Janské Lázně.

Less than a mile beyond Janské Lázně the road meets the Úpa Valley at Svoboda nad Úpou, from where one can continue north for 12km (7 miles) to **Pec pod Sněžkou**, another important Krkonoše resort. This valley, again, is ✳ attractive. A short distance before Pec pod Sněžkou is reached a short chairlift runs up the mountain side to Portašovy Bouda. The name Pec pod Sněžkou means 'Furnace beneath Mount Sněžka', recalling the medieval metal ore mining and smelting that went on in the area. The town is spread out along the Úpa Valley and its tributary the Zeleny, and the parts of the town further up along the banks of the Úpa are indeed overlooked by the rounded peak Mount Sněžka, the highest mountain in Bohemia whose summit can be reached by a well patronised two-stage chairlift from Pec pod Sněžkou, constructed in 1949. A blue-marked track runs along the pleasant Úpa Valley from the bottom station of the chairlift all the way to the Polish border. The confluence of the two mountain rivers is overlooked by a tall hotel, the local landmark (or eyesore) of Pec pod Sněžkou. The town's main skiing grounds are to be found a short way along the valley of the smaller river, the Zeleny, where there are over a dozen ski tows. One cannot continue by road beyond Pec pod Sněžkou.

❄ The Jizera Valley

A road leads west from Vrchlabí to **Harrachov**, 29km (18 miles) away. Harrachov is set in the valley of the River Mumlava, though for most of its length the road runs along beside the River Jizera, another important river that rises in the Krkonoše. Harrachov is the main centre of the western part of the Krkonoše and is very accessible, both along the main E65 road to Prague, and along another main road that runs west to Děčín via Jablonec and Liberec. Beyond Harrachov there is a road crossing into Poland. There is a strong local tradition of glass making in the town. The local glassworks was founded in the eighteenth century by Lord Harrach, the local feudal landlord, and the factory is still producing cut, painted and etched glass under the Crystalex trade mark. There is a small museum and shop in the town where one can buy the factory's products. In the local church of St Wenceslas there is a glass chandelier and altar. Less than a mile from the town is a 10m (33ft) high waterfall (Mumlavska Vodopadé) on the River Mumlava. From here one can continue on along the blue marked track for 10km (6 miles) to Pramen Labe, the source of the Elbe (see under Špindleruv Mlyn, above). There is a chairlift from the town up to Čertova Hora (1,020m, 3,346ft), and on the slopes of this mountain there are five ski jumps of various lengths and heights. There are dozens of ski lifts around the town, and in the smaller winter resort of Rokytnice nad Jizerou, which is situated in the valley of the Jizera a short distance to the south of Harrachov.

The Bohemian Paradise (Česky Ráj)

Like the Elbe Sandstone Area near Děčín, the Bohemian Paradise is a natural wonderland, featuring bizarre rock formations, ruined castles and steep valleys and gorges, which are spread over a wide area between the towns of Turnov and Jičín. The Bohemian Paradise is only about 30km (19 miles) south-west of Vrchlabí, which makes a visit to the area a very convenient day-trip from the Krkonoše on one of the frequent wet days in the mountains. The region also receives many day-trippers from Prague, less than 100km (62 miles) away on good roads, and for this reason it can get very crowded. Many of the sandstone walls in this area are sheer vertical faces, and the area provides for some of the most difficult rock climbing anywhere in Czechoslovakia. Those who do not happen to be qualified rock climbers can buy the map entitled *Česky Ráj Poděbradsko* from bookshops or hotel receptions, and head out on foot, although most of the attractions discussed below are also accessible by car. The uninspiring town of Turnov, on the main road between Prague and the western part of the Krkonoše, is probably the most convenient place to stay, although accommodation can also be found in hotels in Jičín and in smaller villages in the area. Campsites and private rooms to let in villages are other options those wishing to stay in the region may wish to consider.

Turnov And The Surrounding Area

Turnov itself is a real turn off, the only point of interest in the town being the Česky Ráj Museum; it's far better, of course, to see the rocks of this area in their natural state, rather than small lumps of shiny mineral in glass cases, and the best place to start doing this is the area immediately to the south-east of Turnov, around Valdštejn Castle and Hrubá Skála.

Valdštejn Castle is a 2km (1 mile) walk from Turnov-Město station on the Turnov-Jičín railway line. This dramatic pile has lain in ruins for over 400 years, a sad but apposite memorial to the Wallenstein (Valdštejn) family, whose ancestral castle this was. The most famous member of this very minor Protestant noble family was Albrecht of Wallenstein, who became the commander of the Imperial Forces during the Thirty Years War, but who was murdered at Cheb in 1634 by his master the Emperor Ferdinand II, who considered him too ambitious. A path leads from here to the rock formation Hrubá Skála, 2km (1 mile) distant. This is one of the two 'sandstone cities' of this region, where paths lead over, between and around the giant sandstone rocks which have been weathered into bizarre forms. Visitors can climb up to several viewpoints which look out over the whole site.

The most distinctive landmark in the Bohemian Paradise is **Trosky Castle**, a twin-towered ruin perched on top of a steep-sided, conical volcanic hill that is visible from all over the surrounding area, and which, in turn, allows visitors a fantastic view over the whole of the Bohemian Paradise from one of its towers. Trosky Castle is accessible by road or by walking the 2km (1 mile) uphill from Ktová Station on the Turnov-Jičín railway line.

Kost Castle, Jičín And Prachovské Skály

Sobotka, on the southern edge of the Bohemian Paradise, is far less useful as a base from which to see the area, and is only worth mentioning as being the nearest large settlement to **Kost Castle**, situated above the village of Podkost 3km (2 miles) to the north-west. Kost is popular and attracts large crowds, who come to see one of the best preserved medieval castles in Bohemia, the exterior of which has been almost untouched since the early seventeenth century. A short guided tour of the castle is complimented by a visit to the Gallery of Czech Gothic Art, also installed in its rooms, the collections of which is part of the Czech National Gallery in Prague.

❋ Local boy Albrecht of Wallenstein decided to re-invest some of the wealth heaped upon him by Ferdinand II in his own place of birth, and he chose **Jičín**, on the road between Prague and the Krkonoše Mountains, as the showpiece town of the Wallenstein lands. He was responsible for the reconstruction of the town's main square in the 1620s, and also for the château which is on one side of it. The building now houses a museum and art gallery. Next door there is a Baroque Jesuit church. The upper gallery of the old medieval gateway into the city, called the Valdická Brána, gives visitors a view over the town.

❋ Jičín's main attraction, however, is its proximity to the rock town **Prachovské Skály**, only 3km (2 miles) away, the largest 'rock town' in the Bohemian Paradise. It is popular with both climbers and walkers, who come to see and scale the enormous lumps of basalt rock which tower above the surrounding forest in a wide area.

ADDITIONAL INFORMATION

Places of Interest

Bohemian Paradise
(Česky Ráj)
The rock towns *Hrubá Skála* and *Prachovské Skály* are open at all times.
Trosky Castle: Open weekends only, April to September.
Kost Castle: Open April, September, October, 9am-4pm, daily except Monday; May to August, 8am-5pm, daily except Monday.
Valdštejn Castle: Open May to mid-September only, daily except Monday, 9am-4.30pm.

Elbe Sandstone Region
The rock arch Pravčická Brána, and the 'rock town' at Tisá, are open at all times.

Hradec Králové
Art Gallery
Žižkovo Náměstí
Open: daily except Monday, 9am-12noon, 1-6pm.

Kutná Hora
Italian Court (Vlašsky Dvur)
Havlîckovo Námestí
Open: daily, 8am-5pm (4pm in winter).

Hrádek (Mining Museum)
Barborska street
Open: April to October only, daily except Monday 8am-12noon, 1-5pm.

Litoměrice
(Severočeská Galerie)
Michalská Street
Open: daily except Monday, 9am-12noon, 1-5pm.

Mělník
Castle
(with museum, gallery, restaurant)
Open: March, April, September, daily except Monday, 9am-4pm. May to August, daily except Monday, 8am-5pm. Closed October to February. Veltrusy Château, nearby, has the same opening times.

Pardubice
Castle
Open: April to October only, daily
except Monday 10am-5pm.

Poděbrady
Castle
Entrance on main square
Open: May to October only, 9am-5pm,
daily except Monday.

Terezín
Fortress and Museum
Just outside Terezín on the road to
Prague
Open 8am-4.30pm daily, all year.

Ústí nad Lábem
Střekov Castle
On road along east bank of Elbe, south
of the town centre
Open: April to October only, daily
except Monday 9am-5pm (4pm in April
and October).

Vrchlabí
Krkonoše Museum
Krkonošska Street
Open: daily except Monday, 9am-
12noon, 1-4pm.

Zoologická Zahrada
In park behind palace on the main
square
Open: mid-May to mid-October, 9am-
5pm.

Festivals And Events

The Drak Theatre Company in Hradec
Králové is the most famous puppet
theatre company in Czechoslovakia.
They perform at the Drak Theatre on
Hradební Street, a few blocks beyond
the main square.

Tourist Information Centres and Accommodation Offices

Děčín
Prokopá Holého 88
405 00 Děčín
☎ (0412) 28653/22062

Hradec Králové
Leninova Třída 63
501 39 Hradec Králové
☎ (049) 32586, 32321-5

Kutná Hora
Palackého Náměstí
284 01 Kutná Hora
☎ (0327) 2069

Pardubice
Třída Míru 67
530 02 - Pardubice
☎ (040) 23340

Ústí nad Lábem
Hrnčířská 9/3
400 75 Ústí nad Lábem
☎ (047) 26251-5

Krkonoše Mountains

Vrchlabí
Krkonošská 148
543 01 Vrchlabí
☎ (0438) 3181-3

Information office for Krkonoše Mountains:
Krkonošská Street, Vrchlabí
Open: 9am-12noon, 1-4pm, closed
Monday and Sunday (closed Saturday,
Sunday and Monday in winter).

Čedok - Špindleruv Mlyn
543 51 Špindleruv Mlyn
☎ (0438) 93225, 93280

4

SOUTHERN BOHEMIA
AND THE ŠUMAVA MOUNTAINS

Despite Southern Bohemia's strong connections with John Huss, the Czech Nationalist and reformer, there is a definite Germanic feel about this region. Visitors to Southern Bohemia may feel as though they have one foot in Czechoslovakia, and one in Austria. Historically, the region has been under the control of Austrian aristocratic families for centuries; hundreds of their castles and country houses are strewn liberally over the picturesque South Bohemian countryside. The Austrian Schwarzenberg family was responsible for building (or, at least, rebuilding) many of the region's most popular attractions, such as Hluboká, Zvíkov and Orlík castles, and the picturesque towns of Česky Krumlov and Jindřichuv Hradec. Members of the Austrian aristocracy, including a nineteenth-century Austrian prime minister, are buried in an impressive mausoleum in Třebon. Medieval towns that still have a Bavarian or Austrian flavour — such as Tábor, Prachatice, or Jindřichuv Hradec — were established on the old trade routes that ran between Prague and Upper Austria. The region prospered through its connections with the German lands to the south.

In more recent times, the first horse-drawn railway line in continental Europe was built between České Budějovice, the largest town in Southern Bohemia, and the Austrian city of Linz. The medieval trading routes and the railway are forerunners of the modern road and rail routes that run through Southern Bohemia from Prague to Linz and Vienna, and many English speaking visitors may visit the region while travelling between Austria and the Czech capital. Before World War II, much of the population of this region was German speaking, including half the population of České Budějovice, and their presence in what they knew as the 'Sudetenland' encouraged Hitler to annex Bohemia in 1938. A few inhabitants in the region still speak German as a first language, and many of the older generation still understand and speak a fair amount. The German influence still lingers in the region's famous beer and hearty food. The Šumava Mountains, and towns such as Česky Krumlov and Jindřichuv Hradec, are very popular destinations for Austrian tourists, and it is often the Austrian Schilling rather than the all-pervasive Deutchmark which is the 'unofficial' second currency of this region.

In addition to the Austrian inheritance of towns and castles, there is much peaceful scenery and countryside in Southern Bohemia waiting to be discovered by travellers. The whole region is sparsely populated (in part because all the German speakers were deported to Germany after the war), and it is very easy to get away from the towns and into the tranquil forested hills and small secluded lakes of this region, particularly in the heights of the beautiful Šumava Mountains in the south-west. The River Vltava rises in these hills and flows north through the region to Prague. Three artificial lakes, Orlík, Slapy and Lipno, have been created on the river for hydro electric purposes, and many Czechs spend lazy summer holidays on their shores swimming, fishing or sailing. There are so many lakes, castles, historic towns and areas of pleasant scenery, that the region is almost overflowing with attractions. Many visitors to Czechoslovakia will want to make Southern Bohemia one of their primary destinations.

Prague To Česky Krumlov

Between Prague And Tábor

Tábor, 34km (55 miles) south of Prague, is linked to the capital by road (motorway D1, and then the E55/road 3), and by good express trains. There are a number of attractions in the area between Prague and Tábor, but only one of them, Konopiště Castle, lies near this road. One must deviate from the road a short distance in order to visit Slapy Lake or Česky Šternberk Castle. All three attractions described here can be easily and probably most conveniently seen on day or half-day excursions from Prague.

Both road and rail routes pass through Benešov u Prahy, exactly half way between Prague and Tábor. At Benešov one can catch a bus or drive 2km (1 mile) along a road that leads west from here to **Konopiště Castle**, the first of the many Habsburg country houses in Southern Bohemia described in this chapter. In the eighteenth century an Austrian count bought the Gothic castle that stood here and adapted it from a fortress to a country house. In 1887, the Austrian Archduke Franz Ferdinand bought it and expanded and rebuilt it again; now only the old moat around the castle betrays its medieval origins. The park, with its Italian statuary and landscaped gardens, is very attractive. Franz Ferdinand was a noted huntsman and used Konopiště as a hunting lodge, a base for expeditions into the surrounding forests and hills. Thousands of his hunting trophies can be seen in the castle, as well as pieces of his extensive collection of medieval and more modern armour and weaponry, one of the best in Europe. Franz Ferdinand was the last owner of Konopiště. Austria's defeat meant that all the houses and possessions of the Habsburg aristocracy were confiscated and nationalised by the new state of Czechoslovakia, which rose from the ashes of the Austro-Hungarian empire after 1918.

One can continue west along the road that runs past the castle to **Slapy Lake**, created when a dam was built on the River Vltava in the 1960s, thus flooding the valley behind it for more than 32km (20 miles) or so. Visitors can reach this area by car or bus, or in summer, by boat along the Vltava from Prague, should one be lucky enough to obtain a ticket, and if the water level in the river is high enough for the boats to operate. The principal town and resort on the lake is Rabyně, but people sail, windsurf, canoe, swim or fish from many places along its shores, and take walks in the wooded hills nearby.

Twenty two kilometres (14 miles) east of Benešov, along minor roads, is the village and castle of **Český Šternberk**, a very different affair to Konopiště. The

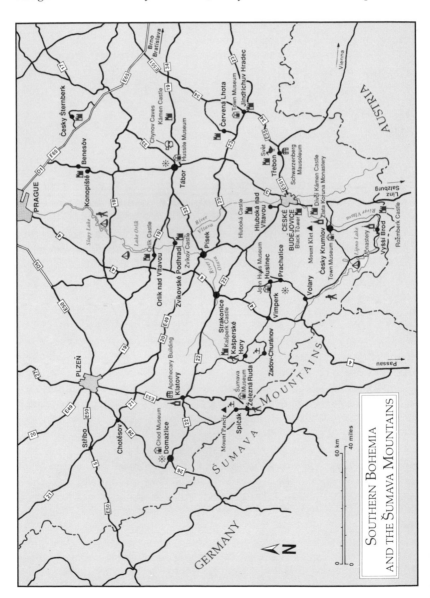

SOUTHERN BOHEMIA AND THE ŠUMAVA MOUNTAINS

Konopiště Castle

Slapy Lake is a popular recreation area

Gothic fortress glares down from a rocky promontory over the River Sázava, which flows through the village below. The castle was founded in 1240, but the decorations inside, which include elegant furnishings and chandeliers, date from Baroque times. Other attractions include a library, another collection of hunting trophies and armour, and, like Konopiště and Karlštejn, good possibilities for walking in the forest-covered hills in which the castle is set. Note that the castle is less than a mile from a junction on the Prague-Brno motorway, from where it is signposted.

❋ Tábor

Eighty-nine kilometres (55 miles) south of Prague, on road E55/3 and also a stop on the Prague to Vienna railway line, is the pleasant little town of Tábor, set above the deep valley of the River Lužnice which is crossed by an impressive modern road bridge. Tábor is the place most associated with the reform movements of John Huss. Huss was burned at the stake in Germany in 1415, and soon after the death of this fiery religious reformer and Czech Nationalist, the Hussite movement that he founded split into two factions. The more militant ones were soon known as the Táborites, because they had chosen Tábor as their headquarters. In 1420 they took over a town called Hradiště, which had existed on this site since Celtic times, and renamed the town after the Biblical Mount Tábor, in Galilee, where the Israelites won a great victory over the Caananites. The old town was completely rebuilt to withstand Catholic assaults on this protestant enclave; its narrow streets were laid out on a crooked ground plan, in order to hinder the progress of any Catholic attackers, and strong bastions and fortifications were put in place. The town's society was organised on a medieval form of Marxist collectivism, with no private property and everything in the common ownership of the people who lived here. Tábor became a haven for medieval idealists intent on establishing a home in such an egalitarian, utopian world, divorced from the Catholic, semi-feudal society that existed everywhere else in Bohemia at the time. The town soon found itself in an invidious position, exciting the jealousy of the Catholic Habsburg aristocracy, who rightly saw all these activities as a vehement defiance of both their authority and also that of the Catholic church. Despite repeated Catholic crusades against this embarrasingly steadfast group of 'heretics', it was the moderate Hussite King, George of Poděbrady, who finally succeeded in capturing the town, in 1452, thus ending its self-imposed political and economic isolation from the rest of Bohemia.

In the centre of the old town is the main square, Žižkovo Náměstí, which honours Jan Žižka, the one-eyed Hussite military chief; there is a statue of him in the square. Various Baroque and Renaissance burghers houses surround the square, but its most obvious building is the **Town Hall**, which houses a museum of the Hussite wars; its most impressive room is the vast ceremonial chamber, built in the fifteenth century and completely unsupported by columns. Chamber concerts are sometimes held here. From the Town Hall, one can descend into the tunnels and cellars that were dug beneath the square by the Hussites for use in a siege, of which 800m (2,624ft) are open to the public. Also on the square is the Church of the Transfiguration of Our Lord on Mount Tábor, dating from the fifteenth century and more interesting on the outside than the inside.

One of Tábor's crooked medieval streets, Klokotská Street, runs down from the Town Hall to the **Bechyně Gate**, which controlled the south-west entrance into the town. A round tower (called Kotnov) is all that remains of a four-teenth- century castle that stood by this gate, but there is a good view from the top of this tower over the red roofs of the old town of Tábor. Inside this building is another part of the Hussite Museum. Most of the rest of the old castle buildings are now incorporated into the town's brewery. This gate is part of the extensive system of fortifications around the town, other parts of which can still be seen. The road leading on from here runs down to the gorge of the River Lužnice.

In the eastern part of the old town, between the main square and the station, is a large artificial lake, the oldest in Czechoslovakia, called **Lake Jordan**, which was constructed in 1492 by the Hussites to supply the town with water. Baptisms were given in this lake, hence its name. It is possible to hire small boats on the spacious lake in summer. To reach it, take Střelnická Street, which leads from the square.

Excursions From Tábor

East From Tábor: Chynov Caves, Kámen Castle, Pelhřimov

Road 19 runs east from Tábor towards the Moravian towns of Pelhřimov and Jihlava. Nine kilometres (5 miles) along this road is the village of Chynov; a minor road from here leads to **Chynov Caves** (Chynovská Jeskyně), a small system of limestone caves which include several small lakes. The guided tour round the narrow, claustrophobic system of caves takes about 20 minutes.

Back on the main road, 17km (11 miles) further on is **Kámen Castle**, situated above the village of the same name on a huge granite rock. The castle was founded in the fourteenth century, but modifications turned it into a Baroque château which now houses the principal museum of the International Motor-cycling Federation, part of the National Technical Museum of Prague. Veteran motorcycles the oldest of which date back to the last century, and other associated mechanical paraphernalia, is displayed in the old rooms of the castle. The International Motorcycle Federation was founded at the nearby town of Pacov in 1904, hence the reason for the museum being situated here.

Beyond Kámen, the road crosses the old boundary between the kingdoms of Bohemia and Moravia, and the Moravian town of **Pelhřimov** is reached after 18km (12 miles). Attractions here include two enormous gates, part of the original fortifications, a fourteenth-century church and a former château, which later became the Town Hall and is now a museum. The large Moravian town of Jihlava is 30km (19 miles) east of Pelhřimov — see Chapter 5.

West From Tábor: Orlík And Zvíkov Castles, And Písek

The most obvious excursion from Tábor takes in the twin castles of Orlík and Zvíkov, on the River Vltava, to the west of the town. Here, the River Vltava is not so much a river as an elongated lake; the construction of the 90m (295ft) high Orlík Dam in the 1950s has meant that the Vltava Valley behind its wall was flooded for a length of over 64km (40 miles), creating **Lake Orlík** which in many places is used for water sports and other forms of recreation. Orlík and Zvíkov Castles are built above this lake, both in impressive positions. Orlík is best visited first; it is reached by taking road 19 from Tábor towards Plzeň, via Milevsko. After 40km (25 miles) this road crosses over Lake Orlík by the **Ždákov Bridge**, which, when it was completed in 1965, had the widest and highest bridge arch span in Europe. It is 540m (1,771ft) long and the road is carried 50m (164ft) above the surface of the lake. At the west end of the bridge there is a viewing point over the swollen river and its wide, stately valley. Because of the Orlík Dam about 13km (8 miles) north of here, the river does not flow in a channel at the bottom of the valley but instead the wooded sides of the valley rise straight out of the water, although the height of the river varies according to the controls of the water flow. After the bridge, the next major turning to the right leads through the village of Orlík nad Vltavou to Orlík Castle.

Orlík Castle was founded in the thirteenth century but after reconstructions in the 1850s it took on the appearance of a grandiose country château, picturesquely situated above the shores of the lake, which is visible from many of its rooms. The yellow-coloured château, which still betrays its origins as a fortified castle, was, like many others in this area, owned by the Schwarzenberg family of Austria. The conducted tours of its interior take one through beautifully furnished rooms, period collections of hunting trophies, and a library. There is a large park attached to the château, with pleasant walks which take in views of the lake, and of the château itself. There are lots of deer in the woods nearby, descendants of the animals that the Schwarzenbergs hunted from this castle.

Zvíkov Castle is a great contrast to Orlík. Unlike the latter, it was not converted into a château, and still retains the appearance of a medieval castle. Moreover, it is stunningly situated on a high V-shaped bluff which is at the confluence of the River Otava with Lake Orlík. This part of the Otava has also been flooded because of the Orlík Dam. Two more impressive bridges near the castle take roads over the Otava and the Vltava (Lake Orlík). The most distinctive part of the castle is the rounded turret, guarding the only possible land access to the castle. From one of its ancient courtyards, a door leads into the Royal Palace, which includes a chapel.

Those visiting Zvíkov separately from Orlík will need a good map to find it. It is immediately north of the village of Zvíkovské Podhradí, approachable on a road that joins the Písek-Tábor road (road 33) at the village of Záhoří. However, those visiting in June, July or August have a number of options for journeying between Orlík and Zvíkov Castles. During these months, a tourist boat service along Lake Orlík links the two castles; there are landing stages on the lake shores just below each castle. The boats pass underneath the Ždákov Bridge and provide great views of it, and the Vltava valley itself. A marked walking track, following the valley all the way, also links the two castles. For those who only wish to walk or go by boat one way only, during the summer months indicated a bus service also links Zvíkov and Orlík, running between the car parks of each castle. It is, of course, possible to drive between the castles, using a good map.

Písek, 46km (29 miles) west of Tábor, and south of the two castles, is a pleasant town on the River Otava, here in its normal state as a river rather than its swollen state further upstream at Zvíkov. There is a good hotel in the town. Gold-bearing sand used to be dug from the river bed of the Otava here — the word *písek* in Czech means sand. Some people still pan for gold along the banks of the Otava around Písek, while there may be enough gold deposits under the ground near the town to make its commercial extraction a possibility. The 74m (243ft) high spire of the thirteenth-century church is a distinctive

Orlík Castle

local landmark, visible from the road from Tábor as it descends into the valley of the Otava. Unsurprisingly, there is a good view from the gallery at the top. In the main square of the town is another distinctive building, the twin-towered Town Hall, which dates from the eighteenth century. Písek's main sight is, however, the bridge over the Otava, built in the thirteenth century and the oldest bridge in Czechoslovakia. Although not nearly as big or grand as the Charles Bridge in Prague, the row of statues along the parapets of the bridge, and its seven wide arches, make it faintly reminiscent of the former bridge, which it predates by almost a century.

Tábor To České Budějovice

The 60km (37 miles) between Tábor and České Budějovice, the regional capital of South Bohemia, can be covered by the fast road E55/3, or by an hour's train journey. Following the route described below is a slightly longer option — entailing a journey of 104km (64 miles), but it takes the visitor through the old towns of Tábor and Třebon and to the château at Červená Lhota, one of the prettiest in South Bohemia.

Head south from Tábor on the E55/3, towards České Budějovice. After 22km (14 miles), soon after passing through the town of Soběslav, turn left at the major crossroads onto road 23, towards Jindřichuv Hradec. After 11km (7 miles) the town of Kardašova Řečice is reached; a sign at the major road junction in the middle of this village points the way to **Červená Lhota**, a tiny agricultural settlement situated on flat plains, which would not be signposted were it not for its château, hidden in trees just outside the village. The château is tiny, and its pink walls, broken up by small square windows and ornamental gables, are perfectly reflected in the still waters of a pond that completely surrounds it, a scene that is faintly ridiculous because of its chocolate-box cover innocence. The first structure built on the island in the middle of this pond was a medieval castle, protected by a drawbrige. In the sixteenth century the castle was replaced by a château, and the drawbridge by a stone arched bridge, which now takes visitors across the pond to the front entrance. The interior houses period furniture and other collections, but the 'fame' of the château still rests on the fact that the generally unheard of German composer, Karl Ditters von Dittersdort, died here in 1799.

Jindřichuv Hradec is 15km (9 miles) south-east of Červená Lhota. This town was founded in the thirteenth century and soon became established as the principal seat of the Lords of Hrádec, one of the most prominent families of the Czech aristocracy. In the centre of the town is its huge castle, a testament to the strength of the Hrádec family; the castle is currently undergoing reconstruction but its reflection in a small pond provides for a good photograph. The town's main square, Náměstí Míru, is lined with Renaissance houses, and in its centre is a grandiose Plague Column of the eighteenth century. Just off the main square is the Church of the Assumption of the Virgin Mary, with a high spire; Jindřichuv Hradec prides itself on having 'exact' Central European Time, because it lies on the line of longitude of 15° east of

Greenwich. The place where the line of longitude passes through the town is marked in the paving in front of the church. Other churches worth seeing include the Baroque Church of St John the Baptist and St Catherine's church dating from the fifteenth century. In the Town Museum, just down from the main square, which includes displays relating to the history of the town, is an interesting and unusual 'find': a fabulously imaginative working model of the Nativity Scene, the result of a lifetime's work by one of the inhabitants of Jindřichuv Hradec in the last century. The model contains 1,756 tiny wooden figures, many of which move, all minutely detailed and controlled by the original mechanisms.

Those deciding to stay at Jindřichuv Hradec will find the Moravian town of Telč, 41km (25 miles) to the east, makes a good excursion destination from the town; see Chapter 5.

Twenty-eight kilometres (17 miles) from Jindřichuv Hradec, on the E551 (road 34) Třebon also offers the visitor a few curiosities. In the area around Třebon there are dozens of artifical ponds and lakes of various sizes, which have been developed since the Middle Ages to allow for the breeding of carp. The ponds are all linked by a system of canals and waterways which were constructed in the Middle Ages; the ultimate source of the water in the ponds is the River Lužnice. These original waterways are still incorporated into the modern, mechanised fish breeding and harvesting industry. The development of Třebon is connected with these ponds, the produce of which is still marketed widely in Czechoslovakia. At one end of the town's main square is the big **Třebon Castle**, which was built in the sixteenth century as a home for the local Rožmberk family. Soon after its construction, the Rožmberks were succeeded by the Schwarzenbergs as the principal noble family of the area. The castle's rooms can be seen on a guided tour. Behind the castle is a small park, and on one side of the park is the oldest of all the artificial lakes constructed in this region, called **Svĕt**. Boats can be hired from the banks nearest to the park and castle. Like all the fish ponds in the region, Svĕt is a major sanctuary for birds and other waterfowl. From the boat houses, walk around the lake, heading left; on the left are the small tanks used for breeding and harvesting the carp that live in the lake. Harvesting and fishing out of the ponds is carried out in September and October — an interesting process to watch, should visitors be here at this time. Those visiting Třebon in November or December, after harvesting has taken place, will find that the water of the lake has been almost drained as a result of the harvesting process, leaving uninspiring mudflats as a result. Carp (*kapr* in Czech) is a famous Bohemian dish, eaten everywhere at Christmas, and, of course, consumed in large quantities in Třebon's restaurants. Walking past the fish tanks, and continuing on around the lake, one reaches the **Schwarzenberg Mausoleum** (Schwarzenberská Hrobovká), a huge neo-Gothic building situated in an unlikely position for such a rich and noted family, shrouded in trees a short distance away from the lake shore. This building dates from the 1870s, and inside there are twenty-six tombs containing the remains of some of the most important members of the Schwarzenberg family. Some of the coffins are still draped with the Austrian and Schwarzenberg colours. The group of deceased incumbents includes a nineteenth-century Austrian Prime Minister. Třebon is also well-known as a spa. The spa buildings are uninteresting modern constructions, situated in the town's suburbs. České Budějovice is 36km (22 miles) from Třebon.

České Budějovice

České Budějovice, the administrative and industrial centre of South Bohemia, is 40km (25 miles) south of Tábor on E55/3. There is a good train service to Prague via Tábor. There are trains from here to Vienna, via Linz. The town is not so interesting in itself, but is an ideal place from which to make a number of excursions. It is a large town, with a good number of hotels, including two directly opposite the station, and one on the magnificent central square. Drivers should head for the central part of the town, overlooked by the high Black Tower, which stands just off the central square, and is visible from many parts of the town. Those arriving by train should turn right as they come out of the station, then take the first road on the left which leads directly towards the main square.

The town was founded in 1265 by Ottokar II who wanted to strengthen Royal power to counter the rapid increase in the strength of the local feudal lords. After a period of growth in the sixteenth century, which resulted from the brewing of beer in the town, and its position as a stopover place on trade routes between Salzburg and Prague, it declined, particularly after the Thirty Years War. In 1832 České Budějovice achieved fame as the starting point of continental Europe's first horse-drawn railway, which ran from here to Linz in Austria. Industrial development followed, including important engineering industries and the establishment in 1894 of an important brewery, producing Budvar beer. Before 1945 half the town's population spoke German, which is perhaps the reason why this beer is known more by its German name, Budweiss. It is often claimed that this is the original American Budweiser, though in fact the two beers are somewhat different. Nevertheless, Budvar beer competes with Pilsner Urquell beer from Plzeň in West Bohemia as the country's most famous beer. Although it is not possible to tour the brewery, one can drink its product in *pivnice* and bars all around the town.

The central square, **Žižkovo Náměstí**, is magnificent and is the largest in Czechoslovakia, and one of the largest in Europe. Though founded as a medieval square, the buildings round it all date from after 1641 when most of the town was destroyed in a fire. Each of its four sides is 133m (436ft) long. In the middle of the square is Samson's Fountain, dating from 1727. One of the most striking buildings on the square is the **Town Hall**, the current appearance of which is a result of reconstruction of an earlier building in the eighteenth century. Just off one corner of the square is the town's main landmark, the **Black Tower**, 72m (236ft) high, and recently restored. The stairs up it are badly lit and very steep, and it is probably not a good idea to take young children up. Climbing to the top provides for stunning views of České

The square at České Budějovice is one of the largest in Europe

Hluboká Castle

Budějovice and the surrounding scenery of South Bohemia. One can borrow binoculars at the top. At the top is the mechanism which controls the workings of the clock and of the bells which one passes by on the way up to the top of the tower. There is a short description of its workings in English. The tower was originally built as a belfry for the seventeenth-century **St Nicholas' Cathederal**, which is next to it. The tower and the church were founded in the thirteenth century, though both have been rebuilt and restored over the centuries. Note that very close to the main square is another square which is also very large, called Náměstí 1 Máje. This is what many people think of a typical East European square — large, modern, angular and grey; avoid it.

A quick inspection can be made of the other interesting parts of the town, as follows: from the north (tower) side of the square, running parallel with the short street that leads to the tower, but coming off the opposite side of the square to the tower, is a street called 5 Kvetna. One hundred metres (328ft) up this street on the left is an interesting triple-naved building which was built in the sixteenth century to house a row of butcher's shops; there is now a stylish restaurant here. Turning left along Hroznová one reaches the River Vltava after a short distance. Just before the river, set back a bit from the road, on Piaristické Náměstí and on the left, are the Dominican Monastery and its associated church, built when the town was founded. Turning left and walking along the river for a few minutes one reaches on the left the **Bishop's House**, with its pleasant gardens open daily in summer. Immediately beyond this is the so-called **Iron Maiden**, a castle tower which is part of the city's fortifications. The next street from here on the left, Biskupská Street, leads back to the central square.

Excursions From České Budějovice

České Budějovice is well-placed for a number of excursions into the surrounding region. To the north and east, Třebon, Jinřichuv-Hradrec and Červená Lhota (see above) and to the south Klet, Dívčí Kámen and Zlatá Koruna (see below) are possibilities for excursions. It is also an excellent base for a day's excursion to Česky Krumlov, 23km (14 miles) to the south (see separate section, below). However, the most obvious excursion from České Budějovice is to the castle at **Hluboká nad Vltavou**, 9km (5 miles) due north of the town, at the village of the same name. It is reached by driving north on the E49/road 20 (towards Plzeň and Písek) and turning off this road at the second junction of the dual carriageway onto a more minor road that leads to Tyn nad Vltavou. This passes through the village of Hluboká nad Vltavou. Just after the road curves round to the left to get into the village, there is a parking area with restaurants, a hotel and the village church. A short path leads up from here to the castle. Frequent buses link Hluboká with České Budějovice, depositing passengers just below the castle. Ignore the two railway stations called Hluboká nad Vltavou — both are some distance from the castle.

Travelling across the flat plain of the River Vltava to Hluboká the castle looms gleaming and white on the top of a hill. It was built as a small copy of Windsor Castle in England and it is from here that the resemblance is most striking. Once in front of the building itself, most similarities to its unlikely English double quickly vanish, but it is still none the less interesting. A castle was founded here in the thirteenth century at the same time as České Budějovice, and for the same reasons as that town. The site, on a steep hill high above the River Vltava, was seen as being very strategic. One of its earliest owners, called Záviš of Falknštejn, fell from political grace and was executed in front of the original castle in 1290. Charles IV and a Spanish general named Balthasar Marradas also owned it briefly. It was rebuilt and reconstructed many times, and all traces of medieval and Renaissance castles on this site have now gone. Its present appearance dates from between 1841 and 1871, when it was owned by the Schwarzenberg family of Austria. They built a remarkable, picturesque folly, with mock battlements, towers and crenellations, which were constructed for their own sake rather than as defences against potential attackers. The rooms of the castle, sumptuously decorated, must be seen on a guided tour. There is an excellent leaflet available with information in English. All the rooms have beautiful ceilings, and have antique tapestries and furniture and collections of arms, glass, and porcelain.

Other parts of the castle are not seen with a guide. These include the chapel of the castle, and a small museum, which are accessible from a door on the right hand side of the main passageway. Next to the castle itself is the South Bohemian Gallery, accessible through the greenhouse-like structure of the Winter Garden. Here are exhibited Dutch and Flemish seventeenth-century paintings, and Czech Gothic and contemporary art. Around the castle is a pleasant park.

Two kilometres (1 mile) south of Hluboká, on the road leading back to České Budějovice, is a small hunting lodge called **Ohrada Castle** that is associated with Hluboká Castle. It was built between 1708 and 1718. It now houses a museum of hunting, and exhibits include the last bear (stuffed) to be shot in the Šumava Mountains. Next to the lodge is a small zoo. Those who wish to walk to Ohrada should consult the map posted up next to the church at Hluboká nad Vltavou. The route to Ohrada from here passes through trees and lakes rather than along the road.

Česky Krumlov

Česky Krumlov, one of the undoubted stars of Southern Bohemia, is a beautiful, well-preserved medieval town set in a tight curve in the River Vltava and overlooked by a huge, forbidding castle which rises above the river, built on the top of a precipitous cliff. The town is situated 24km (15 miles) south of České Budějovice, approached by following the E55/3 towards Linz and turning off after 11km (7 miles) on a more minor road that leads towards Česky Krumlov. There is a rail link between the two towns, but the main line between Prague and Linz that passed through Tábor and České Budějovice does not pass through Česky Krumlov, which is on a branch line. There are very few direct trains between Česky Krumlov and Prague. No international trains pass through the town.

Česky Krumlov is a small town. Although it is possible to drive in many of the streets of the old town, it is better for those just passing through or visiting on a day trip to park outside the medieval part in the designated car parks. The railway station is in the modern suburbs, away from the medieval core; the bus station is much closer. Photographers should head for the bus station regardless of whether they plan to catch a bus or not, as the bus station provides for the best views over the town! The interesting part of town is very small, and it attracts a lot of visitors, so avoid visiting Česky Krumlov on summer weekends. Those who wish to stay in the town in spring or summer must be sure to book well in advance — there are only three hotels in Česky Krumlov! It is very easy, and possibly advisable, to visit the town on a day's excursion from České Budějovice.

The town was founded in the early thirteenth century underneath the castle built by the Vítek family. However, it quickly passed into the hands of the

(Opposite) One of the beautiful rooms in Hluboká Castle

Church of St Vitus, Česky Krumlov

Rožmberk family, and achieved its greatest period of prosperity in the six-teenth century. In 1591 a French historian and chronicler wrote that the Rožmberks 'have so much land and such a vast estate that they can travel from Prague to Linz almost all the way on their own territory'. The castle at Česky Krumlov was the seat of the Rožmberks. From 1719 until 1945 it was in the hands of the Austrian Schwarzenberg family; however, in the middle of the nineteenth century this family moved their principal seat from Česky Krumlov to Hluboká Castle near České Budějovice. There has been little modern industrial or residential development, and the character of the old town survives.

The Old Town is set on a slight rise tightly constrained by the curve of the River Vltava. The tiny central square, such a contrast to České Budějovice's grand, expansive affair, provides the introduction to Česky Krumlov's per-fectly preserved medieval ground plan. The square is named Náměstí Svornosti (previously Klement Gottwald Square) and buildings lining it include the Renaissance Town Hall and the cosy (and usually full) Krumlov Hotel, parts of whose building reputedly date back to 1309 when they were owned by the monks of Zlatá Koruna Monastery, near the town. More use-fully, on the other side of the square, there is a Čedok office and a bank. The Marian Plague Column dates from 1718. All the streets off the square are worth exploring — Česky Krumlov is a place to wander in. Be sure not to miss the narrow back alleys, too. Virtually all the buildings in the old part of town are medieval, with seventeenth- or eighteenth-century frontages. The writer Karel Čapek summed it up in 1925, when he wrote that 'You can see all around picturesque, ancient beauty and historic glory'. Paths along either side of the Vltava are particuarly pleasant, and give one good views over the castle.

The most impressive building in the town itself, also perched above the Vltava, is the **Church of St Vitus**, built between 1407 and 1439. Even if it is locked its exterior is quite impressive — it is best viewed from the nearby bridge over the river. Inside is the Mausoleum of Vilem of Rožmberk, the head of the Rožmberk family in the fifteenth century, when the church was built and when Česky Krumlov enjoyed its greatest period of prosperity. There are also the remains of Gothic paintings. From the church, a street called Horní leads uphill. On the left is the town's main **museum**, which is good and has an English text one can borrow. One of its most important exhibits is a large-scale model of Česky Krumlov as it looked in 1800, created by an architect and a ceramic artist and completed in 1985 after 8 years of work. There are also exhibits of archaeological finds from the ruined castle at Dívčí Kámen.

The former **Convent of the Minorites and Poor Clares**, on the other side of the river near the entrance to the castle, is closed, but it is quite interesting to walk round the outside. The cloisters of the monastery date from the fifteenth century. Next to it is the former armoury of the Rožmberks, now the town's brewery. Nearby are some remains of the town's fortifications, dating from the sixteenth century. Up from this area, past the entrance to the castle, is the České Budějovice Gate, also of the sixteenth century, which forms the outer limit of the Old Town.

The **Castle** glares down over the Old Town from a prime defensive position at the top of steep cliffs. There are normally some miserable looking bears roaming around in what used to be the moat. The castle is the second largest in Czechoslovakia, after Prague Castle. It was founded in the thirteenth century by the Vítkovec family. The round turret that forms the most distinctive part of the town's skyline dates from this time, though it has been rebuilt and altered over the centuries. The oldest parts of the castle are found in the lower courtyard, though the whole complex has undergone much rebuilding. The interior of the castle can only be seen on a guided tour, which is well worth taking. On the tour one can see furnished rooms, the beautiful Golden Carriage made in Rome in 1638, the interior of the castle's chapel, and also many paintings and tapestries. The most interesting room is the Hall of Masks (Masquerade Hall), with its wall frescoes dating from the eighteenth century.

Other parts of the castle are not seen with a guided tour. Beyond the main courtyards is the unique structure of the **Castle Viaduct**, three storeys of covered corridors crossing over a narrow, steep valley, that was built in 1767. Having crossed over this, and walked up a slight rise the extensive **Castle Gardens** are entered through a gate on the right. These were laid out in Baroque style, with fountains, a summer house and modern theatre, which has seats that move around during the performance to follow the actors. Nearby is a Baroque theatre with its original stage, though this has been closed for many years for restoration.

Česky Krumlov is in the foothills of the S"umava Mountains and there are a number of excursions that can be made from the town into the surrounding picturesque countryside.

North-East Of Česky Krumlov: Zlatá Koruna, Dívčí Kámen, And Mount Klet

Taking the road from Česky Krumlov back towards České Budějovice, after 6km (4 miles) one should turn left on a minor road towards Zlatá Koruna and Křemže. **Zlatá Koruna** is the first village along this road. In the village is Zlatá Koruna Monastery, founded in 1263 by King Otakar II — the founder of České Budějovice and Hluboká Castle. The king founded it ostensibly to commemorate his victory over the Hungarian armies at the Battle of Kressenbrünn in Austria, but the real reason for its foundation was his wishes to strengthen royal power in this part of South Bohemia. Zlatá Koruna literally means 'Golden Crown'. The main period of building activity was between 1300 and 1370, though there were many adaptations made to the original Gothic buildings in the eighteenth century. The chapel, the oldest part of the monastery, and the chapter hall of 1290 can be seen.

At **Dívčí Kámen** are some of the most extensive castle ruins in Bohemia. The name means 'Maiden's Stone', and the castle was built in the fourteenth century. It is now completely in ruins, but these ruins are quite extensive, with clearly discernible rooms, storeys and outer defensive walls. Part of the castle's charm is its isolation, set on a high, steep bluff overlooking the River Vltava, and inaccessible by road. The nearest village to the castle is Třísov.

Třísov is 5km (3 miles) beyond Zlatá Koruna (in a northerly direction), along the road towards Křemže. The marked track to the castle starts from the railway station in Třísov, which is on the right as one enters the village from Zlatá Koruna, set back 200m (656ft) from the road. After crossing the railway lines, one comes to a small shrine next to a large tree; turn left here, then follow the markers, which are clearly shown. The walk is very pleasant, through a forest and then down over the River Křemžsky, which is crossed on a small

Typical South Bohemian countryside near Česky Krumlov

Castle ruins at Dívčí Kámen

bridge, and then up to the ruins. The distance from Třísov railway station is 1¹/₂km (1 mile).

Mount Klet (1,083m, 3,552ft) is the highest point in the melancholy hills of this part of South Bohemia. On its summit are an observatory, a pub, hotel, and an observation tower, built in 1825. It is sometimes possible to see the Austrian Alps from here. It is not possible to drive a car up. From Třísov, one can continue on to the next village, Holubov, and from here drive a further 3km (2 miles) through the village of Krasetín to the bottom station of a chairlift that runs up the mountain.

It is possible to see the three places mentioned above by public transport. The following stations are on the railway line between Česky Krumlov and České Budějovice: the monastery at Zlatá Koruna is ¹/₂km (1 mile) from Zlatá Koruna station; Dívčí Kámen is conveniently approached from the station at Třísov (see text); and it is a 3km (2 mile) walk from the station at Holubov to the start of the chair lift up Klet.

South Of Česky Krumlov: Rožmberk And Vyšší Brod

A road from Česky Krumlov leads south towards Větrní and Vyšší Brod. The road by-passes the village of Větrní, without actually going through it. For much of the way the road is quite scenic, following the valley of the Vltava and hugging the river tightly for much of the time. After 24km (15 miles) this road passes through the picturesque village of **Rožmberk**. In the village itself is a Gothic church and several Renaissance houses. Rising above the village is a castle, founded in the thirteenth century by a member of the Vítkovec family, who also held the castle at Česky Krumlov. The oldest part of the present castle is a round tower dating from the fourteenth century. Other parts of the castle date from the mid-nineteenth century. The interiors of the castle contain collections of weapons and paintings.

Follow the road on from Rožmberk. After 4km (2 miles) is a junction where one should turn right; after another 5km (3 miles) one reaches the town of **Vyšší Brod**. Just past the centre of this small town, on the left, is Vyšší Brod Monastery founded in 1259 by the Lords of Rožmberk Castle who wanted to bolster their control of what at that time were sparsely populated borderland forests. The church of the monastery is thirteenth century; there is also a library, picture gallery with paintings by seventeenth- and eighteenth-century Dutch masters, and a museum of postal history. Peter Vok, who died in 1611, was the last member of the Rožmberk family, governors of the castles at Rožmberk and Česky Krumlov, and is buried here. Vyšší Brod is the starting point for the suggested itinerary for seeing the Šumava Mountains.

The Šumava Mountains

The Šumava Mountains, on whose central plateau the River Vltava rises, lie in the south-western part of Bohemia. The main ridge of the Šumava stretches from Česky Krumlov in the south-east to Domažlice in the north-west, and it marks part of Czechoslovakia's borders with Austria and Germany. Many parts of the Šumava have been closed to the public for decades, for military reasons; the border between Czechoslovakia and West Germany was one of the most sensitive parts of the old 'iron curtain'. However, these areas are now gradually being reopened.

The highest point in the range is Mount Gross Arber (1,452m, 4,763ft), which lies in German territory (the same range is known to German speakers as Bayerischer Wald — literally, the Bavarian Forest). The highest point in the Bohemian part is Mount Plechy (1,378m, 4,520ft), on the Austrian-Czech border. Much of the Šumava forms a broad, high plateau, above which the main peaks rise, thus making many peaks seem lower than they actually are. Pine forests (some of the most extensive in Czechoslovakia) form the usual vegetation cover, and in fine weather the sweet smell of pine seems to thicken the air, like a natural kind of incense. In many places, mature trees have been cut down for timber, and one can see large areas in the forest where new trees have been planted to replace them. Many towns in the Šumava have saw mills and timber-working plants, and an extensive network of logging tracks run through many parts of the Šumava forest. In contrast, many other parts of the Šumava are under stringent nature conservation measures. These include dozens of peat bogs, high in the hills, from where many streams rise; and Boubínsky Prales, an area of virgin forest on the slopes of Mount Boubín, in the central part of the range, which has been closed to the public since 1858 to protect the unique forest ecosystems of the area. Some of the individual beech, spruce and fir trees in Boubínsky Prales are several hundred years old.

Tranquil rather than spectacular, the Šumava are an ideal place in which to unwind after the rigours of sightseeing in Prague or the towns of South Bohemia. In summer, the mountains offer ample opportunities for lengthy, but fairly easy walks through pleasant countryside. In winter, there is downhill and cross-country skiing at Železná Ruda-Špičák and at Zadov-Churáňov, although the skiing season is fairly short — most of the snow has melted by the beginning of March. The Šumava are a popular holiday destination for Czechs and Germans, but few English speaking visitors to Czechoslovakia come here. Because they cover a relatively large area, the Šumava rarely become as crowded as other mountain regions in the country. However, it is often difficult to find accommodation, which should, if possible, be booked in advance. The main centres are Klatovy, Železná Ruda-Špičak, Prachatice, Domažlice, Zadov-Churáňov, and the resorts on Lipno Lake in the southern part of the range. The settlement in many parts of the Šumava is sparse, and the road and rail network is not extensive. The large scale walking map *Šumava Prachaticko*, available from bookshops, is a worthwhile investment for those who wish to walk or tour by car in this area, since it shows many of the tiny hamlets and minor roads not shown in road atlases or smaller scale maps. Some roads and walking tracks are closed periodically or permanently for military reasons, particuarly those near the German border (this does not apply in the Železná Ruda-Špičák area), so motorists or walkers should ask for up-to-date information before planning trips in border areas.

Southern Šumava: Cesky Krumlov And Vyšší Brod To Volary

The main feature of Southern Šumava is the artifical resevoir **Lipno Lake**, one of the largest lakes in Czechoslovakia, situated at an altitude of 726m (2,381ft) and picturesquely surrounded by the high, forested, rounded peaks that are typical of the Šumava. The road continues from Vyšší Brod to Lipno nad Vltavou, where the lake's comparatively inconspicuous dam (only 25m [82ft] in height) is situated. There is often no water flowing along the river channel between Vyšší Brod and Lipno nad Vltavou, as the bulk of the water that comes through the dam sluices is piped underground, to be fed back into the natural channel at Vyšší Brod. The dam, and hydro electric plant built underneath the ground near it, were completed in 1960; Lipno is the first of the three lakes on the Vltava that have resulted from daming the river for HEP purposes (the other two are Slapy Lake and Lake Orlík). Despite its tiny dam wall, the lake it supports is 40km (25 miles) long and up to 16km (10 miles) wide in places. A number of resorts have been built along the eastern shore, all linked by the Vyšší Brod-Volary road. There are also a lot of camping grounds in the area. The resorts themselves are not very interesting, being mostly bland and plain and are simply bases from which to enjoy the recreation possibilities of the lake. The road from Lipno nad Vltavou passes through the resorts in the following order: **Frymburk** (situated on the promontory of the lake; there is a Gothic church and seventeenth-century fountain in the village); **Černá v Pošumaví** (from where rowing boats can be hired), and then across a causeway to **Horní Planá** (the largest resort on the lake's shores). Frymburk and Černá v Pošumaví are linked to Česky Krumlov by separate roads which do not pass through Vyšší Brod. In summer, these resorts are linked by tourists boats, and Lipno becomes popular with anglers and swimmers, and with users of boats of all types, including sailing vessels and rowing boats. There are passenger ferries from Frymburk, Dolní Vltavice and Horní Planá to the other side of the lake, although there is little or nothing to see or do on the western shores, and there are no settlements or resorts here, only isolated farms. There are also very few roads.

After Horní Planá, the road and railway (the latter having come from Česky Krumlov) continue along the broad valley of the River Vltava to Volary, the principal centre of the Southern Šumava.

Central Šumava: Volary To Klatovy

Volary is a useful starting point for the central Šumava, but its only hotel (the Hotel Bobík, on the main square) is often completely booked up by groups! Anyone wishing to stay in Volary should make a reservation well in advance. Alternatively, the accommodation at Prachatice or Churáňov could be used as a base from which to see the central area of the Šumava. Cheap hotels can be found in many of the villages described in this section. A few of the houses in Volary, and in other villages of the central Šumava, are built in 'Alpine' style, constructed entirely of dark timber, with a wide, squat roof and an extensive balcony on the first floor.

One of the most popular walks in the Šumava is to follow the yellow-marked path known as the Medvědi Stezka (the Bear Trail) from the railway station at Ovesná, near the top end of Lipno Lake, to the station at Černy Kříž, close to Volary — a distance of 15km (9 miles). From Ovesná, thick forest and boulders are encountered on the way up to the summit of Perník (1,049m, 3,441ft), before the path drops down past a small, pretty lake (Jelení Jezírko) to the village of Jelení. Here one can see one of the few visible parts of the disused Schwarznberg Canal, built 200 years ago to transport Šumava timber south to the Danube. Between Jelení and the end of the walk at Černy Kříž one can see the stone called Medvědí Kamen (Bärenstein in German), which marks the spot where the last bear in the Šumava was shot in 1856 (this beast is now in the hunting museum at Ohrada, near České Budějovice). Now there are lynx and wild cats in the Šumava, but no longer any bears. This walk, if completed in its entirety, should take around 6 hours.

There is little to see in Volary; the town is an important road and rail junction, and like many Šumava towns, it is home to a timber-working mill. A road and railway line lead north from Volary to Prachatice, 18km (12 miles) distant. The road goes over the pass Libínské Sedlo, before dropping down into Prachatice around a number of hairpin bends. From the village of Libínské Sedlo, at the highest point in the road, a blue marked walking track (2km, 1 mile) leads up to the summit of Mount Libín (1,086m, 3,562ft), where there is a lookout tower.

Mount Libín overlooks the town of **Prachatice** itself, set in a large bowl in the foothills of the Šumava. The historic core of this small town is attractive and has been well preserved. The town was founded in 1323, on the trading route known as the 'Golden Trail': salt passed through the town from Bavaria,

This building in the town square at Prachatice is decorated with sgraffito art

while Bohemian grain was transported in the other direction. The town flourished in the sixteenth and seventeenth centuries, the period from when many of its monuments date. The town's small medieval square is lined with Renaissance buildings, including the Old Town Hall (1570) with its interesting *sgraffito* (etched) designs, which depict biblical and other legendary scenes. Other buildings on the square are faced in the same way. There are also two hotels on the square. A narrow street runs down from the square to the Písek Gate, one of the few remaining parts of the town's fortifications. Nearby is the town's most noteworthy monument, St James' Church, founded in the fourteenth century and completed in 1513. Its two stone towers form the town's landmark, while the steep roof of the church is built of timber. Visitors who find the church open can see the carved wooden decorations and late Gothic altar inside.

Only 5km (3 miles) north of Prachatice is the village of **Husinec**, where the preacher and reformer John Huss was born, sometime in the 1370s (historians are not sure of the exact year of his birth). Although Huss spent most of his adult life in Prague, where he was rector of the Charles University, Husinec is rather proud of its famous son, and a memorial stands outside the church in which he preached. The house in the village in which he was born is now a museum of his life and work, and the history of the Hussite movement, which he founded.

The significance of the Hussites and their founder is very easily lost amidst the interminable complexities of medieval religious history, with its schisms and counter-schisms and the burning of so many martyrs and heretics at the stake. However, those who have already visited Tábor or seen the enormous monument which celebrates the Hussites in the Old Town Square in Prague will have gained some idea of the important part the Hussites played in Bohemia's history. The location of Husinec on the old ethnic boundary between Czech and German speakers is the background to the Nationalistic dispute that Huss started at Charles University in Prague, where he was rector. His disdain for the largely German-speaking, Catholic aristocracy that ruled Bohemia became inexorably linked with his calls for an independent, and Protestant, Bohemian church. His fiery sermons became well-known, and the Bohemian leaders, fearing his followers would spark a revolt, brought him to trial at the Council of Constance in 1415. The Emperor had originally promised him safe conduct, but then reneged on this and allowed the German Council to sentence him to be burned at the stake, thereby immediately making him both a Nationalist and a religious martyr. Later, the Hussite movement split into various waring factions, including the most radical group which set up camp in Tábor, but in doing so it effectively destroyed itself, and even 50 years after Huss' death the Hussites were in many ways a spent force, although they resurfaced again 100 years later as a reaction to the Counter Reformation. The influence of Huss on the following centuries of Bohemian and European history has been fiercely debated, but there is no doubt that to some extent he laid the way for teachings of Martin Luther and the start of the Reformation, only 100 years after his death.

The main road in the Šumava continues on from Volary. The next village along this road is **Lenora**, where there is a glass making factory. In an orange-coloured building beside the road, above the factory, is the Glass Making Museum. Beyond Lenora the road meets road 4 (also the main Prague-Passau road) and one can turn north to Vimperk. The road to Vimperk passes through the village of Kubova Hut. The railway station serving the village (it is next to the road) is situated at an altitude of 995m (3,264ft), and is the highest in Bohemia. Near Kubova Hut is Mount Boubín, on the slopes of which is the nature reserve Boubínsky Prales (see the introduction to this section). From Kubova Hut the road decends to **Vimperk**, which is overlooked by an austere castle. There is also a railway from Volary to Vimperk, which passes through Lenora and Kubova Hut. Both road and rail travellers are treated to fine Šumava scenery on this route.

At Vimperk, motorists can join the main Prachatice-Klatovy road, one of the most important Šumava roads. North-west of Vimperk, heading in the direction of Klatovy, minor roads lead off from the main Vimperk-Klatovy road up to **Zadov-Churáňov**, the main resort in the central part of the Šumava, where there are a number of hotels. Often, the resort is called only 'Churáňov' on maps, but is signposted only as 'Zadov'! The two resorts form one settlement. Zadov is the lower resort; it is linked to Churáňov by a chairlift and by a road which twists up the hill side. This is the only road access to the resorts; the road terminates at Churáňov. There are a couple of small ski jumps at Churáňov, and it is an important starting point for many walking and cross-country skiing tracks. There are a couple of ski-lifts, and opportunities for skiing.

The Vltava rises in the central part of the Šumava. The spring itself lies deep in the hills, on the German border, and is inaccessible. The pretty hamlet of **Kvilda** is the first settlement on the Vltava (here called the Teplá Vltava, *tepla* meaning 'spring'). The river at this point is no more that a mountain stream. The Vltava Valley east of Kvilda also makes for a pleasant drive.

The next major settlement on the Vimperk-Klatovy road is **Kašperské Hory**, in whose square is a colourful Renaissance Town Hall, embellished with eighteenth-century gables, a Gothic church, and part of the Šumava museum with an excellent display of more local glass and crystal products. Entering Kašperské Hory it is possible to see a castle on a hilltop, way above the town to the right, its two distinctive square towers poking up over the tree tops. This is **Kašperk Castle** (Hrad Kašperk), an extensive ruin situated at an altitude of 886m (2,906ft) above sea level. There is no road to it, but it can be reached by a number of marked tracks which lead up through the forest. The most convenient way to reach the castle is to take the green-marked track, which leads up to the castle from the village square, first over a hill and then through a docile Šumava Valley, and then up through the trees. This is a very agreeable 3km (2 miles) walk. The castle was closed for restoration at the time of research and those intending to visit it should check if it is open before setting off (perhaps at one of the two hotels in Kašperské Hory). Klatovy, the main centre of the Northern Šumava, is 43km (27 miles) further on from Kašperské Hory.

Northern Šumava: Klatovy To Železná Ruda And Domažlice

The northern part of the Šumava range is the highest, most accessible and most visited part of the mountains. Železná Ruda is the most important summer and winter resort in the Šumava, and Železná Ruda, Klatovy and Domažlice are all linked by good road and rail routes to Prague, all of which run via Plzeň (see Chapter 2). Public transport, roads and accessibility are all generally better in this part of the Šumava than in the central or southern parts. The map to use for walking in this area is called *Šumava Klatovsko*, available from bookshops, but it is not very easy to find. Bookshops in Plzeň or Klatovy may be the best place to look.

Klatovy, the biggest town in the Northern Šumava, lies midway between ✳ Plzeň and Železná Ruda, a geographical location which appealed to the founder of the town in the thirteenth century, since it is situated on the old trade routes between Bavaria and the West Bohemian industrial and commercial centre. Today, the main E53 Prague-Munich road follows the same route, running south from Plzeň through Klatovy to the German border at Železná Ruda. Although it is outside the main area of the Šumava, Klatovy's position as a road and rail junction means many travellers are likely to pass through here. There are a few hotels here, and all the places of interest in the Northern Šumava can be comfortably visited from Klatovy, whether by road or by public transport. Those who are staying here, or just passing through, could afford the town a short visit. Forming a dominant position on the skyline of Klatovy are the twin towers of the Baroque Jesuit church, which is situated at △ one corner of the town's expansive square. The church dates from the latter half of the seventeenth century, and there are some interesting furnishings inside. More interesting, however, is the grisly collection of mummified bodies of Jesuit monks, which lie in special air and temperature controlled catacombs beneath the church (entrance is via a side door). The catacombs are part of a sizeable network of interconnected three-storey passages that run under the square and outside the old town walls, which were built to allow the medieval inhabitants of Klatovy to withstand medieval sieges; however, only the catacombs under the church are open to the public. Another of Klatovy's oddities is an old Apothecary Building (U Bílého Jednorožce), next to the church on the square, with good and quite gruesome displays of the ancient medicines which were once made up and sold here. Also in the square is Klatovy's Renaissance Town Hall (1559), and another landmark, the 76m (249ft) high Black Tower, topped by four clock faces and a spire. There is a good view from the outside gallery at the top. There are other Gothic and Renaissance buildings in the square and adjoining streets; set back a little from the square, on the opposite side of it to the Town Hall, is the Church of the Nativity of our Lady (founded in 1260, but rebuilt in 1560), and next to it another tower, the White Tower (1758), which serves as a belfry of the church. Some of the fortifications around the town have survived. Eight kilometres (5 miles) to the south-west of Klatovy, in the village of **Klenová**, are the insub- ✳ stantial ruins of a Gothic castle, which now house an art gallery.

From Klatovy, one can either head south, to Železná Ruda, or west, to Domažlice. Domažlice is dealt with after the journey to Železná Ruda has been described. Two roads lead south from Klatovy to Železná Ruda, 40km (25 miles) to the south. The more interesting route is along the more minor of the two roads, which runs via Nyrsko. The main railway line also follows this road, and both run along the scenic valley of the River Úhlava. After Nyrsko, road and railway enter the Šumava range, and begin to climb. They pass by a pretty lake in the valley, before reaching **Hojsova Stráž** (900m, 2,952ft), an important winter resort, on the slopes of Mount Mustek. There are a couple of ski lifts above the town, to the left of the road. Beyond Hojsova Stráž the road goes over the low pass Špičácké Sedlo (973m, 3,192ft), before descending into the resort of Špičak. At the top of the pass is a track signpost, which points the way to the two pretty glacial lakes that lie near here, **Černé Jezero** (Black Lake), which is a 4km (2 mile) walk away along the yellow-marked track, and the smaller lake **Čertovo Jezero** (Devil's Lake), a 2km (1 mile) walk away along another yellow-marked track. A green-marked track runs between the lakes themselves. People swim in the lakes in summer and in winter, when they freeze over, they are used for skating. Both lakes, only accessible on foot, are tarns, associated with the beginnings of a glacier (though there were few glaciers in the Šumava in the Ice Age, and very little of today's landscape in the mountains is a result of glaciation).

The resort of **Špičák** stretches along the roadside from the top of the pass. The main part of the resort is at the bottom of the pass, around the railway station, and it is from here that a two-stage chairlift runs up to the summit of Mount Pancíř (1,214m, 3,983ft), via a middle station at Hofmanky Mesiztance, where there are a few more hotels. From the summit of Mount Pancíř there are good views of the northern part of the Šumava; the rounded, flattish mountain to the south, with the distinctive silhouettes of military installations and aircraft navigation towers on its summit, is Mount Gross Arber (1,457m, 4,799ft), the highest peak in the Šumava, which lies over the border in Bavaria.

Just beyond Špičák is **Železná Ruda** (790m, 2,591ft), situated at an important road junction. Although Železná Ruda is more important as a resort, the greatest opportunities for downhill skiing are actually at Špičák. Železná Ruda is bigger than Špičák, however, and has more character, with some older, wooden buildings, one of which, on the main street, houses a museum of the crafts and woodworking traditions of the people of the Šumava. Further up is the interesting twelve-sided Church of Our Lady the Helper (1732), topped by an onion-shaped cupola. A relatively easy blue-marked path links Železná Ruda with the summit of Mount Pancíř (see above).

Less than 2km (1 mile) south of Železná Ruda is a frontier crossing with Germany, at Železná Ruda-Bayerische Eisenstein on the main Prague-Munich road. Železná Ruda and Bayerische Eisenstein were once one settlement. Both names mean 'iron ore' in Czech and German (iron ore was mined here in the Middle Ages), and Železná Ruda used to be called Markt Eisenstein. There used to be one station for the town, which was situated right on the border; a line drawn down the centre of one of the benches on the station platform marked the boundary between Czech Bohemia and German Bavaria. But when the iron curtain was drawn across the Šumava, the village was split in two, and although the road crossing remained, the rail crossing was closed for 40 years. It was re-opened in the summer of 1991, a result of the sudden desire for greater contact with the West that has existed in Czechoslovakia since 1989.

Domažlice, 37km (23 miles) west of Klatovy on road 22, is the centre of the ❋ **Chod Region**. The Chod people were brought here to guard the ancient boundary between the Czechs and the Germans, and the eleven villages in which they lived were granted many royal privileges, the earliest being made by King John of Luxembourg in 1325. The Šumava forest along which the ancient border runs was a difficult obstacle for any attacker to pass, but the Chods were instrumental in defeating invading Bavarians in 1040 and again in 1431. The Chod folklore and costumes have survived. The Chod Festival is held every year in Domažlice in August, and it is the most important folklore festival in Bohemia. Here, the villagers and townsfolk of the Chod Region wear the traditional Chod costumes (the women wear colourful cotton skirts, an apron, a short jacket, and red stockings and a shawl). Chod music is also played during the festival, on traditional bagpipes, violins and clarinets. Other Chod specialities include distinctive local ceramics, which are characterised by decorative designs which include cornflowers, wild poppies and daisies.

The town square at Domažlice

Those who are not in Domažlice at festival time (normally the first weekend in August, but this varies) will have to make do with just wandering around Domažlice itself, but it is a very attractive town. Domažlice was founded in 1260 and has been the centre of the Chod Region since this time. In addition to many old streets, the arcaded square, called Náměstí Miru, is very attractive, with a solid-looking medieval gateway at one end, which dates from 1270 and which is the only remaining part of the town's medieval fortification walls. On the square is a round tower. It is possible to go up it for a view over the town (the tower leans slightly from the vertical). Another noted building on the square is the Town Hall, dating from 1891. Just down from the square is the Chod Museum, with exhibits relating to Chod culture including the mock-up of an ancient Chod cottage. Another tall round tower in the town is the old tower of the thirteenth-century castle.

Seven kilometres (4 miles) south of Domažlice, along the road towards the German border at Furth im Wald, is a popular holiday resort called **Babylon**, where there are many opportunities for fishing, swimming and watersports.

Additional Information

Places of Interest

Červená Lhota
Červená Lhota Castle
8km (5 miles) north of Kardašova Řečice
Open: April, October, 9am-12noon, 1-6pm, weekends only; May to September, daily except Monday, 8am-12noon, 1-5pm.

České Budějovice
Black Tower
Just off main square
Open: April, October, weekends only, 10am-4pm; May to September, daily except Monday, 9am-5pm.

Česky Krumlov
Česky Krumlov Castle
Open: April to October only, daily except Monday, 8am (9am April, September, October)-12noon, 1-5pm (4pm April, September, October). Gardens and courtyards always open.

Town Museum
Horní Street, just up from main square
Open: Tuesday to Friday, 9am-12noon, 12.30-4pm (6pm on Wednesday); weekends, 1-5pm.

Česky Šternberk
Česky Šternberk Castle
22km (14 miles) east of Benešov
Open: April and October, weekends only, 9am-4pm; May to September, daily except Monday, 8am (9am in September)-5pm.

Chynov Caves (Chynovská Jeskyně)
2km (1 mile) north of village of Chynov, 9km (5 miles) east of Tábor
Open: April to October only, daily except Monday, 10am-5pm.

Dívčí Kámen Castle
Accessible only on foot from village of Třísov ($^1/_2$km [1 mile] on marked path) 10km north-east of Česky Krumlov
Open: access at all times.

Domažlice
Chod Museum
Just down from main square
15 April to 15 October only, daily except Monday, 8am-12noon, 1pm-4.30pm.

Hluboká nad Vltavou
Hluboká Castle
9km (5 miles) north of České Budějovice
Open: daily except Monday, 8am-5pm (3.30pm in April and October).

Husinec
Huss Museum
In main street of village
Open: daily except Monday, 8am-
12noon, 1-4.30pm.

Jindřichuv Hradec
Town Museum
Just down from main square
Open: daily except Monday, 8.30am-
12noon, 12.30-5pm (6pm on Wednes-
day).

Kámen
Kámen Castle
20km (12 miles) east of Tábor on road 19
Open: April, October, weekends only,
9am-4pm. May to September daily 8am
(9am in September) -5pm, except
Monday.

Klatovy
Jesuit Church (catacombs),
and Tower of the Old Town Hall
Both on main square
Open: April, October, weekends only,
9am-12noon, 1-3pm; May to September,
daily except Monday, 9am-12noon,
1-5pm.

Apothecary Building
(U Bílého Jednorožce)
On main square next to Jesuit church
Open: daily except Monday 8am-4pm,
April to October only.

Klenová
Klenová Castle
8km (5 miles) south-west of Klatovy
Open: May to October only, daily except
Monday, 10am-12noon, 12.45-6pm.

Konopiště
Konopiště Castle
2km (1 mile) west of Benešov
Open: April to October only, daily
except Monday, 9am-12noon, 1-4pm
(April, October), 5pm (September), 6pm
(May to September).

Lenora
Glass Making Museum
On main road running through village
Open: Tuesday to Saturday 9am-1pm,
2-4pm; Sunday, 9am-12noon.

Ohrada Castle
2km south of Hluboká Castle, on road to
České Budějovice.
Open: daily except Monday, 8am-5pm
(3.30pm in April and October).

Orlík nad Vltavou
Orlík Castle
41km (25 miles) west of Tábor on road
19. Open: April, October, daily except
Monday, 9am-12noon, 1-4pm; May to
September, daily except Monday, 8am-
12noon, 1-5pm.

Rožmberk
Rožmberk Castle
24km (15 miles) south of Česky
Krumlov
Open: April, October, weekends only,
9am-12noon, 1-4pm; May to September,
daily except Monday, 8am (9am September)-12noon, 1-5pm.

Tábor
Town Hall
On Žižkovo Náměstí (central square)
Check Čedok for opening times. Also
houses Hussite Museum.

Třebon
Třebon Castle
Open: April, October, weekends only
9am-4pm. May to September, daily
except Monday 9am-4pm.

Vyšší Brod
Vyšší Brod Monastery
33km (20 miles) south of Česky
Krumlov
Open: 1 May to 15 October only, daily
except Monday, 9am-5pm.

Železná Ruda
Šumava Museum
On main street in village
Open: Wednesday to Sunday, 9am-5pm
(12noon Sunday).

Zlatá Koruna
Zlatá Koruna Monastery
7km (4 miles) north-east of Česky
Krumlov
Open: April to October only, daily
except Monday, 9am-4pm.

Zvíkovské Podhradíe
Zvíkov Castle
14km (25 miles) west of Milevsko on
Lake Orlík
Open: April, October, weekends only,
9am-12noon, 1-4pm; May to September,
daily except Monday, 8am (9am in
September)-12noon, 1-5pm.

Boating and Sailing

Lipno Lake, Southern Šumava; Orlík
Lake, west of Tábor; Slapy Lake, south
of Prague; all large lakes, boating,
fishing, swimming, campsites and
resorts on shores, also commercial
cruise ships in summer, passenger
ferries on Lipno Lake (all year), cruise
ships along the Vltava between Prague
and Slapy Lake, cruise ships on Lake
Orlík between Orlík and Zvíkov Castle.

Much smaller lakes: dozens of small
lakes around Třebon, limited boating on
Lake Svět in Třebon itself; Lake Jordan,
Tábor; Lake Bezdrev, south-east of
Hluboká nad Vltavou. Also at Špičák
Lakes and at Babylon in the northern
Šumava (see text entries).

A licence is always needed for fishing.
See 'Fact File'.

Tourist Information Centres and Accommodation Offices

There are Čedok offices in most towns
which deal with travel and tourist
information and can advise or book
hotel and private accommodation. The
main offices in the region are:

České Budějovice
Hroznova 21
370 01 České Budějovice
☎ (038) 32381, 34050
In summer, coach tours from České
Budějovice to places of interest in south
Bohemia are organised by this office.

Česky Krumlov
Náměstí Svorností 15 (on main square)
381 01 Česky Krumlov
☎ (0337) 2189, 3444

Domažlice
29 Náměstí Miru (on main square)
344 01 Domažlice
☎ (0189) 2266, 2713

Jindřichuv Hradec
Palackeho 136
☎ (0652) 32321

Tábor
Třída 9 Května 658
390 01 Tábor
☎ (0361) 22235, 23563

Třebon
Náměstí J Fucíka 102
☎ (0333) 2433

Also at: **Klatovy** ☎ (0186) 37419
Prachatice ☎ (0388) 21864, 22531

5

MORAVIA

M oravia is the central part of Czechoslovakia, and considering its size (comprising about a third of the area of the country), it is probably the least interesting part. In fact, most people's impressions of Moravia will be those gained from the window of a car or train as they hurry across its largely featureless countryside travelling east from Prague towards the Slovak capital, Bratislava, the High Tatra Mountains in Northern Slovakia, or even perhaps to Vienna. While not completely condemning this approach — Slovakia and Bohemia are undeniably more interesting than Moravia, with their historic towns and sometimes spectacular scenery — it has to be said that visits to Brno, the limestone scenery of the Moravian Karst immediately to the north of this city, and even perhaps to Lednice and Pernštejn Castles, will undoubtably be memorable episodes in a visit to Czechoslovakia, and should not be overlooked by those who have time to stray off the beaten track.

Most of the principal attractions in Moravia are in the south-eastern part of this ancient kingdom. This is where Brno, the capital of Moravia, is situated. Brno itself is quite interesting, and most of the attractions in the south-east can be seen on day trips from this city. This chapter is structured so that first, attractions on the way from Prague to Brno are described; then, the main part of the chapter describes Brno and the many excursions that can be made from the city; and finally, the few attractions of Northern Moravia are noted.

South-Western Moravia: Prague to Brno

Many people will want to drive straight from Prague to Brno on the motorway, or travel there by express train. However, a more leisurely and diversionary route will take travellers through south-western Moravia, through ancient towns and past a very fine château. The suggested itinerary is between Jihlava, just off the motorway, and Brno. Those travelling by road from Prague to Vienna will also travel this way. As regards travelling between Prague and Jihlava, there is the motorway, but travellers could devise a longer route through the northern part of South Bohemia (Chapter 4), from Prague to Tábor and then from Tábor east to Jihlava via Pelhřimov. The motorway between Prague, Jihlava and Brno goes within a few miles of Český Šternberk Castle.

Jihlava

The motorway from Prague to Brno skirts just past Jihlava, and, since the town is just over half way from Prague to Brno, and almost exactly half way between Prague and Vienna, it might be a good place for drivers to break their journeys between these cities. Those travelling to Vienna will come off the motorway at Jihlava and will have to drive right through the town in any case. Perhaps not so interesting in itself, Jihlava is a large town and has a few hotels in which to eat or spend the night. Motorway distances from Jihlava are 124km (77 miles) to Prague and 84km (53 miles) to Brno.

Jihlava is the principal centre of the Bohemian-Moravian highlands, which surround it to the north and south. It was founded in the twelfth century by Czechs. In 1233 a Royal town was founded very close by and became inhabited by German speakers. At the same time, silver deposits were discovered and Jihlava soon became one of the most important silver-mining centres in Europe; the Czech Royal Mint was situated here until 1400 when it was removed to Kutná Hora (see Chapter 3). In 1523 the town was destroyed in a fire and rebuilt almost from scratch. During the nineteenth century many textile factories were established in the town, giving present-day Jihlava, like many towns in Moravia, a very 'industrial' feel. The town has always had a large German population and the German composer Gustav Mahler (1860-1911) spent his childhood here.

The main square (called Náměstí Míru) in the centre of the town is one of the largest in Czechoslovakia, which is not really a recommendation. This grey, chaotic jumble of architectural styles is finally spoilt by a horrible department store stuck rather foolishly in the middle of it. A seventeenth-century plague column and two eighteenth-century fountains in the middle of the square barely improve the mess. Some of the houses around it are medieval burghers houses; one of them, in the corner of the square near the large Čedok office, houses the **Museum of the Bohemian-Moravian Highlands**, with coins, stuffed animals and other collections relating to the history of the region. On the east side of the square (near the department store) there is the Town Hall (Gothic vaulting inside) and close to it a Jesuit church (from the 1680s).

Things pick up a little once one is away from the square. Clearly visible from the square is the Gothic parish church founded in the thirteenth century, with its distinctive twin steeples. If it's open, visitors can peer into the gloomy Gothic interior and see a wrought iron baptismal font made in Nürnberg in 1599, and also Gothic statues of the Madonna (1370) and St Catherine (1400). Behind the church are Jihlava's old city walls and some woods which contain a zoo. Komenského Street leads off the square from near to the Čedok office; at number 10 is an art gallery. On the other side of the square from the department store is Obráncu Míru Street, leading past the thirteenth-century St Mary's Church to St Mary's Gate, the only remaining gate out of the five that which used to provide a way in to the old town.

Telč

Jihlava is not the best introduction to provincial Moravia, and things get a lot better when one travels south to this small market town. Because of its distinctive and pretty square, views of Telč appear on many a Čedok publicity poster or brochure. This small, friendly little town is 29km (18 miles) from Jihlava, with drivers branching off the main road 38 (E59) at the village of Stonařov, 13km (9 miles) from Jihlava and heading along a minor road through the pleasant countryside of the Bohemian-Moravian highlands. There are a couple of hotels in Telč, and it is probably a more pleasant place to stay than Jihlava, though perhaps less convenient.

Telč was founded in the thirteenth century in the vicinity of a large aristocratic estate. In 1339 this estate fell into the hands of the Lords of Hradec, who laid out the present town. Over the next few centuries, the town's present ground plan, and the two lakes on either side of it, which formed parts of the original fortifications, were laid out. Telč underwent several years of renovation in the 1950s and most of the old parts are still in pristine condition.

The main square (Náměstí Míru) is completely surrounded by medieval houses with distinctive rows of Renaissance arcades built onto the outside of them. There is a Plague Column and fountain in the square. At the narrowest end of the square is Telč Castle, built between 1550 and 1580 on the site of a previous Gothic castle and designed by an Italian architect named Baltazar Maggi of Arogno. Inside the castle grounds are courtyards, one of which is in the form of an arcaded garden; there is a small art gallery and one can see the period collections in the old rooms of the castle. Opposite the castle is the Church of St James; climb the stairs to the top of the tower for a view of the old town. From the castle one can walk down Na Baště street through the Small Gate (part of the town's old fortifications) to one of the two lakes, called Štěpnicky Rybník. A street called Palackého leads off the opposite end of the square from the castle, past the thirteenth-century tower of the Church of the Holy Ghost (the church itself has long since vanished) through the Big Gate to the lake called Ulicky Rybník; the road just along the lake has some very nice Baroque statues.

Those who decide to stay in Telč will find the pleasant South Bohemian towns of Třebon and Jindřichúv-Hradec, and the château at Červená Lhota, are within easy excursion distance; see Chapter 4.

From Telč it is a short way back to road 38 (E59) which continues towards Znojmo. From Moravské Budějovice there is a road to Jaroměřice nad Rokytnou and **Jaroměřice Castle**, a red and white building dating from the beginning of the eighteenth century, set in a very fine Baroque park which contains many statues of mythological gods and godesses. Returning to the main road at Moravské Budějovice, it is another 31km (19 miles) to Znojmo.

Znojmo

Famed for its fine wines and pickled gherkins, Znojmo is the centre of a rich agricultural region, a medieval town in the southernmost part of Moravia very close to the Austrian border. It is situated on the Jihlava-Vienna road, the E59 (road 38), 65km (40 miles) from Telč.

Just under 1,000 years ago, Prince Břetislav I founded a castle above the River Dyje at Znojmo, to protect ancient trade routes, and a town grew up around this; in 1226 it was proclaimed a Royal town. In the thirteenth century three monasteries were founded in the town and fortification walls were built. In the late Middle Ages Znojmo was an important mercantile centre, its prosperity based on wines produced from the vineyards in the surrounding areas. In the 1850s the cultivation of cucumbers and the already thriving wine making activities meant that Znojmo became an important food processing centre.

Fountain in the square at Telč

The old part of the town is immediately to the east of the deep valley of the River Dyje; the two distinctive high spires of the old town are at either end of its main square, called Náměstí Míru. At the north end is the tower of the Town Hall , 69m (226ft) high and dating from 1445; much of the Gothic Town Hall was damaged in World War II, but this remarkable tower remains and there is a good view over Znojmo from the top. Along the square itself are burghers

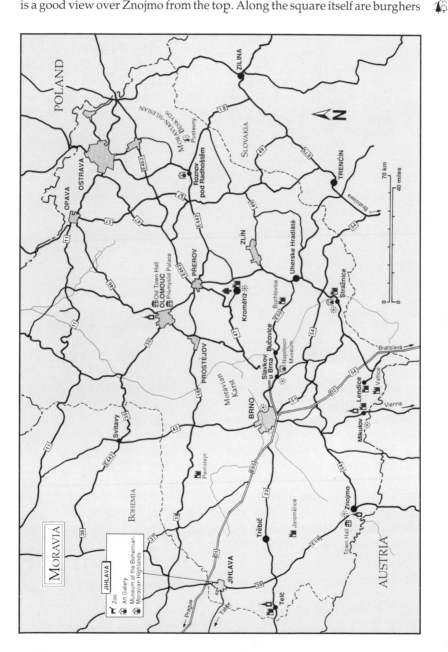

houses from the fifteenth to the seventeenth centuries, many of which were owned by local wine magnates. The wine cellars under the houses were connected by underground passageways, some of which are accessible — the entrance is opposite the Town Hall tower. At the other end of the square is a Capuchin Monastery with Wolf's Tower (or Vik's Tower) next to it; this tower is one of the few remaining parts of the fourteenth-century fortifications. There is an art gallery on the square, close to the monastery.

Take the street called Velká Mikulášska that leads off the square; this road brings one to St Nicholas' Church (built between 1338 and 1500) with St Wenceslas Chapel (completed in 1521) next to it. There is a good view of the deep valley of the River Dyje from here. Finally, there are pleasant walks to be made along the promenades which were once the medieval fortifications, and also along the valley sides immediately below the castle.

The Austrian border is reached 10km (6 miles) south of Znojmo, on the E59; alternatively, Brno is reached after travelling 61km (38 miles) along road 54 (after the village of Pohořelice this road becomes road 52 (E461).

Brno

The south-eastern part of Moravia boasts the biggest concentration of things to do and see and it is to here that visitors who only wish to spend a short time in the region should head. Brno is the main centre of south-eastern Moravia, the capital of Moravia itself and the third largest city in Czechoslovakia. Not only are there a number of things to see and do in Brno itself, it is also a convenient centre from which to see a variety of other places, most notably the fabulous limestone caves and scenery of the Moravian Karst a short distance to the north of the city; these attractions are described in the next section.

Brno is 196km (122 miles) from Prague on Czechoslovakia's principal motorway. There are frequent trains between Prague and Brno which take about $3^1/_2$ hours. Many of these trains are international services: there are through trains from Brno to Berlin, Budapest, Vienna, Warsaw and many other East European cities. Orientation is fairly easy: Brno's two principal landmarks, the cathedral and the castle, overlook the Old Town, which is called Brno-Město. The railway station is at the bottom of the slight hill that the Old Town is built on.

The site of Brno was occupied by Slavic peoples in the fifth century. A thousand years ago an imperial castle was founded here and in 1243 Brno was proclaimed a town; it has been the capital of Moravia since 1643. Its rich industrial heritage dates back to the eighteenth century, when textile works were founded here; now, there are many engineering and electrical works, and important universities. The scientist Gregor Mendel (1822-1884) and the composer Leoš Janáček (1854-1928) lived in Brno. The city was badly damaged during bombing raids in World War II largely because of the high concentration of industry which was located here, a feature in common with most towns in Moravia.

One of Brno's prime attractions are the exhibitions which are held here throughout the year in the specially-built exhibition grounds, which attract hundreds of thousands of visitors from all over the world. There is a great number of hotels in the city to cater for these visitors, but expect prices in restaurants, hotels etc to be higher than in other parts of provincial Czechoslovakia. However, the incidence of English being spoken by staff in hotels, tourist and transport offices and restaurants is very high.

A Walking Tour of Brno's Old Town

Brno's Old Town has precious few medieval monuments, and those who come to Brno looking for old-world charm will be disappointed. Nevertheless, there are some interesting curiosities, and the heart of this city is more bustling and lively than many other provincial cities in Czechoslovakia. There are a number of museums, and there is a lively theatre and nightlife in the town. The town, like Prague, has strong musical traditions. In the 1920s, most of the operas of the composer Leoš Janáček had their premiere in the Mahen Theatre, which still stages concerts and plays. Janáček dedicated a number of works to the city, and made musical arrangements of Moravian folk songs. His name is also remembered in the modern Janáček Theatre, opened in 1965.

A sensible and convenient place to begin a tour of Brno is the main railway station (Hlavní Nádraží), on Tatranská Street at the bottom of Špilberk Hill. Streets leading off Tatranská Street opposite the station lead up through the old town towards the castle on Špilberk Hill. The main street leading up the hill, immediately to the right of the Čedok office, is called Třida Vitězství. Just up this street is Kapucínské Náměstí (formerly the coal market), a small square recognisable by the row of saints along the frontage of the old **Capuchin Monastery**. The monastery church itself is inaccessible, but a door to the right of the church leads to its crypt; here, underground, and ventilated by a specially devised system of air shafts, is a truly bizarre but curiously fascinating collection of dozens of mummified bodies of old members or benefactors of the monastery, and of the local nobility and important Brno citizens. The bodies date mostly from the seventeenth and eighteenth centuries, and are not mummified in the Egyptian manner with layers of bandages but are, for the most part, in a near naked state. Some bodies are in glass coffins, some are just lying on the ground behind wire cages, with their heads supported by bricks. The bodies of monks were laid here wearing their cassocks.

There is an interesting view across the square to the cathedral. The steps up from the square are an entrance to the Moravian Museum (see below). However, a short lane leads up from Kapucínské Náměstí to the square called **Zelny Trh**, which means Cabbage Market — and, true to its name, a colourful fruit, flower and vegetable market is held in this square every morning 6 days a week. This square has been the city's principal market place for over 700 years. On the right, at the point where the lane enters the square, is the **Reduta** **Theatre**, dating from the eighteenth century, with a pleasant façade. Mozart

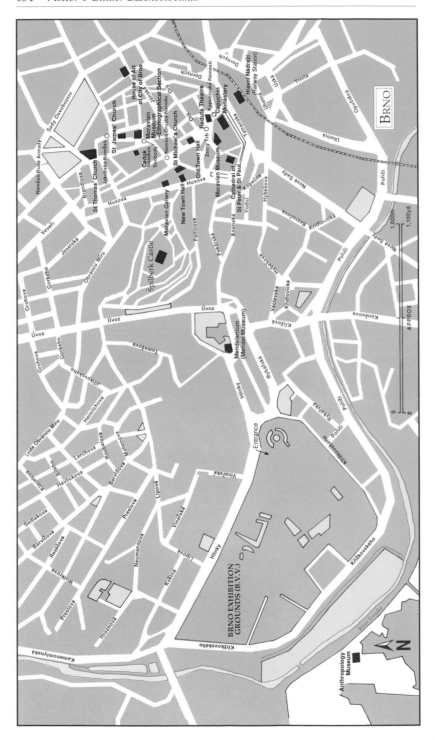

appeared here as a conductor in 1767, when he was 11 years old. Many other old palaces and burghers houses line the square. In the middle of the square, amidst the amiable chaos of the market stalls, is the seventeenth-century Parnassus Fountain. The statue is of Hercules. Carp used to be bred in the fountain's waters and were sold at Christmas time. Also on the square is the Dietrichstejn Palace (1760), housing the main part of the South Moravian Museum (see below). The Russian commander who fought Napolean at the Battle of Austerlitz near Brno in 1805 established his headquarters here.

Paths to the left lead up a steep rise to the **Cathedral of St Peter and St Paul**, on Petrov Hill. This was the site of Brno's first castle, built in the eleventh century, and established by the Moravian branch of the Přemyslid Royal dynasty (who also governed Prague in the early Middle Ages). The present Gothic appearance of this church is deceptive: the Gothic exterior actually dates from the early part of this century, though the cathedral itself dates from the fourteenth century and has been rebuilt and restyled many times. The interior is bright and airy; the oldest object inside is a stone statue of the Madonna and Child, made in 1300. At 11am every day, the cathedral bells always chime. This is associated with the story that, in 1645, the Swedish army (passing this way during the Thirty Years War) tried to take Brno. The Swedish General became annoyed by Brno's apparent unassailability, and vowed that if he did not take the city by midday, he would give up and go home. At 11 o'clock, the city was on the verge of capitulating, but the cathedral bell-ringer suddenly had a fit of inspiration and rung the midday bells, even though he did not know anything of the Swedish general's vow. On hearing

Vegetable market in Brno

the bells, the Swedes gave up their onslaught on the city, the bell-ringer was the hero of the day and Brno was saved. Immediately below the cathederal, on the slopes of the hill, is the tiny **Denis Park**. Here there are preserved medieval walls and a obelisk erected in 1818 to commemorate the end of the Napoleonic Wars.

Walk back to the Cabbage Market. A tiny road called Radnická leads off from the square, on the opposite side to the Reduta Theatre. This brings one very quickly to the **Old Town Hall** (Stará Radnice), on the left as one walks up this street. The Town Hall has been situated here since the foundation of the town in 1243; much of the present-day building dates from the sixteenth century. Look above the main entrance door: one of the pinnacles of the ornamental portal is crooked. The legend behind its curved appearance is that the city govenors did not pay the architect the promised sum for his building work on the Town Hall, so the architect got his own back by sculpting a crooked pinnacle. Just inside the door, hanging from the ceiling, is the Brno Dragon, which is not a dragon at all but a large stuffed crocodile, a gift from the Turkish Sultan Ahmed I to the Archduke Matthias, presented after the signing of a peace treaty between the Turks and the Habsburgs in 1606. Matthias gave it to the city 2 years later as a bribe, to encourage the Czech nobility of Moravia to accept him as the sovereign. Also hanging in the passageway is the Brno wheel, made in the seventeenth century and rolled by its maker the 48km (30 miles) from Lednice, in Southern Moravia, to Brno, in order to win a bet. Both the wheel and the dragon are symbols of Brno; the 'Brno Dragon' appears on the bottle labels of Brno beer. This building ceased its functions as a town hall in 1935. Its medieval rooms are now used for concerts and temporary art exhibitions. The observation gallery of the town hall tower (1577) is open in the summer months.

At the top of Radnická Street is Panská Street; turn left along this road which leads into Náměstí Družby Národu (the old Fish Market). The building that dominates this square is the **New Town Hall**, the oldest buildings of which used to house a monastery that was founded in 1228; the pleasant old court- yard is open to the public. Also in this square is **St Michael's Church**, which was founded as the church of the aforementioned monastery, but which was reconstructed in Baroque style; there are carved figures of saints along the outside.

A street at the far end of the square called Zámečnícká leads to the right and brings the walker to **Náměstí Svobody**, Brno's main square, lined with mostly nineteenth-century buildings that now house shops. Česká Street, the most important shopping street in Brno, leads from the opposite end of the square. 9 Května Street runs parallel to it. Along this street on the right is **St James' Church**, built between 1314 and 1480, with a sixteenth-century steeple 91m (298ft) high. It is celebrated for its pure Gothic appearance. Decoration inside includes an early medieval cross, a stone pulpit dating from 1525 and various tombstones. This road continues on past the church to Náměstí Rudé Armády (Red Army Square). Just before the square is **St Thomas' Church**, a Gothic foundation rebuilt in the seventeenth century. The buildings next to it were once a monastery associated with the church, which now house a gallery. Red Army Square itself is large, with parks in its centre, and, to the right, a large memorial to the Soviet Red Army which liberated Brno from the Nazis.

Other Attractions

Špilberk Castle, is on a hill overlooking the Old Town, which spreads out to the east of it. It was founded by Přemysl Otakar II, the King of Bohemia, in 1270. Through the centuries it was altered from a medieval fortress to a prison and then a barracks. It successfully resisted many seiges but was captured by Napoleon. At the time of research (November 1990) the castle was completely closed for restoration work, and is scheduled for re-opening between 1992 and 1994. When it re-opens visitors can see dungeons, an art gallery, a lookout tower and the Museum of the City of Brno. Whether the castle is open or not, there is a good view over Brno from the ramparts.

Brno's commercial and industrial activities are enhanced by the holding of many trade fairs in the city, in the BVV (Brněnské Veletrhy A Vystavi-Brno Trade Fair) grounds. These lie in the valley beyond Špilberk Castle, on the north side of the River Svratka. The first exhibition took place here in 1928; more pavillions were built in the 1950s. There are about 15 trade fairs each year, attracting 5,000 exhibitors from over 50 countries, and attended by a total of $1^1/_2$ million visitors each year who come from all over the world. The exhibition season is between March and November. The exhibition area is interesting in itself, consisting of modern buildings, fountains and greenery, and normally it is possible to see around the exhibitions themselves. Regular exhibitions are concerned with consumer goods and engineering goods but also include anything from pet shows to book affairs.

Museums and Galleries

There is a rich collection of museums and galleries in Brno. In the **Moravian Museum** one can see geological, zoological and archaeological collections, and exhibits relating to the history of Brno (main part at Zelny Trh no 8); the ethnographical section is at 1, Gagarinova Street, and includes exhibits of Moravian folk costumes; the Anthropology section is housed in a pavillion in a park situated the other side of the Exhibition Grounds. On Mendelovo Náměstí is the **Mendelanium**, an old monastery established in 1322 where the founder of modern genetics, Gregor Mendel, lived and worked. It now houses a museum of Mendel's life and work. One can also see inside the old monastery church. Leoš Janáček started his career as a musician here. The museum is situated between the Old Town and the Exhibition Grounds.

The **Museum of the City of Brno** is situated in the castle. The **Moravian Gallery**, at 14, Husova Street has exhibits of Czech and European art from many periods. The **House of Art of the City of Brno** (Dum Unmění), on Malinovského Náměstí 2, is one of the largest art galleries in Czechoslovakia. A smaller gallery, the **Gallery of the City of Brno**, is situated in the castle.

Exploring South-East Moravia; Excursions from Brno

The south-eastern part of Moravia is definitely the most interesting part of this ancient kingdom, and there are a number of worthwhile excursions that can be made from Brno into the nearby towns and countryside. When considering possible excursions from Brno, do not overlook towns such as Telč or Znojmo in the south-west of Moravia or Olomouc and Kroměříž, further to the north, which although further away than the places described here, still present nonetheless viable and worthwhile possibilities.

The Moravian Karst

The region of limestone caves and scenery of the Moravian Karst (Moravsky Kras) is easily the most popular excursion from Brno. The boundary of the Moravian Karst, designated a Protected Landscape Region, encloses an area about 25km (15$^1/_2$ miles) long and 6km (4 miles) wide, stretching in a north-south direction immediately to the north-east of Brno. Its attractions include steep, forested valleys and ravines, and hundreds of underground limestone caves, four of which have been opened to the public. Both motorists and walkers wishing to see this area should hunt around Brno's bookshops for the map *Moravsky Kras*, which shows all the locations of the attractions described in this section, as well as the walking tracks that link them.

All the caves are seen on guided tours. There are English translations of what the guide says, and other information in English, available at each cave itself and at the information centre. The caves are very popular; be prepared for long waits in summer and try to avoid visiting the caves at weekends in summer. Make use of the fact that the caves open very early in the morning — a couple of early starts from Brno should avoid the worst of the delays. Also note that all the caves close for the day in the early afternoon. The temperature inside most caves is a constant 7°C (45°F).

The starting point for any visit to this relatively small area is the town of **Blansko**, a short distance north of Brno. In the castle in Blansko there is a museum of the Moravian Karst and of the town's history as a mining community. There are hotels in Blansko, and in other places in the area, but the caves are easily and most convieniently seen on day trips from Brno. The most important area of the Moravian Karst is due east of Blansko, reached by a road that runs east from that town into the hills, along the valley of the River Punkva. The roads and walking tracks in the area pass through steep sided limestone gorges, and in many places one can ofter see rivers coming out of the limestone cliff face, or the entrances to caves which have been closed off. The more specific attractions of the area are listed below:

 The **Punkva Caves** (Punkevní Jeskyně), are the largest and most popular caves in Czechoslovakia. The Punkva Caves are a system of caves over 20km (12 miles) in length, though the length open to the public is 2$^1/_2$km (1$^1/_2$ miles). The first part of the tour takes one through fine stalactite and stalagmite features before coming out into the open air and the stunning Macocha Abyss;

this enormous pit is 140m (459ft) deep, with sheer, vertical walls, formed by the collapse of the roof of a former cave, thus leaving the top of the pit, way above, open to the sky. One of the two tiny lakes at the bottom is 25m (82ft) deep! The entrances to more caves, many of them unexplored, open from the walls. The abyss has a unique climate, which is unusually mild and allows many species of plants and insects to thrive here. Earliest records of the abyss being climbed in date from 1723 when two monks lowered themselves down from the top on hoists. The name of the abyss (*macocha* means 'stepmother' in Czech) comes from a seventeenth-century folk tale, which tells of how a wicked step-mother from the nearby village of Vilémovice got rid of her step-daughter by throwing her into the ravine. The girl, however, landed in some bushes on a ledge, and survived; angry villagers then punished the step-mother by throwing her into the ravine.

After the abyss, the tour plunges back into the rock and an incredible trip by boat along the underground River Punkva, the boat barely narrow enough to navigate the twists and turns of the river, the rock ceiling never far above one's head; there is a break of journey along the way for some more stalactites. The boats then emerge from the rock next to the entrance to the cave. After seeing this cave, it is not difficult to tell why it is so popular!

The **Sloup-Šošuvka Cave** (Sloupsko-Šošuvské Jeskyně) is near the village of Sloup in the northern part of the area. This system consits of caves on two different levels, which are connected by holes, and there are many other stalactite and stalagmite forms. Many archaeological finds have been made here, including the skeletons of cave lions and bears, and, in a cave nearby, the jaw bone of a Neandertal man. Concerts are sometimes held in this cave because of its good acoustics.

The main feature of the **Kateřinská Cave** (Kateřinská Jeskyně), which has no water running through it (the streams have long since taken different routes), is the huge dome, 96m (315ft) long and 20m (66ft) high. There are many other beautiful limestone rock formations, which have been given bizarre names such as 'The Dome of Chaos' and 'The Bamboo Forest', and another one called called 'The Witch', which is lit by a ghostly red light and which, with a bit of imagination, resembles a witch flying on a broomstick.

At the village of Ostrov u Macochy is the entrance to **Balcarka Cave** (Balcarka Jeskyně). This is the smallest cave in the Moravian Karst, but still worth visiting.

The bottom part of the Machocha Abyss was seen on a tour of the Punkva Caves, but there is also a road to the top, from where there is a stunning view over this remarkable feature.

The physical geography of this region is a result of the actions of water flowing in underground streams, which dissolves and then carries away in solution the carbonate minerals that make up limestone, a very soft, sedimentary rock that is easily weathered. Moreover, limestone is geologically composed of many vertical and horizontal cracks, which means that the surface streams can easily disappear into the ground through a 'swallow hole' (a vertical crack) that has been dissolved and widened by the actions of water.

In the rock itself, water flows along horizontal cracks, dissolving the rock and hollowing it out to form subterraneous tunnels and channels. Boats take tourists along such an underground waterway in the Punkva Caves. In this way, cave systems are composed of several relatively level storeys that are linked by vertical or near-vertical shafts. Over time, the water may take another route inside the rock, leaving previous channels and tunnels dry; there has been no water in the Katerinská Cave for millions of years, and the old underground channels through which water once flowed can now be walked through by visitors. The limestone in this area is classified by geologists as being 'Devonian' limestone (ie it is about 350 million years old). The features seen take tens of millions of years to form, and are in many cases still being altered and changed by the actions of water. The existance of some of the caves has been known for centuries; other caves have only been discovered more recently, and many parts of the underground waterways are still to be explored. During World War II, the caves were used as a hiding place by members of the Czech resistance, and an illegal printing press was even set up inside one of them. Between Blansko and Brno (and on the railway linking the two towns) is the village of Adamov, from where walkers can get to grips with some of Moravia's best scenery by walking up the craggy limestone valley called Josefovské Udolí for 6km (4 miles) to the village of Křtiny, home to a Baroque church of pilgrimage.

♜ Pernštejn Castle

Pernštejn Castle (Hrad Pernštejn), 32km (20 miles) north-west of Brno, is probably Moravia's most visited medieval castle. It is reached by taking road 43 (E461) which heads due north of Brno, towards Svitavy, Blansko and Boskovice, and turning off this road after 10km (6 miles) and passing through the towns of Kuřim and Tišnov on a more minor road before reaching the town of Nedvědice. Here, a country road leads to the left, and Pernštejn is the first village one reaches on this road. Pernštejn is also linked to Brno by a railway line.

Pernštejn Castle is noted for the fact that it is one of the best preserved and biggest castles in Czechoslovakia. It has a very distinctive skyline and sits on a low spur between two valleys. Founded in the thirteenth century as a fortress by the Lords of Pernštejn, it was enlarged and rebuilt through the centuries but has never been turned into a country house or château, a fate which has befallen many castles in Czechoslovakia. The Swedish Army tried to capture it in 1645, but failed to do so despite a long seige. Barborka Tower is the oldest part of the castle; around the original palace more rooms (including the impressive Hall of Knights) and chapels were built, culminating in the construction of fortification walls. Inside there are period collections from the various eras when the castle was lived in, and some dungeons.

Pody Jí

Pody Jí is the valley of the River Dyje and the picturesque area surrounding it, well to the south of Brno, near the Austrian border. Although this area is a fair distance from Brno, motorists at any rate can accomplish much of the 49km (30 miles) journey between Brno and Lednice, the main place of interest, by motorway. The main points of interest are around the towns of Lednice, Valtice and Milulov, which lie just to the west of Břeclav, the largest town in the region.

At the village of Lednice is **Lednice Château**, for six centuries the family seat of the Austrian Liechtenstein family. The grandeur of their château, one of the most visited in Czechoslovakia, refects the amount of land they once held in this part of Southern Moravia and nearby northern Austria. The present appearance of the château dates from the 1840s, when it was rebuilt in a romantic neo-Gothic style (the Schwarzenberg family did the same thing to Hluboká Castle, in Southern Bohemia, at around the same time). The richly-carved wooden ceilings and other decorations in the interior of the castle are similar to those at Hluboká. There is also a hunting and fishing museum here. Next to the château is a cast-iron glass house, almost 100m (328ft) long, built in 1843, and full of exotic flowers and plants. The castle's garden's are superb; they include a number of fish ponds, now important bird sanctuaries, a tall minaret (1802) and Jan's Castle (Janov Hrad), a romantic folly built as a ruin.

There is another Liechtenstein castle and park at the wine-making village of **Valtice**, 8km (5 miles) to the south; it is older but less interesting than the one at Lednice, and although there is a certain amount of interest in its ornate woodwork and ceiling paintings, more fun might be had in the hotel and restaurant which now take up some of the building, where red wine made from vines grown in the château's gardens can be tasted. The wine-making traditions are also evident in the town of **Mikulov**, 12km (7 miles) to the north-west, and a crossing point into Austria on the Brno-Vienna road. The rebuilt castle above the town houses a museum of viticulture. The town was once in the hands of the Austrian feudal magnates the Dietrichsteins, who built a number of chapels in the surrounding countryside but whose one contribution to the town itself is the Baroque church St Anne (sv. Anna). Mikulov has a strong tradition as a Jewish town, and is home to an old synagogue (Husová Street) and a medieval Jewish Cemetery (Židovsky Hřbitov) on Brněnská Street.

Dolní Věstonice is a village just off the road from Mikulov back to Brno. One of central Europe's most important archaeological sites is situated nearby. In 1950, archaeologists discovered traces of a 20,000-year-old settlement, and found some very early ceramic objects and mammoth and ivory bones that were used by hunters. Many of the finds that were made here are exhibited in a museum in the village but the most noteworthy have been moved to the Moravian museum in Brno.

A circular tour of Brno - Lednice - Valtice - Dolní Věstonice - Brno involves a road journey of about 118km (73 miles), 72km (45 miles) of which is by motorway. Alternatively, those who are travelling by road between Brno and

Opposite: (top) Pernštejn Castle; (bottom) Lednice Château

Vienna or Bratislava could see this region while journeying between these cities. Lednice, for example, is only a short distance from a junction on the Brno-Bratislava motorway. Otherwise, there are a number of hotels and campsites in the area.

East From Brno

A similarly lengthy tour using Brno as a starting point is along the E50 (road 50) which heads east from the city towards Uherské Hradiště and Trenčín. There are a number of places of interest along this road.

Twenty-one kilometres (13 miles) along this road is the small commuter town of **Slavkov u Brna**, better known throughout the world by its old German name, Austerlitz . It was on the rolling hills near here that Napoleon fought the combined armies of Russia and Austria at the 'Battle of The Three Emperors' on 2 December 1805, and won one of his most famous victories: the French army was inferior in numbers to the Austrian-Russian army to the tune of 22,000 men, yet Napoleon lost 9,000 men to the defeated army's 26,000. Napoleon's forces had actually captured Vienna only about 97km (60 miles) to the south, three weeks beforehand, and had pushed the Russian and Austrian armies back towards the town of Austerlitz, where the emperor set a trap for the enemy forces which they were led into with ease. Despite Austrian attempts to cut off Napoleon's supply lines from Vienna, the French leader routed the allies and forced them to surrender 2 days later. The surrender was signed at the Baroque château in the town of Austerlitz, now Slavkov u Brna (a formal peace treaty was later signed at Bratislava). The château is at one end of the main shopping street in the centre of this small town; in it, there is a small but excellent museum of Napoleon in general and the Battle of Austerlitz in particular. One can also see some of the period rooms of the château, now housing an art gallery, and behind it, there are some interesting Baroque gardens. Bones of dead soldiers and a complete skeleton have been unearthed from the actual battlefield, about $8^1/_2$km (5 miles) west of Slavkov: a monument called *Pracky Kopec* (the Mohyla Míru, or Monument of Peace), built in 1912 on a low hill, overlooks the battle site, though unfortunately a good map must be used to find it (it is on a road leading south from the village of Prace). It is clearly shown on the map Jižní Morava, number 11 in the *Poznáváme Československo* series.

The next town one passes through travelling east from Slavkov is **Bučovice**. The unimpressive exterior of the château here yields some surprises inside, where one can see effusive Rococo interiors and ceiling paintings. This château is another country home of the Liechtenstein family, who owned Lednice. Further on again is **Buchlovice**, with another château, this time a smaller one once owned by the Berchtold family, still replete with its Rococo furnishings.

A short distance beyond Buchlovice is Uherské Hradiště, near where there have been many archaeological finds from the Great Moravian Empire, which flourished in the eighth and ninth century and included much of present-day Czechoslovakia, as well as parts of Austria. From Uherské Hradiště, road 50 continues east across the White Carpathians to Trenčín in the Váh Valley (see Chapter 7). Alternatively, one can head south from Uherské Hradiště to Strážnice, home to one of Czechoslovakia's most famous folklore festivals. The festivities are held on the last weekend in June in the grounds of the castle in the town. Those who are not in Strážnice at the time of the festival can see round the folk museum in the castle, which includes exhibits of locally made musical instruments, ceramics, and craftwork. Nearby is an open air museum called Muzeum Vesnice Jihovychodní Moravy, where many houses and other folk architecture of the region have been rebuilt on a growing site in the town.

Northern Moravia

Although there are two pleasant ranges of low mountains, the Beskyds and the Jeseniks, the greater part of Northern Moravia is concerned with industry. The air and water pollution caused by the intense concentration of industrial plants and coal mines here have laid waste to the surrounding countryside, creating the biggest ecological disaster area in the whole of Czechoslovakia. The previous regime simply stamped hard on any complaints made by underground environmental groups, and only now, after 40 years of what could almost be described as environmental rape, is something actually being done about the situation, although many millions of dollars must be pumped into the area to ameliorate the situation. The largest town in the region is Ostrava, near the Polish border, which is the centre of the Czechoslovak iron and steel industry. Many other towns have grown up around it, to form the country's largest industrial connurbation. The first ironworks was founded here in 1828 and now the region produces many steel products, and there are many chemical, textile and engineering factories that are powered by electricity generated by the burning of locally mined coal. It is steadily eating away at the few historic buildings there are in Opava, and, more importantly, the valuable ancient buildings in Krakow, Poland's most historic city, which is a short distance away across the border. There is really very little reason for tourists to visit this region; those that do travel there can reach Ostrava by air from Prague. Opava is a smaller town to the west of this connurbation, and it is similarly industrialised. Opava is the historic capital of the kingdom of Silesia, most of which is now part of Poland.

The two most interesting places to visit in Northern Moravia are the historic towns of Olomouc and Kroměříž. Neither town is close to Ostrava or the steel making area, although Olomouc itself is fairly industrialised. Both can be visited from Brno in a fairly long day's excursion. Alternatively, Olomouc lies on a road route between Prague and the High Tatras, a road which continues on from the city over the Moravian-Silesian Beskid mountains, into Northern Slovakia.

Olomouc

Olomouc is billed in many places as the 'second most interesting town in ❋ Czechoslovakia', which it is not; nevertheless, this industrial city in the centre of Moravia has a fair amount to offer visitors. By road, it is 77km (48 miles) from Brno, virtually the whole distance covered by motorway or dual carriageway (a motorway is steadily being built all the way between the two cities). Fast buses and not-so-fast trains also link the two cities. The growing industrial suburbs of the town now overwhelm its old buildings and its long history. The town has been the seat of a bishop since 1063, and in 1469 King Matthias of Hungary was proclaimed the Czech king here. Olomouc was the capital of Moravia until the 1640s, when it was destroyed by the Swedish army in the Thirty Years War, an event which led to the rise of Brno as the modern capital of Moravia. In Habsburg times, Olomouc was an important garrison town, a tradition which continued into the Communist era when the town was the unwilling (but grudgingly accepting) host to the largest concentration of Soviet troops on Czechoslovak soil. Now, there are important metal working and chemical industries here. One of the most important modern factories produces chocolate, and the smell of gently burning chocolate hangs in the air for much of the time!

Unlike many other cities in Czechoslovakia, Olomouc is very spread out, with the main train and bus stations a fair distance from the town's centre, and the sights themselves sprinkled liberally over a surprisingly large area. Good use could be made of the city's tram system, which at the time of writing, was used differently to other tram systems in the country: tickets are not bought at kiosks or shops, but on the tram itself (use one ticket for each journey taken, whatever the distance travelled). The town's hosting of the summer flower festivals, and also a Spring Music Festival in May, means it has a cultural life and vibrancy to rival that of Brno. There are a number of hotels here, a couple of which are very good, and which may provide drivers with a night's rest on the way from Prague to the High Tatras.

The square at the centre of the town is Náměstí Míru, with the picturesque **Old Town Hall** in its centre. This is a white structure, adorned with gables, ⌂ mini-spires and a tall, square clock tower, that has been expanded and altered from its foundation in the fourteenth century. The most recent addition to the Town Hall is the astronomical clock, beneath the tower. The first clock on the wall of the Town Hall was built in the fifteenth century, but it was completely destroyed in the war, and the present one, built in 1955, is an interesting relic of Stalinist days. It is, in fact, a modern version of the clock in Prague, and it is much easier to read! The other main features of the square are two fountains, and a huge, eight-sided group of statues, called *The Holy Trinity*, which dates from 1754. The neighbouring square, Náměstí Rude Armády, is modern but there are a few Renaissance buildings here, and another Baroque column.

From *The Holy Trinity* group of statues, walk down 28 Října Street, and turn right along 8 Května Street to **St Maurice's Church**, the biggest Gothic building in Olomouc. Its huge organ, built in 1745, has over 2,300 pipes but this does little to lighten the heavy, gloomy aspect of this thick walled building. From the church, continue along Pekařská, which leads into Denisova. A fairly lengthy stroll (or a tram ride) along this street — keep going, across another square (Náměstí Republiky), with a museum on the left, and then along 1 Máje Street — brings one to **St Wenceslas Cathedral**, a very impressive but sombre Gothic building, set back a little from the main road. The present appearance of the cathedral dates from the 1880s, though it was founded in the twelfth century. The steeple is over 100m (328ft) tall. Next to the cathedral is the **Přemyslid Palace**, which was opened to the public in 1989, after extensive archaeological work had been carried out here. It was established in 1063, as a residence for the newly ordained bishop of the city, and many of its finely carved stone Romanesque arches and columns, and a chapel, decorated with early medieval designs and vaulting, remain.

East From Olomouc Into The Beskyds Mountains

Those who are continuing east from Olomouc to Žilina and the mountains in Northern Slovakia (see Chapter 7) will travel through the Moravian-Silesian Beskyds, a low range of mountains on the border between Slovakia and Moravia, south of (and, in terms of contrast, a million miles away from) the

Watching the astro-nomical clock at Olomouc

Ostrava region. The road through the Beskyds is numbered 35 (also the E462), which passes through the town of **Rožnov pad Radhoštěm**, where the biggest *skansen* (outdoor folk museum) in Czechoslovakia has been constructed. Here, old timber buildings and a whole village have been recreated (or moved from their original positions) to show how Moravian hill farming peasants lived in previous centuries. Seven kilometres (4 miles) beyond Rožnov pod Radhoštěm a road leads off from the main road to the left into the hills and the small town of **Pustevny**, a major resort in these mountains, where there is a chairlift up to Ráztoka. A popular walk in these mountains is from Pustevny up to the summit of Mount Radhošt (1,129m, 3,703ft), 3km (2 miles) from the town, where there is a Baroque chapel, a group of statues and an excellent view over the Beskyds. Alternatively, the return trip to Brno could be made via Kroměříž.

South From Olomouc To Koměříž

Kroměříž is 41km (25 miles) south of Olomouc by road, and the town has been the summer residence of the Archbishop of Olomouc for seven centuries. Kroměříž, however, is a very different town to its industrial neighbour to the north, and it is an excellent place in which to unwind for a couple of hours or so before returning to Brno, 54km (33 miles) to the west (along road 47 and then the D1 motorway). The central square, Velké Náměstí, is lined with Renaissance houses, but more interesting is the splendid château nearby, which has a good art collection (including a Van Dyck portrait of the English King Charles I), and paintings by Titian, Cranach and Veronese amongst others. The interior rooms of the château are also well worth seeing. Kroměříž is, moreover, well-known for its Baroque gardens; adjoining the château is the Podzámecká Garden, with many pavillions, colonnades and statues, and the larger Květná Gardens (entrance from Gen. Svobody Street, a short distance from the square, in the other direction), which contain a big Baroque French park, with beautifully laid-out flower beds, arcades, an octagonal garden pavillion and many statues. The Bishops of Olomouc are buried in the Gothic church of St Maurice, just up from the château on Pilařova Street.

Additional Information

Places of Interest

Brno
Moravian Museum
Zelny Trh and Kapucínské Náměstí
Open: 9am-6pm.

Mendelanium
(Mendel Museum)
Mendelovo Náměstí
Open: 9am-6pm, daily except Monday.
Closed in winter.

Moravian Gallery
14, Husova Street
Open: 10am-6pm, daily except Monday.

Anthropology Museum
In a pavillion in Piarky Park, west of city centre. Open: daily except Monday, 8.30am-5pm, closed in winter.

Capuchin Monastery
Kapucínské Náměstí
Open: Tuesday to Saturday, 9-11.45am,

2-4.45pm. Sunday: 11-11.45am, 2-4.45pm.

Castles

Castles described in the text have the following opening times: April, October: weekends only, 9am-4pm. May to August, daily except Monday, 8am-5pm. September, daily except Monday, 9am-5pm. November to March, closed. This includes châteaux and castles at: Telč, Jaroměřice, Pernštejn, Lednice, Valtice, Buchlovice, Kroměříž. Stražnice Castle is completely closed in April and October.

Dolní Věstonice
Archaeological Museum
Open: May to September, daily except Monday, 8am-4pm. Rest of the year: weekends only, 8am-4pm.

Jihlava
Museum of Bohemian-Moravian Highlands
Náměstí Miru. Open: daily except Monday, 9am-5pm (1pm on Saturday).

Kroměříž
Gardens
Open: from 7am to 4.30pm daily.

Mikulov
Castle in centre of town
Open: April to September, daily except Monday, 8am-4pm.

Moravian Karst Caves
(Winter opening times are from 1 October to 31 March).

Punkva Caves
Summer: Tuesday to Friday, 7am-3.15pm; weekends, 7am-2.45pm. Winter: Tuesday to Friday, 7.30am-1.45pm; weekends, 7.30am-2.45pm.

Balcarka Caves
Summer: daily except Monday, 7am-3.30pm. Winter: daily except Monday, 7.30am-2pm.

Kateřinská Cave
Summer: daily except Monday, 7am-3.45pm. Winter: daily except Monday, 7.30am-2.45pm.

Sloup-Šošuvka Cave
Summer: daily except Monday, 7am-3.15pm. Winter: daily except Monday, 7.30am-1.45pm.

Rožnov pod Radhoštěm
Open-Air Museum
Open: daily May to October.

Slavkov u Brna
Napoleon Museum
April, September, October, November: 9am-11pm, 1-3pm, daily except Monday. May to August: 8am-11pm, 1-4pm, daily except Monday.

Events and Entertainments

Many international exhibitions are held in Brno (see text). The exhibition season is from March to November. In Brno, operettas presented at the Reduta Theatre, on Zelny Trh, are popular. Opera and ballet at the Leoš Janáček Theatre, Rooseveltova Street. The Radost Theatre at 32, Bratislavská Street presents puppet shows on a Sunday afternoon. The general theatre ticket booking office is at 32, Dvořákova Street. Music: The Brno Philharmonic Orchestra performs at the Besední Dum, on Komenského Náměstí. Flora Olomouc (Olomouc Flower Show) takes place at the beginning of May in Smetana Park, Olomouc; buying and showing of flowers.

Tourist Information Centres and Accommodation Offices

Brno
Diavelni 3, 662 46 Brno
☎ (05) 23301, 23923
Offers tours (summer only) to Moravian Karst, Slavkov, Pernštejn Castle, Lednice Château, Telč and Jihlava etc.

Jihlava
Komenského 1, 586 01 Jihlava
☎ (066) 22461, 22450

Olomouc
Náměstí Míru 2, 771 03 Olomouc
☎ (068) 28831

Ostrava
Dimitrovova 9, 729 92 Ostrava
☎ (069) 231424, 234287

6

BRATISLAVA
AND THE DANUBE LOWLANDS

T he River Danube (Dunaj in Slovak) is the great river of central and south-eastern Europe. In fact, Napoleon gave the Danube a higher status than the Rhône, the Rhein or the Elbe, by calling it 'the king of the rivers of Europe'. Rising in the mountains of Bavaria and the Black Forest, the 2,737km (1,700 miles) course of the Danube takes the river through eight countries and three capital cities. It finally drains into the Black Sea, forming an enormous delta that covers a large area of Romania. For a large part of its length, the Danube marks many international boundaries, including much of Czechoslovakia's frontier with Hungary, and a small part of its border with Austria. However, for a short distance of less than 32km (20 miles) or so, the Danube flows wholly within the borders of Czechoslovakia, and it is here that the city of Bratislava, the capital of Slovakia, and the second largest city in the country, is built on the river's banks.

Popular culture, at least, often portrays the Danube as romantic; this is the river of Strauss waltzes and idle river cruising, of Vienna, Budapest, and the dozens of other medieval cities that lie along its length. Unfortunately, Bratislava belies this romantic image. Undeniably, there is some charm to be found in the Old Town, admittedly rather lost amidst the modern concrete clutter, but Bratislava is primarily an industrial metropolis, and the city lies rather awkwardly out on a limb in the south-western corner of Slovakia, close to Vienna and Hungary but not really to anywhere else. For these reasons, the city may not feature very prominently on most visitor's lists of important places to visit in Czechoslovakia; but its location, only 64km (40 miles) from Vienna and less than 161km (100 miles) from Budapest, and its connection with these cities by express trains, fast roads and Danube hydrofoils, means that Bratislava should perhaps be regarded more as a gateway into or out of Czechoslovakia, rather than as a destination in its own right. However, those who do decide to visit the city, or merely have cause to pass through it, will find that it offers a fair amount to see and do, and that there is an intriguing, if sometimes slightly off-putting, blend of Czechoslovakia's past and present to be discovered there.

Although the modern aspects of Bratislava now tend to overwhelm its more ancient monuments, there is a long history of human occupation of this site, including Stone Age, Celtic, Roman and Slavonic settlements. In 1536, the Turkish army, which controlled much of the Balkan peninsula for many centuries, captured Buda (now part of Budapest), forcing the Hungarians to withdraw north and make Bratislava their capital. For nearly four centuries, Bratislava was a Hungarian, rather than a Slovak city, known to its native Hungarians as Pozsony. The mid-eighteenth century was the most prosperous era in the city's history, when art and cultural life flourished, and when many Baroque palaces and churches were built. Slovaks were a minority until 1918, when the city was incorporated into the newly-formed state of Czechoslovakia, and re-named Bratislava, after the fifth-century tribal leader B̌retislav who brought the first Slavik peoples to settle here. Since this time, Bratislava's population has increased sevenfold, and vast new residential estates, built in some of the worst styles of Communist functionalist architecture, have grown up on both sides of the Danube, threatening to swallow up the comparatively tiny historic core. Almost denying its Austro-Hungarian roots, Bratislava is now defiantly Slovak, full of youthful university students and migrant workers who come to live in the city from other parts of Slovakia.

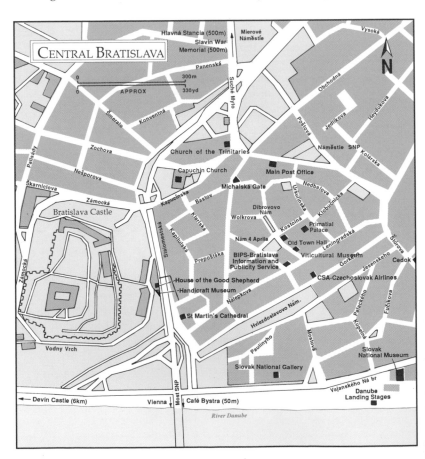

The city's leaders have encouraged a sense of civic pride, and in addition to the many industrial complexes and government institutions (the seat of the Government of Slovakia is here), Bratislava now boasts many cultural facilities, including theatres, concert halls, cinemas, and the hosting of several festivals, all of which seems to make the people who live here more outward-looking and less conservative than the poorer, older people who still inhabit most of the rest of rural Slovakia.

Visitors arrive in Bratislava by car, train, plane, boat or long-distance bus. The motorway from Brno and Prague ends in the city's suburbs and deposits motorists in Mierové Námestie, although those arriving from this direction see nothing of the Danube. There are trains linking Bratislava with Prague, Brno, and many other towns and cities all over Czechoslovakia and Eastern Europe, as well as with Vienna. The uninviting main station (Hlavná Stanica) is half a mile or so north of the city centre; taxis or trams will take one on from here. A few trains stop at Bratislava — Nové Mesto station, which is even further out, in the eastern suburbs. The main bus station, where express coaches terminate, is closer to the city centre. There are flights to Bratislava from Prague, Košice and Poprad-Tatry. Buses and taxis bring air travellers from Bratislava Airport into the city. Those who arrive by boat from Vienna or Budapest will come ashore at the landing stages on the Danube's northern embankment, in the centre of Bratislava. Most of the city's good hotels, of which there are over half a dozen or so, are located in this small central area, and a couple even overlook the Danube itself.

The River Danube at Bratislava

A Walking Tour Of Central Bratislava

Little remains now of the old Bratislava that was the capital of Hungary for over 200 years, and which saw much of Slovakia's cultural and literary renaissance that took place here during the eighteenth and nineteenth centuries. Some of the old town, such as it is, was even destroyed in the 1960s, in the course of the construction of the new showpiece bridge over the Danube (called Most SNP). Presented here, however, is a tour around the central area of the city, which guides the visitor around the oldest parts of Bratislava while also providing for occasional glimpses of the most interesting aspects of the modern city. A city map is a good investment, since Bratislava can be a confusing place in which to find one's way around. It will be useful later on, if the visitor decides to visit some of the attractions in the outskirts of Bratislava. The best map to buy is *Bratislava-Plan Mesta*, available from bookshops, street kiosks and hotel reception desks all over the city. The Old Town lies on the north bank of the Danube.

The tour starts at the **Old Town Hall** (Stará Radnica) on the square Námestie 4 Apríla (4 April 1945 was the date Bratislava was liberated from the Soviet Red Army). The medieval character of this Gothic building, which dates from the fifteenth century, has been preserved, and concerts are often held in its pleasant arcaded courtyard in summer. A fire in 1733 necessitated the rebuilding of the tower, which now forms a Baroque addition to the main Gothic core of the building. Its large and finely decorated medieval halls and rooms house the exhibition rooms of two museums.

Other interesting buildings surround Námestie 4 Apríla, which was the centre of medieval Bratislava, the scene of popular rallies, markets and public executions. Next to the Old Town Hall is a Jesuit Church, which dates from the 1630s and whose interior is richly decorated. Opposite the church is a Plague Column (1675) and in the middle of the square is Roland's Fountain (1572). Other buildings surrounding the square include those housing a wine-making museum and the city art gallery.

Turning the corner from the Town Hall and walking along Kostolná Street (or, simply exiting from the Town Hall via the east gate, if it's open), brings one into the square Primaciálne Námestie. Lining one side of this ancient square is a strawberry-pink coloured building, the **Primatial Palace**, built in the 1770s as a winter residence for the Bishop of Eszertegom, but more notable for being the place where Napoleon and the Austrian Emperor Franz I signed the Treaty of Pressburg in 1805 (after the Battle of Austerlitz, fought near Brno in Moravia; Pressburg is the old German name for Bratislava). Today the building houses various city function rooms, but one can go inside and see the Hall of Mirrors, the room in which the treaty was signed. Upstairs there are some rare English tapestries, housed in a small gallery. The tapestries were woven in the seventeenth century at Mortlake, on the River Thames west of London.

From Primaciálne Námestie, follow Uršulinska Street north. It opens out into the square Námestie Slovenského Národného Povstania (Square of the Slovak National Uprising), normally shortened to **Námestie SNP**. The same name is given to scores of squares, streets, bridges, and other monuments all over Slovakia. They are all named in memory of those members of the armed resistance movement who died in the uprising against the Nazi occupation of Slovakia, which broke out in 1944. Supported by the Soviet Union and its allies, the uprising was Communist in its ideology and, to an extent, provided the impetus for the popular adoption of Socialism in Slovakia after World War II. A stark group of austere statues stands in the centre of the square. They were erected in 1974, the year that marked the thirtieth anniversary of the uprising. An eternal flame burns near by, to keep alive the memory of those who died in this popular revolt against German Fascism.

From the square, walk along the busy street to the left which leads slightly up hill. Then take the first street on the left, Michalská Street. This picturesque lane leads over a stone bridge which crosses a deep fortification ditch, before passing under an arch and turning sharply to the left. The building on the left here is an old pharmacy, now housing the pharmaceutical museum. However, attention is more immediately focussed on the tall **Michalská Gate** (Michael's Gate), under which the street passes a short distance beyond the pharmacy building. The gate is the only remaining part of Bratislava's medieval fortifications. The top part of the tower, and its roof, are later additions. The tower now houses the Armaments Museum; climb the steps inside to the outside gallery at the top, for a fine view over Bratislava's old town.

Immediately after passing under the Michalská Gate, a tiny medieval alleyway to the right, Baštova Street, takes one into Klariská Street, from where there are steps up to Octóbrové Námestie. The central feature of this square is the small **Capuchin Church**; an elegant plague column stands outside the front door. Turning right and heading along the road a short distance, following the tram lines, brings one to Bratislava's most beautiful church, the **Church of the Trinitaries**. Its rich Baroque interior is the work of an Italian painter, and dates from the 1720s. The attached monastery has been adapted to house Slovak government offices. Backtrack now to Klariská Street again, and take any of the streets that lead down towards the Danube and **St Martin's Cathedral**. This church is not so attractive from the outside, but its interior is finely decorated. The oldest parts of the tripple-naved church date from the thirteenth century, when this building was used for defensive purposes. The church was completed in 1445 and has been restored many times since this date. During the seventeenth and eighteenth centuries, it witnessed the coronations of nine Hungarian monarchs. The interior furnishings include a bronze font (1403) and a Baroque statue fashioned from lead, depicting St Martin on a horse, cutting off half his robe for a beggar (1734).

The area immediately surrounding St Martin's is the scene of the most insensitive developments in modern Bratislava since the war. So important was the new bridge, Most SNP, to the city's post-war 'Socialist' look, that the Communist authorities tore down the old Jewish Quarter that was once here, to build the complex set of access roads and flyovers for the bridge. Traffic screaches relentlessly along the main highway, called Staromestká, which has been built literally a couple of metres from the west doorway of the cathedral.

The endless pounding by the traffic has seriously undermined the foundations of St Martin's, necessitating a lengthy and expensive bout of restoration work if the city's cathedral is to be saved.

From St Martin's, head back uphill in the direction of the Old Town, up some steps which lead along old fortification walls. Turn left over a footbridge which crosses the busy highway that leads towards the SNP Bridge, and then left again, to the noteworthy Rococo house called the **House of Good Shepherd** (U Dobrého Pastiera), which overlooks the main road. It houses the museum of historical clocks; the Handicraft Museum is opposite. From here, one can climb up to Bratislava's most obvious ancient landmark, its prison-like **castle**. The steep street leading up to the castle, called Bablavého Street, is lined with innocuous-looking cottages that were once home to the city's infamous medieval red light district, situated just below the barracks that was once set up in the castle. Now these buildings are all rather classy cafés and shops. The earliest, pre-Christian human settlements in Bratislava were situated on this hill, a prime fortification site overlooking the River Danube. In the 1430s a Gothic fortress was built. A hundred years later, the castle was adapted as a base from where the Hungarian rulers of Bratislava could direct their armies against the Turks, who were in control of Budapest. The Hungarian crown jewels were once stored in one of the round towers. Later centuries

The Old Town Hall, Bratislava

saw the castle neglected, turned into a barracks, and, in 1811, almost completely destroyed by fire. It was restored and rebuilt in the 1950s. The oldest part of the castle is its distinctive square core; this and other buildings in the castle complex house government offices, a concert hall, a museum, and a restaurant. There are excellent views from the castle ramparts, especially of the SNP Bridge, which is the next and final stop of the tour. On clear days, it is possible to see the spires of Vienna from here, only 48km (30 miles) away across the Danube plains.

The Bridge of the Slovak National Uprising (Most SNP) is one of the three (shortly to be increased to four) bridges that cross the River Danube at Bratislava. It is a notable and distinctive landmark of the town, an ostentatious showpiece which individuals will either detest or admire. Construction of the bridge was completed in 1972. There is a pedestrian walkway on either side, underneath the traffic lanes. At the other side of the bridge, one may ascend one of the pylons by a fast lift (elevator) which takes one up to the Café Bystrica, situated 80m (262ft) above the river. This is a good place to end the tour; one can buy a drink or meal and, through the tinted windows of the café, contemplate the fine views over the castle and the Old Town, and watch the pleasure boats and industrial barges on the River Danube below; but the view from the other side of the café (and from the toilets!), over the southern suburbs of Petržalka, may leave visitors with a somewhat different impression of Bratislava.

Museums And Galleries

As the capital of Slovakia, and the second largest city in Czechoslovakia, Bratislava has a rich and varied collection of museums and galleries that is second only to Prague's.

Bratislava Municipal Museum (Múzeum Histórie Bratislavy)
The collections of this museum are housed in the Old Town Hall. They provide an extensive and exhaustive survey of the city's history, from Roman times to the present day. Models of how Bratislava looked in medieval and other times help put the rest of the city's sights in perspective. Do not overlook the Museum of Federal Justice, a smaller museum downstairs in the basement. To be seen in the old prison cells here are various medieval torture instruments, and contemporary pictures and engravings which show how they were used, in vivid and lurid detail.

Armaments Museum (Múzeum Zbraní a Mestského Opevnenia)
This museum is housed in Michalská Gate, a point of interest included in the walking tour described earlier in this chapter. It comprises a small exhibition of guns, weapons and armoury that medieval and more modern soldiers wore and used to defend Bratislava.

Museum of Historical Clocks
(Múzeum Bratislavskych Historickych Hodín)
A fascinating and unusual display of historical and ornamental clocks which date from various centuries, housed in the House of the Good Shepherd, below the castle. Visitors should ask one of the curators to wind up and operate the clocks that play tunes.

Handicraft Museum
(Múzeum Umeleckych Remesiel)
This is across the road from the Clock Museum, a large and varied collection of the products of Bratislava's craftsmen, dating from medieval times to the present day. Exhibits include silver and gold ornaments, chalices, and also furniture, porcelain, crystal, toys and jewellery.

Slovak National Museum
(Slovenské Národné Múzeum)
Similar to the Czech National Museum in Prague, this exhibition, housed in a building on the north embankment of the Danube, includes large numbers of stuffed birds and animals, geological collections and a number of skeletons and other archaeological bits and pieces collected from sites all over Slovakia.

Castle Museum
The museum in Bratislava Castle is good, and includes exhibits relating to the history of Slovakia, Bratislava and the castle itself, including many Roman and prehistoric finds.

Slovak National Gallery
(Slovenské Narodná Galéria)
This is probably the best art gallery in Bratislava, given the handicap that there is no unified body of Slovak art, and much of what there is simply isn't very good anyway. Nevertheless, a few themes stand out, most noticably portrayals of Slovak peasant life, and more serious studies which bring to attention the very serious problems of poverty that once existed in many parts of rural Slovakia. There is also the inevitable section on 'Socialist art', depicting the triumph of Communism against Fascism, and, as a contrast, a number of medieval icons plundered from various parts of Eastern Slovakia. The collections of this gallery are housed in an old eighteenth-century naval barracks on the Danube waterfront, which has been brutally modernised to suit the purposes of the gallery.

Bratislava Municipal Gallery
A collection of Slovak and European Baroque art, housed in the much-admired Rococo Mirbach Palace, on Dibrorovo Námestie, just up from the Old Town Hall.

Viticultural Museum
This museum, very close to the Old Town Hall, celebrates the fact that Bratislava is the centre of Czechoslovakia's wine-making industry, but is recommended for wine fans only.

Pharmaceutical Museum
An old medieval building, very close to the Michalská Gate (see walking tour), called U Červeného Raka (At the Red Lobster) once housed Bratislava's oldest pharmacy. Its rooms now house the collections of the Pharmaceutical Museum, with exhibitions devoted to seventeenth-eighteenth- and nineteenth-century Slovak medicine.

The Outskirts Of Bratislava

As seen from the restaurant at the top of the SNP Bridge, Bratislava's suburbs look far from inviting. Nevertheless, there are a number of interesting things to see in the city's outskirts. The following places of interest are all within the city limits of Bratislava, and their locations are clearly marked on the city map. Those not using a private car can reach these places by taxi, or by Bratislava's municipal transport service (buses, trams and trolleybuses); public transport routes and numbers are also indicated on the map.

The **Slavín War Memorial** is actually within walking distance of the city ✳ centre, and is visible from many parts of Bratislava. From the corner of Križkova Sytreet and Obrancov Mieru Street, about ten or fifteen minutes walk north of Namestie SNP, a flight of steps leads up the side of Slavín Hill to a stark memorial erected in 1960 in memory of the 6,847 Soviet soldiers who died during the fight to liberate Bratislava from Nazi control, in the spring of 1945. Six soldiers are buried here. The main pylon of the memorial is 42m (138ft) high, and is crowned with a statue of a victorious soldier. Other statues stand at the base of the memorial, looking out over the city. The dates around the side of the memorial show when each town in Slovakia was liberated by the Red Army as it swept westwards. There is a good view over modern 🏰 Bratislava from this sombre and often windy hilltop, but the overt militarism of the monument, and the fact that 8 years after its construction a second, and unwelcome, Russian 'liberation' of the country took place (the crushing of the Prague Spring), means that a visit to Slavín cannot fail to be accompanied by a rather bitter suspicion of the veracity of it all.

In the western suburbs of the city is the valley Mlynská Dolina. A busy highway of the same name runs along it, in a north-south direction. Towards the north end of Mlynská Dolina is Bratislava's zoo, which has been closed for many years while it is rebuilt. It should re-open in the early 1990s.

Near the zoo is the valley **Zelezna Studnicka**, a peaceful rural area separated from the main part of Bratislava by a limb of the Little Carpathians (Malé Karpaty). The road in the valley leads to a small spa. There are four small lakes in the valley, used for boating and bathing in summer, and for ice skating in winter. Just after the road has passed the fourth lake, a complex of buildings on the right mark the bottom station of a chairlift up Mount Kamzík (440m, 1,443ft) the dominant peak of the Little Carpathians which rises above the 🏰 northern suburbs of Bratislava. At the top of the chairlift are a couple of restaurants and, reached after a short stroll through the forest, an enormously high television tower, visible from all over the city. There is a revolving coffee bar half way up the tower. If the chairlift is not running, it is possible to drive up to the tower from the other direction, by a road leading up through the suburb of Koliba. A city bus route also runs most of the way up to the tower, via Koliba.

Although a separate village some distance away from the city, **Devín**, 10km (6 miles) north-west of Bratislava, is still within the city's administrative boundaries. Take the road that runs along the north embankment of the Danube, or alternatively a bus from the stop underneath the north side of the SNP Bridge. A boat also runs from Bratislava to Devín, along the Danube. The road out to Devín follows the Danube, and once the village is reached the immediate sight that greets the visitor is that of the impressive ruins of Devín 🏰 Castle that rise above it. The castle is situated on a high bluff above a broad curve in the river, at the spot where the Morava meets the Danube. Devín is just one of scores of ancient castles that were built along the 2,737km (1,700 mile) course of the River Danube over the past two millennia. Unsurprisingly, the rock it sits on has a long history as a fortified settlement; some archaeological finds made at Devín show that Stone Age man lived here in 5,000BC. The Romans built one of the first stone castles on this site, and for a long time, both Devín and Bratislava castles marked the northernmost limits of the Roman empire in central Europe. In the ninth century there was a hill fort here and six graves dating from this time, where the bodies were buried with objects such as small tools and jewellery, have been unearthed. Later castles on this site were the scene of fierce fighting between the Hungarians and the Turks. The present castle was left in ruins after being destroyed by Napoleon's army in 1809, and makes for an interesting visit, with good views over the Danube from the castle ramparts. One of the courtyards gives access to a small museum. The middle of the wide river at this point marks the border between Czechoslovakia and Austria. The authorities are still very nervous about the border here, and may ask to see visitor's passports — but if everything is in order, tourists should be allowed to continue about their business undisturbed.

Beyond Devín there are many villages involved in wine making, and vineyards cover many of the slopes of the Little Carpathians here. Many easy, pleasant walking trips can be made in the hills in this part of Slovakia.

Other Attractions In The Region

The area to the east of Bratislava forms the greatest expanse of lowland in Czechoslovakia. Numerous small rivers and streams cross this area and drain into the Danube. The area is very fertile and is very intensively farmed. Most of the land is very flat, and it is the warmest part of the country. Many birds and waterfowl live in the rich natural habitat of the lowlands, in protected reserves which are normally out of bounds to the public. Since 1978, however, their natural habitats have been threatened by the steady constuction of an enormous dam on the Danube, which was originally to have been built jointly by Hungary and Czechoslovakia with Austrian capital. The environmental damage that such a dam would cause, however, has meant that Austria and Hungary have pulled out of the project, bowing to world-wide pressure exerted by conservation agencies, and the Czechoslovak government has yet to decide whether to continue with the half-finished project or to simply build a much smaller dam than was originally planned. This problem merely highlights a world-wide dilemma, by no means confined to Czechoslovakia or Eastern Europe; how to produce large quantities of cheap electricity, by any number of different methods, without somehow threatening the physical environment.

There is little to interest the tourist in this area. However, a couple of places have been described here, which the tourist is more likely to visit while journeying on to somewhere else, rather than making a special excursion to see. **Nitra**, a town 85km (52 miles) north-east of Bratislava, is on the E571 road which motorists may use to drive between Bratislava and the High Tatras (the towns of Zvolen and Banská Bystrica also lie on the same route, and are discussed in Chapter 7). Here, the River Nitra flows south out of the Slovakian hills and onto the Danube Plains. In AD820 the first church in Slovakia was built here. By the eleventh century, Nitra was a bishopric and the town acquired a castle, but in 1663 the Turkish army reduced Nitra and its castle to rubble, and its medieval period of importance was abruptly ended. Nitra is nowadays known chiefly as an agricultural centre and marketplace, and important agricultural exhibitions are held in the town. The castle, located on a hill overlooking the town, inside a tight bend in the River Nitra, was rebuilt in the seventeenth century; inside its walls are a Gothic cathedral, which contains the remains of two tenth-century Slovak saints, and the Bishop's Palace which, like most of the buildings in the castle area, is closed to the public. The Plague Column (1750) outside the entrance to the castle, is one of the most admired in Slovakia. Buildings in the street Ulice Samova below the castle house the collections of two rather dull museums, the Agricultural Museum and the Town Museum. The town is overlooked by Mount Zobor (588m, 1,929ft), one of the most southerly of the hills of central Slovakia. There is a chairlift to the summit, taking people over fields covered in vineyards.

Komárno, 100km (62 miles) south-east of Bratislava, is the second most important Slovak town on the River Danube. The lowlands around here are completely flat and the vegetables and fruit produced in this mild region are sent to all parts of Czechoslovakia. Komárno itself lives off the Danube; it is an important river port and there is a small boat building industry here. The river at Komárno marks an international frontier, and cuts the town in half, with the northern part (Komárno) lying in Slovak territory, while the southern part (Komárom) is in Hungary. A road bridge across the Danube allows one to cross between the two countries. The town is worth mentioning as boat trips along the Danube operate between here and Bratislava. The River Váh, the principal river of Slovakia, which rises in the High Tatras, joins the Danube at Komárno. A fortress, most of which dates from the 1660s, and which successfully withstood Turkish onslaughts, lies in the Slovak part of the town. The whole town is surrounded by bastions and forts from Napoleonic times. There are also numerous old houses and a museum devoted to the River Danube, exhibiting archaeological finds from the Danube Valley.

Additional Information

Places Of Interest
In And Around Bratislava

Armaments Museum
(Múzeum Zbraní a Mestského
Opevnenia)
Michalská Gate, Michalská Street
Open: 10am-5pm, daily except Tuesday.

Bratislava Castle Museum
Open: 9am-4pm, daily except Monday.
The castle grounds are open daily.

Bratislava Municipal Gallery
Mirbach Palace, between Dibrovo
Námestie and Zámočnicka Street
Open: 10am-5pm, daily except Monday.

Bratislava Municipal Museum
(Múzeum Histórie Bratislavy)
In the Old Town Hall (Stará Radnica),
Námestie 4 Apríla.
The Museum of Federal Justice is in the
basement of the same building.
Open: 10am-5pm, daily except Monday.

Handicraft Museum
(Múzeum Umeleckych Remesiel)
Beblavého 1
Open: 10am-5pm, daily except Tuesday.

Museum of Historical Clocks
(Múzeum Bratislavskych Historickych
Hodín)
Židovská 1 (corner of Beblavého Street)
Open: 10am-5pm, daily except Tuesday.

Pharmaceutical Museum
In the house called U Červeného Raka,
on Michalská Street
Open: daily except Monday, 10am-5pm.

Slovak National Gallery
(Slovenské Národná Galéria)
Rázusovo Nábrezie 2
Open: 10am-5pm, daily except Monday.

Slovak National Museum
(Slovenské Národné Múzeum)
Vajanského Nábrezie 2
Open: 9am-4pm, daily except Monday.

Viticultural Museum
Next to the Town Hall, on the square
Námestie 4 Aprilá
Open: daily except Monday, 10am-5pm.

Devín Castle
10km (6 miles) north-west of Bratislava
Open: May to October only, 9.30am-
5pm, daily except Monday.

Café Bystrica
Top of SNP Bridge
Open: daily. Opens at 10am (1pm
Monday); closes at 11pm (10pm winter).

Boating and Sailing

Boat Services On The Danube
Routes and other details change annu-
ally. Some services are operated by

cruise boats, others by faster, closed-in
hydrofoils. Places served by boat or
hydrofoil from Bratislava include
Vienna, Hainburg (Austria); Devín,
Komárno (both in Czechoslovakia; see
entries in this chapter); and Budapest.
Enquire at the ticket and information
office on the Danube waterfront, or at
Čedok. There are also much shorter
cruises which just go a short way up
and down the Danube from Bratislava.

Lakes
Boating and sailing on the lake Zlaté
Piesky in the north-eastern suburbs of
Bratislava.

Events and Festivals

Bratislava has a strong and varied
cultural life:

Bratislava International Music Festival,
first two weeks of October; classical
music festival which attracts many
international performers.

Bratislava Lyre Festival, May, Popular
songs.

International Flower Show, April.

Bratislava Biennial of Illustrations,
September every odd year, illustrations
for childrens books.

Puppet Theatre, 36, Dunajská Street;
Slovak Philharmonic Orchestra performs in the ornate Reduta Theatre at 2,
Palackého Street; the Slovak National
Theatre, 2, Gorkého Street, stages opera
and ballet. Contact Bratislava Information and Public Service for information
on 'what's on'.

Transport

ČSA-Czechoslovak Airlines
Mostová 3
☎ (07) 311217
Flights from Bratislava to Prague,
Košice, Poprad-Tatry.

Bratislava's municipal transport system
is excellent. The extensive tram system
is similar to that in most Czechoslovak
cities, ie tickets should be bought from

kiosks, hotels, automatic machines etc and stamped on entering the tram. Only trams can use the tunnel which runs under the castle. Trolleybuses and buses operate in the same way. Some buses run at night, and leave hourly from Námestie SNP. 'ZZ' at a bus stop indicates a night bus. In summer only, there is a passenger ferry across the Danube which operates immediately downstream from most SNP. Taxis can be hailed in the street or found at ranks by the big hotels or the railway station.

Tourist Information Centres and Accommodation Offices

(Numbers before the names of towns are town postal codes).

Bratislava
Main Čedok office
Čedok-Bratislava
Štúrova 13
813 83 Bratislava
☎ (07) 55280, (07) 23696
Deals with accommodation and information. Cars can be hired from this office. Tours are operated from this office, between May and September: eg, walking tour of Bratislava; half-day coach tour of the Little Carpathians, including wine tasting and visits to local vineyards.

Bratislava Information and Publicity Service (Bratislavská Informačná a Propagačná Služba — BIPS).
Leningradska 1
☎ (07) 33 44 15
(If this street name has changed, see map for location). Similar services to Čedok. Advises on events, concerts etc, organises tours, provides interpreters, general information on Bratislava. No accommodation service.

Komárno
Čedok-Komárno
Pohraničnej Stráže 4
945 01 Komárno
☎ (0819) 3654

Nitra
Čedok-Nitra
Leninova Trieda 72
949 75 Nitra
☎ (087) 28250, (087) 28248

7

THE CARPATHIAN MOUNTAINS

B ratislava, despite being the capital of Slovakia, really provides travellers with a very false window into this land. Despite the modern, youthful appearance of Bratislava, urbanisational and industrialisation have come to this region relatively recently. Slovakia is a mountainous country, and Slovaks are, by tradition at any rate, a mountain people, more at home in wood-timbered hillside villages than amidst the industrial throng of a place like Bratislava, whose history and culture is linked to that of the Danube Valley rather than to the mountains of the north. It is no accident that the two largest towns in Slovakia (Košice and Bratislava) both have strong cultural and historical links with Hungary, rather than being purely Slovak creations. Whereas Czech culture is traditionally centred on Prague and the Vltava, Slovaks do not hold their capital or the Danube in such high esteem. The title of their national anthem, *Lightning Is Flashing Above The Tatras*, admirably highlights the fact that Slovaks look to the mountains as the true heartland of their country.

Bratislava, and the Danube lowlands on which it lies, are geographically an extention of the plains of northern Hungary. At Nitra and Trnava, these plains suddenly give way to the massif of the Carpathian mountains, which are the principal geographic feature of Slovakia. The Carpathians are also a prominent feature of the geography of eastern and central Europe, stretching round in a broad arc through half a dozen countries, from Vienna to Bucharest. All the mountain ranges in Slovakia — the White and Little Carpathians, Malá Fatra, The Low Tatras, The High Tatras and others — are part of this extensive range. The High Tatras themselves, the primary goal of most visitors to Slovakia, include the highest mountains in the Carpathians as a whole, with a few peaks in this range soaring to over 2,500m (8,200ft) in height.

The itinerary around which this chapter is structured is a very obvious one, running along the Váh Valley virtually all the way from Bratislava to the High Tatras (where the Váh rises). The Váh is obvious on any map, as its valley forms the major communications corridor of Slovakia, with principal roads and railways running through it, linking the towns that have grown up on the banks of the river. Thus, the suggested itinerary presented here can be followed by both road or rail travellers. Virtually all the most important towns

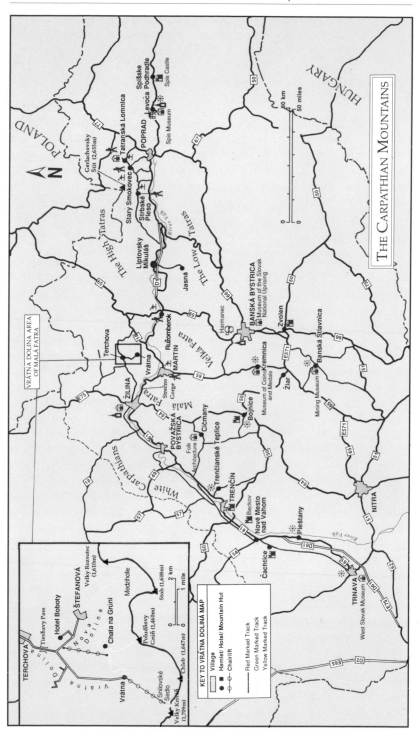

THE CARPATHIAN MOUNTAINS

HUNGARY

POLAND

Spišské
Podhradie
Spiš Castle

Spišské
Podhradie
Levoča
Spiš Museum

Tatranská Lomnica
POPRAD

Gerlachovský
Štít (2,655m)

Starý Smokovec
Štrbské
Pleso

Vah River

The High Tatras

The Low Tatras

Liptovský
Mikuláš

Jasná

D1

65

Harmanec

BANSKÁ BYSTRICA
Museum of the Slovak
National Uprising

Zvolen

Banská Štiavnica

Veľká Fatra

Ružomberok

Terchová

Vrátna

MARTIN

Strečno
Gorge

Malá Fatra

ŽILINA
Fatra

E75

POVAŽSKÁ
BYSTRICA

Čičmany

Bojnice

Kremnica
Museum of Coins
and Medals

Žiar

Mining Museum

E571

Trenčianske Teplice
Folk
Architecture

TRENČÍN

Beckov

Nové Mesto
nad Váhom

Piešťany

River Váh

NITRA

Čachtice

TRNAVA
West Slovak Museum

E75

D2

VRÁTNA DOLINA AREA
OF MALÁ FATRA

KEY TO VRÁTNA DOLINA MAP

▭	Village
■ ●	Hamlet/ Hotel/ Mountain Hut
⊸⊙⊸	Chairlift
—	Red Marked Track
—	Green Marked Track
—	Yellow Marked Track

TERCHOVÁ

Hotel Boboty

Tiesňavy Pass

ŠTEFANOVÁ
Veľký Rozsutec
(1,610m)

Medziholie

Nová
Dolina

Chata na Grúni

Poludňový
Grúň (1,460m)

Stoh (1,608m)

Vrátna Dolina

Snilovské
Sedlo

Vrátna

Veľký Kriváň
(1,709m)

Chleb (1,647m)

0   1 mile
0   2 km

80 km
50 miles

of Western Slovakia — such as Trenčín, Žilina, Ružomberok and Martin — are situated in the Váh Valley. Often, visitors will find accommodation in these towns before heading out into the surrounding mountains on day excursions.

The Carpathian Foothills

 The White and Little Carpathians are the foothills of the major part of the range. They rise to a comparatively modest altitude of only 970m (3,182ft), at Mount Velká Javorina. They are important for ethnic reasons, however, as for more than a thousand years they have formed the natural boundary between Moravia and Slovakia, and the separate cultures of the Czechs and the Slovaks.

Bratislava To Žilina

The distance between the Slovak capital and Žilina, the most important town in north-western Slovakia, is 202km (125 miles) by road. The main road (E65, also road 61) and railway line follow each other along the Váh Valley. The following is a step-by-step guide to the major points of interest between the two centres.

Road travellers will do the first part of this journey by motorway, which just bypasses the town of **Trnava**, one of the oldest in Slovakia, and on the boundary between the plains and the mountains. Trnava is 36km (22 miles) from Bratislava; most trains on the Bratislava-Žilina line stop here, as it is also an important rail junction. The town was founded in 1238, and after Buda fell to the Turks and the Hungarians headed north, Trnava assumed an intellectual and religious importance. The Hungarians established a university here, and the town became the seat of the Hungarian Bishop of Eszertogom, whose seat encompassed much of the area to the north and south of the Danube. Later the town became a crucial centre of the Counter Reformation, bringing with it the Jesuits and a Catholic University. Although the town's rich ecclesiastical heritage has survived, modern Trnava gives few hints at its previous periods of wealth and importance. Its main square, Trojinské Námestie, is lined with a number of modern and ancient buildings, the latter dating from the sixteenth and seventeenth centuries. One road off the main square, Divadelná Street, leads to the St John the Baptist (Svatého Jakub), which dates from 1380 and is the oldest church in the town. Next to the church is the Bernolakova Brana, the only remaining gate in the city's old town walls, which here run along the banks of the River Trnavka. In the other direction, Hviezdoslavova Street runs

 off the main square to the twin-towered St Nicholas' Cathedral (Sv Mikulaše), once the most important church in Hungary during the Turkish occupation of the lands south of the Danube. Staromestká Street runs down from here to the

 West Slovak Museum (Západolovenské Muzeum), the exhibition rooms of which feature examples of Slovak folk art and pottery.

After Trnava the road and railway join the Váh and run along the broad

valley which is cut through low lying hills. Thirty-three kilometres (20 miles) further on from Trnava, is **Pieštany**, one of Slovakia's most famous spas. The motorway skirts past the western suburbs of this town, and ends just a short distance beyond it; there is also an important railway station here. The main part of the spa area, and the most pleasant part of town, is on an island in the Váh called Kúpelny Ostrov, comprising modern hotels and areas of pleasant greenery. The Romans knew about the warm, sulphurous mineral springs that are found here, and the therapeutic mud which is nowadays applied to the skin of patients in mud packs. All spas specialise in the treatment of one ailment or another, and Pieštany's best known curative treatments are for muscular and nervous diseases. By the colonnade bridge (Kolonádovy Most) over to the island there is a statue of a cured man breaking his crutches, which is the symbol of the town.

Road and railway continue along the valley, still very broad, for another 20km (12 miles) to **Nové Mésto nad Váhom**, a small industrial town, which can be used as a base from which to see two of the many fine castles with which this part of Slovakia is particuarly well endowed. A road leads back from this town, southwards along the valley, to **Čachtice**, which has a nice-looking village church. From here, one can walk up to Čachtice Castle (Hrad Čachtice). There is also a shorter, steeper path up from Višňové, the next village along this road. The castle is now in ruins, but there is a good view over the Váh Valley. This now peaceful spot belies the castle's bizarre and gruesome history, when it was the prison of the Romanian Countess Elizabeth Báthori (1560-1614), who sought eternal youth by bathing in the blood of girls and young peasant women, whom she murdered just for this purpose. In the other direction from Nové Mesto nad Váhom, a short distance away on the other side of the river, is **Beckov Castle**, which is perched on a precipitous rock above the village of the same name. Since being destroyed by fire in 1728, this castle has also lain in ruins, although they are very substantial.

Neither of these two castles, however, come close to matching **Trenčín Castle** in splendour or size. Any road or rail traveller entering Trenčín, another 22km (14 miles) on along the Váh Valley from Nové Mesto nad Váhom, cannot fail to miss the sight of its castle, as the main road through the town is built right beneath the castle rock, and the railway station also lies very close by in the shadow of its towers and thick walls. The first castle on this easily defendable rock was built in the ninth century, at the time of the Great Moravian Empire. By the thirteenth century, however, the castle was in the hands of the Hungarian aristocrat Matthias Čak, also the owner of Beckov Castle, and he added a Royal palace to the original Romanesque fort. Čak was noted for setting up an independent kingdom here in the fourteenth century, with Trenčín as its 'capital' and himself as 'king'. Although the kingdom was short lived and Čak, little more than a feudal lord, is celebrated as a folk hero in Slovakia because he stood up to the ruling Hungarians. Subsequent owners in the ensuing centuries expanded and rebuilt the place, until it was destroyed in a disastrous fire in 1790. Now, much of the castle has been restored, and many of its small rooms house exhibitions relating to the history of the castle.

The town below the castle has a few points of interest as well. The square is lined with old Renaissance buildings, and there is a tall gateway which is one of the few remaining parts of the town's medieval fortifications. Trenčín was one of the most northerly points of the Roman Empire in central Europe; they established a military camp and town here called *Laugaricio*. There is a Roman inscription hewn into the rock on which the castle sits, which records the victory of the Roman Emperor Marcus Aurelius over the Germanic tribe of the Kvads, in AD179. The only way of seeing the inscription is from a viewing window in the Tatra Hotel.

Nine kilometres (6 miles) beyond Trenčín, road and railway pass through Trenčianské Teplá, from where a road (and a nice little metre-gauge electric railway) lead into the hills for a couple of miles to the picturesque spa town, ❊ **Trenčianské Teplice**. The spa is slightly reminiscent of Mariánské Lázně, in its woodland setting and its rows of turn of the century buildings and spa sanitoria, which line the narrow River Teplička. The sulphurous springs and mud here, like those at Pieštany, are used to treat muscular and nervous disorders. Well worth seeing in the centre of town (the entrance door is not very obvious) is the interior of one of the spa sanitoria, the Hamman bath, which was built in the late nineteenth century and is decorated in Turkish style with ornate carpets and Moorish arches. This sanitoria is a working bathhouse, so ask first before trying to see its main room, which is reached from the entrance along a number of dim corridors. A 10-minute walk away from the centre of the town, hidden in a wood, is an artificially-dug pond called Zelená Žaba (The Green Frog), the warm waters of which are natural and are used for public swimming every afternoon. Paths from here lead up to Královec, the main viewpoint over the spa and the valley.

Returning to the main valley, road and railway continue on to Žilina, 69km (43 miles) from Trenčianské Teplá. The mountians get gradually higher until by Žilina one is in the Malá Fatra, the first of the most important mountain ranges of Slovakia. A more interesting, but longer, route to Žilina is via ❊ **Čičmany**, a small village in the mountains which is reached by a road which leads off from the main road in the Váh Valley from just beyond Ilava. The village, set high in the Strážovské Hills at an altitude of 973m (3,191ft), boasts interesting folk architecture in the form of a number of wooden houses, the outside walls of which are decorated with dazzlingly intricate folk designs and patterns. Čičmany is also famous for its colourful folk costumes and embroidery, which are decorated with the same emblems and motifs as the houses. Brightly-coloured footwear called *válenky*, made from felt and cloth, is manufactured in the village. There is a museum and shop, which exhibit and sell the village's traditional folkloric products.

Malá Fatra And Velká Fatra Ranges

Malá Fatra is the first of the high mountain ranges that stretch in a west-east direction along the northern borders of Slovakia. Žilina is the principal town,

Folk architecture at Čičmany

Winter scene at Trenčianské Teplice

and the Malá Fatra are the first relatively high mountains that those arriving in the town, whether from Bratislava (following the itinerary already described in this chapter) or from Prague, will encounter. The highest peak in the range is Mount Velky Kriváň (1,709m, 5,606ft), in the northern part of the range and surprisingly accessible, by chairlift and then a short walk on foot. Many peaks in the Malá Fatra are rounded, but there are a number of more rocky and jagged mountains, such as Mount Velky Rozutec and Mount Stoh, and walking in these areas provides for more challenging excursions. To the east of Malá Fatra is the lower Velká Fatra range, which has been less developed; the highest peak is Mount Ostredok (1,592m, 5,222ft). Bears still live in the thick forests that cover the lower slopes of Velká Fatra. Accommodation in the region can be found in the towns of Žilina, Martin and Ružomberok, but more preferably in the towns and villages in the mountains themselves, where there are hotels and private rooms (most are controlled and reserved through Čedok at Žilina). All those planning to walk or tour in this area should buy the detailed map *Malá Fatra*, number 11 in the series *Edícia Turistickych Máp*.

❋ Žilina

Žilina itself is a largely unexciting industrial town in the Váh Valley; but many visitors to the Malá Fatra will choose to stay here, in one of a number of its good hotels. Žilina's position at the crossroads of the E85 and the E16 roads, and its role as one of the most important rail junctions in Czechoslovakia, means that virtually all visitors will at least pass through the town. Road and rail routes run south-west to Bratislava (202km, 125 miles); east along the Váh Valley to Poprad and the High Tatras, and the important East Slovakian towns of Prešov and Košice; north to Ostrava and Warsaw; and west to Prague (396km, 246 miles) and Brno (212km, 131 miles).

Žilina's origins are medieval, but the real growth in the importance of the town came in the last decades of the nineteenth century, when the railway along the Váh Valley was built. Over 1,700 Russian soldiers who died fighting for the town's liberation in 1945 are buried on a hillside outside the town. There are two main squares in the centre of Žilina. Námestie SNP, the lower of the two squares, is fairly modern and uninteresting. A ramp and stairway lead up from this square past the pink-coloured Gothic Church of the Most Holy Trinity, with its distinctive belfry, dating from the fifteenth century. Continuing along a narrow alley from the church (Pučikova Street) brings one out into Námestie Dukla, a more pleasant square surrounded by Baroque and Renaissance houses with arcades. In the western suburb of Budatín is Budatín Château, founded in the thirteenth century to guard an ancient ford across the River Váh, which houses a museum of the Váh Valley. In another suburb, Zavodie, is Zilina's most noteworthy building, St Stephen's Church, which was founded in the thirteenth century and whose interior is decorated with medieval wall paintings. The church is also surrounded by a medieval wall.

Excursions From Žilina Into The Malá Fatra

The mountains in the immediate vicinity of Žilina are neither very high nor very interesting. One must travel about 24km (15 miles) to the east to reach the most popular part of the Malá Fatra, the Vrátna Dolina area which is centred on the three villages of Terchová, Vrátna and Štefanová.

The village of **Terchová** is 22km (14 miles) east of Žilina. It must be reached by crossing the road bridge over the River Váh at Žilina, and then following the roads which run along the north side of the Váh. Terchová is the birthplace of Juro Sánošík (1688-1713), a Slovak folk hero who, Robin Hood style, robbed from the rich to give to the poor. A road leading south out of Terchová takes one past a small memorial to him (on the left-hand side of the road), and then through the spectacular **Tiesňavy Pass**, which is at the entrance to the Vrátna Dolina Valley. The road winds up past craggy ridges which come right down to the banks of the fast-flowing River Vratnanka, which rises just beyond Vrátna. After a mile or so of fine scenery, there is a road off to the left to the village of Štefanová (see below). The main road continues along the valley, past popular skiing areas on both sides, to terminate at **Vrátna**, 750m (2,460ft). From here, a popular chairlift (arrive early in the morning to avoid the worst of queues) takes one up to Snilovské Sedlo (1,500m, 4,920ft). There are good views from the top over the peaks of Malá Fatra. There are more skiing grounds around Snilovské Sedlo. From the top station of the chairlift it is a five minute walk along the green-marked track to Snilovské Sedlo itself (1,520m, 4,986ft), a high pass on the main ridge of the Malá Fatra. From here it is an easy walk to the summit of **Mount Chleb** (1,647m, 5,403ft) or, in the other direction, to **Mount Velky Kriváň**, at 1,709m (5,606ft), the highest mountain in Malá Fatrá (both are about half an hour's walk from Snilovské Sedlo, on the red-marked track).

The turning off the main Vrátna Dolina Valley, mentioned above, takes one through the Nová Dolina Valley. On the right, almost immediately after the road junction, is the bottom station of a chairlift up to **Mount Grúň** (1,000m, 3,280ft). This chairlift is not so interesting, running through forest, but there is pleasant scenery at the top, dominated by the solid-looking peak **Poludňovy Grúň** (1,460m, 4,789ft). Visible from the top station of the chairlift, to the left, and a short walk away, is the mountain hut Chata na Grúňi, which should sell refreshments in season. Poludňovy Grúň rises ominously above the wooden chalet, and one can ascend the peak from here; it takes 1-1^1/$_2$ hours on the yellow marked track, up a fairly steep path.

The road along Nová Dolina from the chairlift continues to **Štefanová**, (625m, 2,050ft), a pretty mountain village with shops and a good restaurant. The road terminates in the village, which is a very popular starting point for walks. Among the wide variety of walks from Štefanová are ascents of two Malá Fatra peaks, Stoh and Mount Velky Rozsutec. A green-marked track leads from Štefanová to (Sedlo) Medzieholie, a pass on the main ridge of the Malá Fatra (1 to 1^1/$_2$ hours). From Medzieholie, walking in either direction along the red-marked track takes one up fairly steep paths: either to the right, up **Mount Stoh** (1,608m, 5,274ft) or in the other direction, to the left, up the distinctive rocky peak of the summit of **Mount Velky Rozsutec** (1,610m, 5,281ft); both walks take 1 to $1^1/_2$ hours from Medziholie.

Žilina To Ružomberok

It is 64km (40 miles) from Žilina to Ružomberok, on road 18 (E50), part of the Žilina-Poprad-Košice road. The railway follows the road along the Váh Valley, and both road and railway give travellers fine views of mountain scenery, especially in the Strečno Gorge.

Eleven kilometres (7 miles) from Žilina the flattish land of the Váh Valley is suddenly interrupted by the main massif of the Mála Fatra, which road and railway pass through by means of the steep sided **Strečno Gorge**, which has been cut through the mountains by the River Váh. Both the main road and the railway run along the complete length of the gorge, competing with the river for space on the narrow valley floor (the railway goes through a tunnel for a short distance). The entrance to the gorge, at the village of Strečno (which the road bypasses), is overlooked by the ruins of Strečno Castle, situated on a sharp, precipitous rock right above the road; the best view of the castle is actually from the railway, which is on the other side of the river at this point. The castle was founded in 1321 and guarded the trade routes that passed along the valley. It was destroyed on purpose in 1678, to prevent anti- royalists from using it as a base from which to attack the forces of the Austrian emperor. When it re-opens, after a lengthy period of restoration, access to the castle will be from the minor track that leads behind the rock it is situated on.

Another, less noted ruined castle overlooking the Váh Valley is accessible from here. The village of Strečno is situated immediately below the castle, bypassed by the main road. A metal foot bridge in the village takes one over to the north bank of the river. From here, it is a 45-minute walk along the red-marked track to the castle, **Stary Hrad**, founded a century before Strečno Castle to protect an ancient crossing place over the Váh.

The main road and railway continue through the gorge, from Strečno. A mile further on, Stary Hrad can be seen from the road, on steep cliffs on the opposite bank of the river; it is inaccessible from here, because there is no bridge over the river (for access, see above). The gorge soon widens out and the road runs through the northern part of the town of **Martin**, bypassing the town centre and continuing on to Ružomberok. Martin is set in the broad valley of the River Turiec, which devides the Malá Fatra (to the west) from the Velká Fatra (to the east). The Turiec Valley is another important communications corridor through the mountains, affording road and rail access to southern and central Slovakia (including Banská Bystrica). This ostensibly unremarkable town is surprisingly rather proud of itself, and its present industrial facilities (until recently, it was an important centre for Warsaw pact tank component production) belie a political history that has given the town a prominent place in Slovak history. In the 1860s, the first, muted demands for Slovak independence from Hungary came from this town, which was even

The main ridge of the Low Tatras provides good skiing in winter

Touring by car through the spectacular scenery of the Low Tatras

considered by Nationalists as a viable capital of an independent Slovakia in preference to 'Hungarian' Bratislava. In 1918, the Martin declaration proposed that Slovakia should join with Bohemia and Moravia, to form a united Czechoslovakia. It was a major centre of the Slovak National Uprising and its brewery produces the strongest beer in Czechoslovakia (12 per cent proof). Having said all this, the town itself is of little interest to tourists (although there are a couple of art galleries and, in the south of the town, an open-air museum), and the main reason to come to Martin is to take the chairlift up through the forest to **Martinské Hole**. The bottom station is in the western part of the town, and drivers will find themselves crossing the railway and the River Turiec by a modern road bridge to reach it. There are skiing grounds at the top. From the top station, carry on along the road to the red marked track which runs along the mountain ridge, and take this track to the left to ascend Mount Velká Lúka (1,476m, 4,841ft).

The main Žilina-Poprad road and railway line continue east from Martin to cut through another, steep-sided gorge formed by the River Váh, this time through the Velká Fatra. A sign on the road here points the way to the **Šutovo Waterfalls** (Šútovsky Vodopad), a 38m (125ft) high waterfall set deep in the mountains, accessible on a very minor road. The main road continues on to **Ružomberok**; just before entering the centre of this town, a sign points the way to Hrabovo, a small village just south of the main valley, where there is an outdoor swimming pool and a hotel. A cable car runs up from here to **Málinô**, a low ridge set above a dry valley. The slopes on the other side of the valley are used for downhill skiing, and are the most important winter sports areas in the Velká Fatra. A number of walks are possible from the Hotel Málino, to the left and down a little from the top station. One can walk back down to Ružomberok ($1^1/_4$ hours, blue track), or along the red track up to the summit of **Mount Sidorovo** (1,099m, 3,605ft) and then, following the same track, on down into Ružomberok (3 hours in total from Hotel Malino). These walks bring one down into the centre of Ružomberok.

Ružomberok itself is a small industrial town, and a fairly important road junction, with a road leading south to Banská Bystrica and central Slovakia. There is a certain amount of accommodation here, and the town is an excellent base from which to visit those places described in this section, and the valley Demänovská Dolina in the Low Tatras.

The Low Tatras (Nízke Tatry)

The Low Tatras form the second highest mountain range in Czechoslovakia. The range covers a comparatively large area, stretching from Banská Bystrica and Ružomberok in the west to Poprad and Švermovo in the east. To the north and south the range is bordered by the broad, deep valleys of the Rivers Váh and Hron, through which run main roads and railway lines. Although there has been development in some areas of the mountains — Jasná, for example, is one of the top ski resorts in the country — much of the Low Tatras is unpopulated, and it is much easier for walkers to get away from the crowds in the Low Tatras than in the other ranges in Slovakia. Czechoslovakia's greatest numbers of bears, lynx and wolves live in the thick pine forests that cover the lower slopes of the mountains. Like Malá Fatra, the peaks of the Low Tatras are typically rounded, rather than jagged or sharp. The Low Tatras are primarily granite mountains, though the number of caves in the area also point to limestone being an important component in their geology. There is a certain amount of evidence that the area was glaciated during the last Ice Age. The main ridge of the mountains runs in an east-west direction and culminates in the highest peaks, Mount Ďumbier (2,043m, 6,701ft) and Mount Chopok (2,024m, 6,639ft). The only road to cross the Low Tatras from the Váh to the Hron valley does so at the lowest point of the ridge, over the Čertovica Pass (1,238m, 4,061ft). No railways cross the main ridge. Many streams rise in the vicinity of the ridge and flow perpendicular to it — north to the River Váh, or south to the Hron — and the steep valleys they have eroded are often very picturesque. The most developed part of the Low Tatras is along two of these valleys, Demänovská Dolina in the north, and Bystrá Dolina in the south. The main ski resorts are Jasná, on the northern slopes of Mount Chopok, Bystrianská Dolina on the southern slopes of Mount Chopok above Hotel Srdiečko. There is also the much smaller resort of Čertovica at the summit of the Čertovica pass, which is more popular with less advanced skiers. Jasná is also an important centre for cross-country skiing. In summer, all these resorts and others provide accommodation for those who want to walk or tour by car in the mountains.

Ružomberok To Liptovsky Mikuláš

The main road and railway lines continue eastwards from Ružomberok to **Liptovsky Mikuláš**, 26km (16 miles) further on along the Váh Valley. This part of the journey is not so interesting as the valley here is much broader, a contrast to the steep-sided gorges that the river has cut through Malá Fatra. Liptovsky Mikuláš, like so many of the settlements in the Váh Valley, is more of a place to stay than see, and road travellers at least can safely avoid it since it is bypassed by a short motorway. From the town a road leads into the heart of Low Tatras, along the Demänovská Dolina Valley to the summer and winter resort of Jasná, 16km (10 miles) to the south. The only approach to this valley — which is a 'dead end' (one cannot continue beyond Jasná) — is from the north, via Liptovsky Mikuláš. Users of public transport can make use of the frequent buses that run from Liptovsky Mikuláš to Jasná, which stop at all the principal attractions in the valley. Accommodation in the area can be found in many centres, including Liptovsky Mikuláš and Jasná, but many people come here on day excursions from the High Tatras or Malá Fatra.

Excursions From Liptovsky Mikuláš Into The Low Tatras

The following is a step-by-step guide to the attractions in the Demänovská

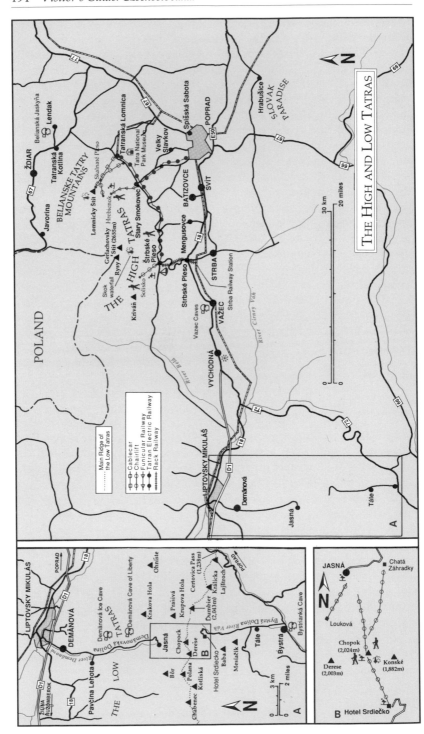

THE HIGH AND LOW TATRAS

Dolina-Bystrá Dolina area. Although it is laid out as a continuous itinerary, those who want to see all the attractions here will need to set aside more than a day to cover it. Those intending to enjoy some serious walking or skiing at Chopok or other centres could easily spend two or three days exploring this relatively small area.

The main road through Demänovská Dolina to Jasná runs south from Liptovsky Mikuláš, and the junction on the motorway bypass, through the village of Demänová and then into the Low Tatras National Park. The lower part of Demänovská Dolina is a beautiful limestone valley cut by the River Demänová, with steep sides and many steep bluffs which tower above the road. Clumps of trees grow on the sides of the valley that are not sheer rock faces. Water has also been at work inside the cliffs themselves, and the total length of the nine storeys of interconnected caves here is 19km (12 miles). Two of the caves in the valley, which are part of this system, have been opened to the public.

Soon after entering the National Park, 8km (5 miles) south of Liptovsky Mikuláš, a car park on the left hand side of the road is for the **Demänová Ice Cave** (Demänovská Ladová Jaskyna), reached by a short walk up the hillside. This cave, cut by the River Demänová over four levels, boasts many bizzare ice patterns and flows, as well as stalactites and other limestone formations on the upper storeys. Spring is the best time to visit the cave, when the melting ice means that the formations are at their best. Its existence has been known since medieval times. A circuit 680m (2,230ft) in length has been open to the public since 1952.

A little further on along the valley is a second cave, the **Demänová Cave of Liberty** (Demänovská Jaskyna Slobody), so named because partisans hid weapons here during the Slovak National Uprising against the Nazis in 1944. It can be reached by walking up the hillside from the carpark on the road, but there is also a short chairlift which runs up to the entrance. The cave, also a result of the actions of the River Demänová, was discovered in 1921, and it boasts many limestone formations and beautiful subterranean lakes.

Beyond the latter cave, the gradient of the road increases and from Chatá Záhradky, on the left hand side of the road, as it curves around, there is a chairlift up to Mount Chopok. Just beyond here the road terminates at **Jasná**, at the top end of Demänovská Dolina, which in winter becomes one of the most important skiing resorts in the country, with fine downhill skiing on the slopes of Mount Chopok, where there are many ski lifts and tows. From Jasná there is a two-stage chairlift up to the summit of Mount Chopok (2,024m, 6,639ft). This chairlift is the principal lift up to the summit of Chopok, and like many other lifts in the mountains, a ride up it often entails waiting in a long queue. Another chairlift from Jasná goes up to Louková which really only gives access to more skiing grounds, rather than a specific summit. Jasná has hosted many international skiing championships and many of the downhill runs, particuarly those further up towards the summit of Chopok, are used by very advanced skiers.

There are excellent views from Mount Chopok, partly because it is on the main ridge of the Low Tatras, so one can look one way over the Demänovská Dolina, and the other way over another valley, the Bystrá Dolina. A red-marked track runs all the way along this ridge, so one could walk along this in either direction, over more peaks and past mountain chalets. One popular option is to walk for about 2 hours from Chopok along the main ridge of the Low Tatras to the summit of Mount Ďumbier (2,043m, 6,701ft) the highest mountain in the Low Tatras. From Ďumbier, another track brings one, after five hours, to the campsite at the bottom of the Demänovská Dolina, very close to Liptovsky Mikuláš. One can also walk back down to Jasná (blue markers).

A chairlift also runs down from Mount Chopok to Hotel Srdiečko, in the Bystrá Dolina Valley, on the opposite side of the ridge to Jasná. One can also ski on these slopes, although they are south-facing compared to the north-facing slopes on the Jasná side of Chopok, and conditions and facilities here are generally not as good as those at Jasná. By now it must be assumed that those who have driven to Jasná will be without their cars, since there is no road access between Jasná and Hotel Srdiečko. The shortest distance by road between the two places is about 81km (50 miles), back through Liptovsky Mikuláš and then over the Čertovica Pass! So those who want to continue on from Hotel Srdiečko must make use of the regular bus service that runs along the valley. Bystrá Dolina is a similar valley to Demänovská Dolina, although it is not quite as attractive. Six kilometres (4 miles) from Hotel Srdiečko the valley broadens out at **Tále**, another important winter resort. A short distance south of Tále the minor road in the Bystrá Dolina Valley meets the more important road 66, at the village of Bystrá. In the village, just along the road towards Banská Bystrica, is **Bystrianská Cave** (Bystrianská Jaskyňa), the third of the limestone caves in the area.

This itinerary could easily be followed, in reverse, by those approaching from the direction of Banská Bystrica: one could drive to Hotel Srdiečko, via the Bystrianká Cave, then go up to Mount Chopok by chairlift and down the other side into Jasná, from where one can catch a bus along the Demänovská Dolina Valley to the two caves. Those planning to stay in the Low Tatras should book accommodation in advance. The hotels rooms at Jasná and in the Demänovská Dolina are controlled by Čedok at Liptovsky Mikuláš; those in Bystrá Dolina, to the south, by Čedok in Banská Bystrica.

The High Tatras (Vysoké Tatry)

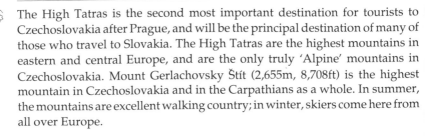

The High Tatras is the second most important destination for tourists to Czechoslovakia after Prague, and will be the principal destination of many of those who travel to Slovakia. The High Tatras are the highest mountains in eastern and central Europe, and are the only truly 'Alpine' mountains in Czechoslovakia. Mount Gerlachovsky Štít (2,655m, 8,708ft) is the highest mountain in Czechoslovakia and in the Carpathians as a whole. In summer, the mountains are excellent walking country; in winter, skiers come here from all over Europe.

Geologically, the Tatras were formed about 35 million years ago, at the same time as the Alps and the Pyrenees. This makes them (in geological terms, at least) very young mountains — the Scottish Highlands and the Appalachians are both about ten times older than the Tatras. There are no glaciers here today, but much of the landscape is a result of glacial erosion of the granite rocks during the last Ice Age, which has produced many sharp, pyramidal peaks, high, jagged ridges and dozens of tiny lakes which are situated high up in the mountains. The lower slopes of the mountains are very thickly forested; bears and deer live here. Higher up there are chamois and marmot, and there are also many beautiful Alpine flowers, which it is forbidden to pick. Other animals which live in the Tatras include rock eagles, wolves, lynx and wild cats. Above an altitude of 2,300m (7,544ft), there is no vegetation or animal life, just bare, steep, rocky slopes.

Tourism began in the High Tatras in the late eighteenth century, but until the war it was mainly rich Hungarians who were able to afford to travel to and stay in the three fashionable resorts of Štrbské Pleso, Tatranská Lomnica and Stary Smokovec. Many lifts were built in the 1940s, including the cable car up to Lomnicky Štít, the second highest mountain in Czechoslovakia. The greater accessibility that resulted from the building of the railway to Poprad, and the Tatran Electric railway that links the three resorts themselves, meant that the Tatras grew in popularity as a holiday destination. In the 1960s and 1970s, more hotels, and many skiing facilities (especially at Štrbské Pleso) were built. The Tatras have long been popular with East European tourists, but they receive relatively fewer visitors from Western Europe.

Many will be surprised by the small area that this range covers. In fact, the High Tatras are the smallest range of Alpine-type mountains in the world. There are only three resorts, which lie very close to one another. The main ridge of the High Tatras is only 26km (16 miles) long. Moreover, a smaller, and lower, part of the range is in Poland. This means that the High Tatras cannot really be seen by car. Unlike other mountain ranges — the Low Tatras or the Krkonoše, or even the Alps — there are no roads that run *through* the mountains. The only road in the High Tatras runs *around* the main massif of the mountains, providing road travellers with views of pine forest rather than of mountain scenery. There are no road passes over the mountains. It is a truism of mountains anywhere in the world that the only way of seeing them properly is on foot; but it is truer of these mountains than of others, and the aim of this chapter is to get people out of cars or trains, and into the mountains by chairlift, funicular and cable car, and then to continue on foot.

Because of their popularity, it is advisable to book accommodation in the High Tatras well in advance, at any time of year; each of the three resorts has dozens of hotels, many of them very plush and, by Czechoslovak standards at least, very expensive. There are also hotels in Poprad. The whole region is so compact it is easy for visitors to stay in one centre (Poprad or one of the three resorts) and see all they want to of the High Tatras from there. This applies both to motorists and those using public transport. The main Čedok office in the High Tatras is at Stary Smokovec, just up from the station and on the main road through the resort. They can advise travellers who turn up without having booked a room on which hotels have space left. They are also the main source of tourist information for the region.

When To Visit: The Weather In The High Tatras

The weather in the High Tatras is variable and unpredictable, as it is in any other mountain area. The first snow arrives in November and does not melt completely until May or June. The main skiing season is from January to March. In winter, days will often start grey and misty, but as the sun gets higher in the sky it will evaporate the mist away, resulting in fine, bright and often very cold afternoons. Spring may not start until April or May. In summer, it can get very hot in the High Tatras, and there will often be short, sharp thunderstorms in the late afternoon, which then clear very quickly to give fine evenings. In summer, walkers should always get an early start, to avoid the heat of the day and the ensuing storms. August, September and early October are more settled months. Late October and November are damp and rainy, and are the slackest season in the High Tatras, so far as tourists are concerned.

Since they cover such a small area, and are so popular, the High Tatras can often get very crowded. It may even be advisable not to visit the area in July and August, when it may seem that much of Eastern Europe is taking its holiday here. The same goes for January and February, which are the main skiing months. September or May are probably the best months for walkers to visit the High Tatras, when they can avoid the worst excesses of the heat and the crowds.

Getting To And Around The High Tatras

The main town in the region is **Poprad**. Poprad is not in the mountains, but the peaks are visible from it, on the near horizon. Poprad is an industrial town, and can safely be avoided by those with their own transport, but see further on in the chapter, under 'The Spiš Region' for points of interest in Spišska Sobota, a suburb of Poprad. However, it is the main centre in the region, and the focus of all the public transport routes in and to the High Tatras. In fact, those who are using public transport will find it almost impossible *not* to pass through Poprad at one time or another. The main airport for the High Tatras, Poprad-Tatry, is near the town; ČSA fly there from Prague, via Bratislava. Fares are very cheap. Poprad is on many internal and international rail routes and the station here (also called Poprad-Tatry) is one of the most important railheads in Slovakia. There are many trains to Prague (about 9 hours) and Bratislava (6 hours), both of which run via Žilina (the Bratislava-Poprad trains will follow the complete itinerary described in this chapter). The journey from Prague is best and most conveniently done overnight, in couchette (sleeping berth) or sleeper trains.

Poprad is also the centre for public transport within the High Tatras. There are many buses up to the resorts, which leave from the bus station next to the main railway station. More entertaining, if slower, is the Tatran Electric railway, a metre-gauge railway which winds its way along the northern slopes of the mountains, linking the three resorts with each other and with Poprad. The narrow gauge tracks next to the main railway lines at Poprad-Tatry station mark the lower terminus of the line. Another part of the line is a rack section, from Tatranská Štrba up to Štrbské Pleso, one of the main resorts. Many trains on the Poprad-Žilina line stop at Tatranská Štrba (the station here is just called Štrba).

Poprad is an important road junction as well, but motorists approaching from the west will branch off the main Váh Valley road before reaching Poprad, probably at Tatranská Štrba, to take the road up to the three resorts. Poprad (and the Tatran resorts) are about 540km (335 miles) from Prague. There is a choice of routes from Prague to Žilina: for instance, through Brno, or through Olomouc (for both, see Chapter 5). Between Žilina and the High Tatras, road travallers will follow the itinerary presented in this chapter — through the Strečno Gorge, and through Martin and Ružomberok. The roads in the mountains are good, and are cleared in winter.

Walking In The High Tatras

The High Tatras were designated a National Park in 1949. National Park rules must be followed by walkers: do not pick flowers, do not disturb the wildlife and do not stray off the marked paths. Route-finding in the High Tatras is, in fact, very easy, since all the paths are obvious, well signposted and marked,

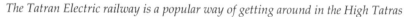

The Tatran Electric railway is a popular way of getting around in the High Tatras

and well trodden on. However, some more basic rules should be followed. Do not walk too far from the settlements, or too far up, if the weather is bad. If the weather changes (and it can change *very* quickly), turn back immediately. Try to find out the weather forecast before setting out on a long walk. Take the following things: warm clothing — even on a hot day in summer, it may be cold at high altitudes, or it may become cold later in the day or if the weather changes; protection from the sun — sun hat, sun glasses, sun cream; some food and drink; basic first aid; wear good shoes, particularly for walking on paths above the tree line, which are often rocky; and take a whistle, which can be used in an emergency to attract attention (the normal 'distress call' is to blow six times every minute). It may be possible to buy food in one of the huts in the mountains, but check if they are open before setting off. One last indispensable piece of equipment is the walking map *Letná Turistická Mapa :Vysoké Tatry*, which is number 21 in the series *Edícia Turistickych Máp*. This shows all the colour-coded marked walking tracks described below, as well as dozens of others, which walkers can obviously use to plan their own trips. As well as the three main resorts, and all the walking tracks and lifts that start from them, the map shows all the other places mentioned in this section — Vychodná, Važec, Poprad and Ždiar. The map is sold at news stands, tourist offices and hotel receptions all over the High Tatras. However, demand for this map can sometimes outstrip supply for short periods, so it is a very wise move for those who see the map in a shop or kiosk in another part of Czechoslovakia to buy it then, before travelling to the Tatras. Note that most of the high-altitude paths are closed in winter, and that some of the best paths are only open from 1 July to 30 October; they are closed during the rest of the year for environmental reasons (mainly to prevent walkers disturbing animals during the breeding season.

More ambitious walkers might want to spend the night in one of the many mountain huts (called *chata*) in the Tatras. Unfortunately, these are often booked up, and it is definitely advisable to reserve a bed in a chalet in advance, before setting off. The place to do this is at Slovakotour, who have an office in the MS 70 hotel in Novy Smokovec, very close to Stary Smokovec. A couple of the chalets are sizeable hotels, with private rooms, but others such as Pod Rysmi (2,250m, 7,380ft) and Téryho (2,015m, 6,609ft) are ancient stone-built huts a long way up in the mountains, which only sleep a dozen or so people in very basic dormitories. Most chalets will sell food, but walkers should not rely on them doing so, and should always take an adequate supply of food and drink with them. Many of the highest peaks in the Tatras do not have marked trails leading up to their summits. Nevertheless, these can be ascended by walkers and climbers who hire a mountain guide. Guides can be hired from Horska Služba, the mountain service, who have an office in Stary Smokovec. In fact, anyone considering doing a lot of high-altitude walking, with or without a guide, should seek information from this office on planning trips, to find out, for example, the weather forecast, whether any paths have been closed, what mountain huts are open, etc.

This section describing the High Tatras continues from Liptovsky Mikuláš, where the last section left off, and looks at each of the three Tatran resorts in turn, in a logical order.

Liptovsky Mikuláš To The Tatran Resorts

It is 35km (22 miles) from Liptovsky Mikuláš to the road up to the Tatran resorts at Tatranská Štrba. From Liptovsky Mikuláš, road and railway continue eastwards, passing through the village of **Vychodná**, where the largest folk festival in Slovakia is held, at the end of July. Since there is no accommodation in the village, visitors usually camp out in haylofts belonging to local farmers, which they specially let out for this purpose. The next village on from Vychodná is **Važec**. The road bypasses the village (there is also a railway station) but, on the opposite side of the village to the road is the entrance to **Važec Caves** (Važecká Jaskyňa). The caves were formed by the actions of one of the tributaries of the River Váh, and they boast many stalagmites and stalactities. The caves were discovered in 1922, and the length of the circuit open to the public is only 230m (754ft), making the cave much smaller than those in the Low Tatras. There is a good view of the High Tatras from the entrance to the caves. Važec used to be one of the most beautiful villages in the Tatras until 1931, when most of the buildings were damaged in a fire, but a small folk museum in the town shows how things used to be.

The next village beyond Važec is Tatranská Štrba, served by Štrba railway station. Here, rail travellers will change onto the rack railway, and road travellers will take the road to the left, which lead up to Štrbské Pleso, the first of the Tatran resorts.

Štrbské Pleso

Road and railway wind up the side of the hill, crossing each other a number of times, until they reach Štrbské Pleso (1,355m, 4,444ft), the highest and flashiest of the three resorts. The town is overlooked by two dominant ridges, with a glacial valley running between them. The town was founded as a spa; bronchial and respiratory diseases are treated here, not by spring waters but by the fresh mountain air. However, in recent years the town has become better known as a ski resort and has hosted many international skiing championships including the 1970 World Alpine Ski Championships. Very few people, if any, actually live here; Štrbské Pleso is basically a collection of hotels, some of which are nice old wooden buildings but many of which are grey concrete-box affairs, local eyesores built in association with the town's function as a premier ski resort. But Štrbské Pleso is very spacious, with many parks, and it covers a fairly wide area.

The station, and the road entrance to the town, are just below its centre. Above the station, and slightly to the left, is a big glacial lake, also called Štrbské Pleso, which is used for boating and swimming in summer and, in winter, when it freezes over, for skating. Many of the town's hotels are built on its shores, including the distinctive triangular-shaped Patria Hotel, which has one of the town's best panoramas. Beyond the lake, near the Hotel Fis, there are two ski jumps. The larger one, whose triangular silhouette is visible for miles around, was built in 1970 when the resort hosted the 1970 World Ski Jumping Championships. It is still used for international competitions. In winter, it is often possible to see people using the smaller jump, next to it. The main downhill skiing areas are beyond the jumps. Near the jumps is a chairlift up to the mountain ridge of **Solisko** (1,830m, 6,002ft). Beware of the queues to go up the chairlift, which form at busy times in summer, when a time-booking scheme may operate. Get to the lift early to be sure of booking a time.

Opposite: Štrbské Pleso is one of the most popular resorts in the High Tatras

Walking in the High Tatras

A mountain hut at the top station serves refreshments.

 There are dozens of possibilities for walks from Štrbské Pleso. The following are a few suggestions. All times stated are one-way rather than round-trip times (unless otherwise indicated).

Easy Walks From Štrbské Pleso

1. The walk from Štrbské Pleso to the tiny lake **Jamské Pleso**, along the red-marked track, takes 1 hour 5 minutes.

2. The walk from Štrbské Pleso to the **Skok Waterfall** (Skok Vodopády), along the yellow-marked track, takes 1 hour 20 minutes. This track runs along the bottom of the Mlynická Dolina Valley, between the two ridges which overlook the town. Just above the waterfall is another tiny lake, **Pleso nad Skokom**.

3. The walk from Štrbské Pleso to **Popradské Pleso**, a much larger glacial lake, set in a bowl in the mountains, takes 1 hour 5 minutes, on the red-marked track. There is a mountain chalet on its shores, called Chata Morávku, where one can stay in dormitories or private rooms. This walk is justifiably popular, and the crowds of people taking picnics by the lake in mid-summer reduces the tranquillity of this otherwise peaceful spot.

4. The walk from Solisko (at the top of the chairlift) to the glacial lakes at **Nišné Wahlenbergovo** on the blue, and then the yellow marked track, is a bit harder, and takes 1 hour 30 minutes. The lakes are beautifully situated, in the valley Furkotská Dolina.

Harder Walks From Štrbské Pleso

1. The walk from Solisko (at the top of the chairlift) to the peak above it, **Predné Solisko** (2,093m, 6,865ft) is a short but very sharp climb up the red-marked track.

2. From Solisko, walk along the blue, then yellow marked track to Nišné Wahlenbergovo (see immediately above). From here the yellow-marked track gets much steeper and ascends the pass **Bystré Sedlo** (2,314m, 7,590ft); one reaches the top from the lakes after $1^1/_4$ hours. From the top of the pass, the path takes one down into the next valley, Mlynická Dolina. The walk back to Štrbské Pleso from here, still following the yellow markers, goes past the Skok Waterfall. The walk from Solisko to Štrbské Pleso over the Bystró Pass takes 5 to 6 hours. This is a good walk, as it is a circular walk, rather than one which requires the walker to use the same track twice.

3. The ascent of **Mount Rysy** (2,499m, 8,197ft) from Štrbské Pleso is a 9 hour return trip. This is one of the toughest and most rewarding trips in the Tatras that can be undertaken by the average walker, and the view from the top is one of the very best the High Tatras can offer. From Štrbské Pleso, take the red marked track to Popradské Pleso (see above). After Popradské Pleso the paths are much steeper and it is another $3^1/_4$ hours to the summit: follow the blue markers for a while then branch off to the right, on the steep red-marked path up to the top. The highest mountain hut in Czechoslovakia, **Chata pod Rysmi**, is a short distance below the summit. It is built of stone and has dormitory accommodation for about a dozen people. Mount Rysy is on the Polish border (it is actually the highest mountain in Poland). The red marked track continues on down into Poland from the summit, but it is not possible to cross the border; the return trip to Štrbské Pleso must be made along the same paths as the ascent. Lenin walked up Rysy in 1914, and from 1957 the 'International Ascent of Youth' up Rysy was organised every year, to commemorate this remarkable event in the history of world Socialism. It was discontinued in 1989, after the demise of Communism.

4. The ascent of **Mount Kriváň** (2,494m, 8,182ft) is also fairly tough, a 7 hour return trip from Štrbské Pleso. The first part of the walk is along the red markers to Jamské Pleso; from the lake, take the blue-marked track for another $2^1/_2$ hours to the summit of Kriváň. Kriváň is a distinctive pyramdial peak and often features in Slovak folklore and poetry.

Stary Smokovec

From Štrbské Pleso, the main road in the Tatras continues east for 17km (11 miles) through thick forests to Stary Smokovec (1,010m, 3,313ft), another spa, and the largest resort in the High Tatras. Views from the road (and electric railway, which follows the road) are of pine trees rather than mountains.

Stary Smokovec forms a whole with Horny-, Dolny- and Novy- Smokovec, nearby. There is more character to this resort than to Štrbské Pleso: only a few of its buildings are modern, and many of the hotels still retain the elegant grandeur of the nineteenth century, when the place was a favourite holiday resort of wealthy Hungarians. Stary Smokovec was established in 1797 and, along with the spa of Horny Smokovec nearby, soon became very fashionable. Some buildings from the village that used to stand here still remain; for example, opposite the Grand Hotel, just above the station, there is a nice wooden church, typical of many in the Carpathians. The Grand Hotel itself, right in the middle of the town, is a half-timbered building dating from 1905 and is one of the most expensive and popular places to stay in the High Tatras. Next to the church is the bottom station of a funicular railway up to **Hrebienok**, 1,263m (4,143ft). The funicular is not very long, and one can also reach Hrebienok by a half-hour stroll along the green-marked track that runs up through the forest beside it. There are a few skiing grounds at Hrebienok.

Stary Smokovec is overlooked by the bulky Mount Slavkovsky Štít (2,452m, 8,043ft), which can be ascended from the town along a blue-marked track; this is a 9 hour return trip.

Alternatively, many walks are possible from Hrebienok. From the track marker post just above the top station of the funicular, one can walk for 20 minutes past Bílikova Chalet and down to the waterfall **Studenovodské Vodopády**. From here, follow the blue marked track (signposted to Zbojnícka Chata) for five minutes to a track junction in a forest clearing; then, take the red marked track from here for fifteen minutes to the waterfalls **Obrovsky Vodopády**. Carry on along the red marked track for another 20 minutes, as it climbs the side of a hill; a track junction in the forest points to the Nálepkova Chalet, a minute's walk away along a green-marked track. This chalet is a picturesque wooden building, set in trees and overlooked by a sharp, high ridge. From here, the green marked track becomes gradually steeper, as it climbs slowly out of the forest and into more rocky terrain to **Téryho Chata**, a 2 hour walk from Nálepkova Chalet. The last part of the walk is the steepest, as it zig-zags up the head of the valley to the chalet. Téryho Chata is a stone-built mountain hut situated at 2,015m (6,610ft), near a number of small lakes. The lakes here (called tarn lakes) are situated in a small saucer-shaped bowl that has been formed by the start of a glacier, which flowed down from here and eroded the valley which walkers have just come through. Virtually all the landscape of the Tatras is a result of glaciation in the last Ice Age, which ended 10,000 years ago.

From Téryho Chata, one can of course go back to Hrebienok the way one came, but a more adventurous way back is to walk for about 2 hours along the yellow-marked track to **Zbojnícka Chata**, over the pass Priečne Sedlo, 2,352m (7,715ft). This chalet is also situated at the head of a rocky valley, near many small lakes. From here, it is a 3 hour walk along the blue-marked track back down to Hrebienok.

The above round trip takes about 8 hours. One can, of course, just do the first part of it (past the waterfalls to Nálepkova Chalet), which is easy and takes an hour, one way. An alternative from Nálepkova Chalet is to walk back to the red marked track for one minute, and continue on along this for one hour up to **Skalnaté Pleso**, 1,751m (5,744ft). From here, there is a cable car down to Tatranská Lomnica, from where, if necessary, one can take the train back to Stary Smokovec. This latter option may be a good idea in bad weather, as

The lake at Štrbské Pleso

Skalnaté Pleso is 600m (1,968ft) lower than the aforementioned pass higher up in the mountains. However, it is still above the tree line, and is quite exposed.

Tatranská Lomnica

Tatranská Lomnica is only 4km (2 miles) east of Stary Smokovec, along the main road in the Tatras. It is linked to Stary Smokovec by a branch of the Tatran Electric railway. Like Stary Smokovec, it has a slight air of faded grandeur about it, and many of the hotels were built over 100 years ago. The landmark of the resort is the Grandhotel Praha, which dates from 1905. There are a number of parks, and the resort is overlooked by the pointed peak Lomnicky Štít. The excellent Tatra National Park Museum, housed in a grey building below the Grandhotel Praha, has exhibits on the plant and animal life of the Tatras, and on the people who first lived in and explored the mountains.

Tatranská Lomnica is not such a good base for walkers or skiers, but it is from here that the greatest number of lifts in the High Tatras operate. Next to the Grandhotel Praha is the bottom station of a cable car to Skalnaté Pleso,

1,751m (5,743ft), a tiny lake situated below Lomnicky Štít. From here, a single-cabin cable car takes 15 people at a time up to the summit of Lomnicky Štít, 2,632m (8,633ft), the second highest mountain in Czechoslovakia. The lift was installed in 1941 and some of the cars operating on it are Swiss-built. There are often very long queues to ride up on this cable car, as it is the most popular tourist attraction in the High Tatras, and a time-booking system is often in operation. If the weather is fine, and the queues are bearable, the views from the top are, of course, fantastic. There is an observatory and a meteorological station at the top, as well as the usual place selling food. One can walk around outside at the top, though not very far. One must remain at the top for 35 minutes, until the next car comes up.

There is another cable car from Tatranská Lomnica to Skalnaté Pleso, which runs from the other end of the town, from near the Hotel Horec. The top stations at Skalnaté Pleso are, however, next to one another. It is normally possible to approach Lomnicky Štít by using this second cable car — one has to change at Skalnaté Pleso, in any case — but check first. In addition to the Lomnicky Štít cable car, there is another lift from Skalnaté Pleso, a chairlift up to Lomnické Sedlo, 2,190m (7,183ft). Lomnické Sedlo is a pass, not a peak, but there is no marked track back down the other side. A long, steep green-marked track links Lomnické Sedlo with Skalnaté Pleso. From Skalnaté Pleso one can also walk to Hrebienok, above Stary Smokovec, in 2 hours, along the red-marked track. Most of the walk is downhill, and it passes two mountain chalets and two waterfalls before reaching the top station of the funicular at Hrebienok, for the ride down to Stary Smokovec. Simply follow the walk described above under 'Stary Smokovec', in reverse.

Beyond Tatranská Lomnica

The main road in the High Tatras continues east from Tatranská Lomnica. After 9km (6 miles) it meets road 67. Turning left here, towards Zakopane, in Poland, one reaches the village of Tatranská Kotlina. At the far end of the

village there is a path up to the entrance to the caves **Belianská Jaskyňa**, where water has created many stalagmites and stalactite features in the limestone rock here. It was discovered in 1881 and in 1896, the cave was opened to the public and lit with electric lighting, only 12 years after the invention of the light bulb. The caves are very substantial and the sightseeing circuit is fairly long. Fewer people hike from Tatranská Kotlina, so those who want to get away from the crowds could use the map to plan some walking in this area. A

popular place to walk to is the chalet Brnčalova Chata on the shores of the tarn lake, Zelené Pleso, a 3 hour walk from Tatranská Kotlina.

A short distance on along the road that leads past the caves, one passes a turning on the right, which leads to the bottom station of a chairlift up to Spišska Magura (1,134m, 3,720ft) — there are excellent views from the top. However, the main road continues on into the village of Ždiar, which is well-known for its many wooden houses, similar to those built in Alpine areas. One of the buildings is a folk museum, open every day. The valley here is very

scenic and provides road travellers with some good views: the ridge on the left
is the Belianske Tatry, an area of the Tatras that has been closed to all walkers,
climbers and skiers as a nature conservation measure. The Belianske Tatry are
limestone rocks (hence the caves at Tatranská Kotlina), rather than granite,
which is the rock that forms the High Tatras. Just beyond Ždiar, on the left
hand side of the road, is a small skiing ground which is very popular with
families and less advanced skiers. From here, the road meanders down
through Javorina to the Polish border.

Excursions East Of The High Tatras

As in any mountain area, there are always likely to be wet days in the Tatras,
but these can be profitably spent seeing the attractions that lie immeditately
to the east of the mountains. In addition to those excursions described below,
do not overlook the Low Tatras (primarily the Demänovská Dolina Valley) as
a possible day trip from the High Tatras.

The Spiš Region

The Spiš region lies immediately due east of Poprad and the High Tatras. In
fact, the region includes a small part of the High Tatras. In the thirteenth
century, this region was devastated by the Tartar invasions, and most of the
local population fled or were killed. Later, the ruling Hungarians encouraged
Saxon (ie German) and Slavik peoples to colonise the area laid waste by the
Tartar invasions from the East, and they founded, in all, twenty-four new
towns, which gradually became a semi-autonomous kingdom within a kingdom, where the inhabitants all spoke German rather than the Slovak of the
indigenous population. The towns had special military and administrative
rights which lasted up until the nineteenth century, which frequently brought
them into conflict with the church and with the local Hungarian magnates.
The colonists originally came to work in the mines in the area; later, the towns
they founded grew very wealthy through trade, and metal and wood working
industries. Many towns in the area are prefaced with the word *spiš*, including
an ancient suburb of Poprad, called **Spišská Sobota**, where the richly decorated Gothic church and belfry testify to the previous prosperity of the region.
Most people take one look at Poprad, decide quite rightly that it is an ugly,
industrial place, and head on to the Tatras; but this ancient suburb, less than
a mile from the centre of Poprad, is very different from its larger neighbour.
Its square is similar in style and the age of the buildings to that of Levoča, the
archetypal Spiš town; burgher's houses, once owned by the rich merchants of
the Spiš region, line the square, in whose centre is a Renaissance Town Hall
and belfry, and late Gothic church, where a carved wooden altar similar to that
at Levoča and carved by Master Pavol sit beneath some beautiful vaulting.
That said, there is less to see here, and far less to see in Spišská Nová Ves,
nowadays the largest town in the Spiš region, than along the road leading east

(road 18) from Poprad towards Prešov, which passes through Levoča and Spišske Podhradie.

✳   **Levoča** is 20km (16 miles) due east of Poprad along this road. Users of public transport should travel to Levoča (and to Spišské Podhradie, below) on the frequent Poprad-Prešov buses that run along this road. In the Middle Ages, Levoča was the centre of the Spiš region, its wealth built on trade and craft industries which in turn led to a flourishingof fine art and rich architecture, paid for by the rich German merchants who settled here. The trade and the merchants have gone, but the rich aristocracy legacy is left for today's travellers to appreciate. The main road that runs through Levoča skirts the medieval walls that surround the Old Town before opening out into Námestie Slobody, the main square of the New Town. Buses also stop here. From the square it is possible to go through the Košice Gate (Košická Brána) through the walls and into the Old Town. From the gate, and the colourful New Minorite Church next to it, Košická Street runs into the main square of the Old Town, a large rectangular medieval showpiece nowadays called Mierové Námestie. Levoča's medieval ground plan, a chess-board pattern of straight streets built around a central rectangular square, has survived, as have its medieval burgher's houses which line the square. However, it is the cluster of buildings in the centre of the square which more immediately command attention.

⌂   The first building is an undistinguished and now rather neglected old merchant's house, with the town's coat of arms above the door; it was in this unlikely building that most of medieval Levoča's money was made, however, for it was the old trading centre of the medieval town. The money was made

The summit of Lomnicky Štít in winter

here by the Levoča merchants funded the building of the church behind it, dedicated to St James, now the principal attraction of the town and the second most important church in Slovakia after St Elizabeth's Cathedral in Košice.

Inside the church, the outstanding work amongst all the late Gothic decoration is the remarkable high altar, created by an architect named Master Pavol of Levoča and carved out of the wood of lime trees between 1507 and 1517. It is $18^1/_2$m (61ft) high, a unique work which is purportedly the largest Gothic High Altar in the world. The carving is entitled *The Last Supper*. Such was the egotism of Master Pavol's patrons, the Levoča merchants, that it was they who posed as models for the portrait of the disciples. The altar was fully restored in the 1950s. One can put a coin into the machine in the central isle of the church, which gives a good tape-recorded description of the altar, and other decorations in the church, in English.

Just below the church is another distinctive building, the Renaissance Town Hall, with its distinctive arches, the final appearance of which dates from 1615. It now houses the Museum of the Spiš Region; other parts of the museum are housed in another building on the square, opposite, at number 20, the house in which Master Pavol is supposed to have lived. There is an exhibition here devoted to his life and works. The other church in the square, an uninspiring Protestant church, dates from the early nineteenth century. The whole of Levoča is surrounded by its old medieval walls, most of which can be walked along. Those who walk round the walls will pass a nineteenth-century German monastery called the Gymnazium. On a hill overlooking the town, called Marianska Hora, is the distinctive domed church called Kostel Marie Katédralá, from where there is a good view over the town. On the first Saturday in July the church plays host to the biggest Marian festival in Slovakia, when over 200,000 Catholics from all over the country descend on the church for a night of prayer, feasting and dancing.

Road 18 continues east from Levoča for 15km (9 miles) to **Spišské Podhradie**, another ancient Spiš town overlooked by Spiš Castle (Spišsky Hrad), one of the biggest ruined castles in Europe. The main road bypasses Spišské Podhradie, but entering the town itself the first thing one comes to on the road that runs through its centre is the complex of buildings that make up Spišská Kapitula. This is a fortified ecclesiatical settlement, still surrounded by a high wall, which was the religious centre of the Spiš region. Its main feature is a twin-towered thirteenth-century basilica of St Martin, a remarkable Romanesque building. The Bishop's Palace, in the same complex, dates from the eighteenth century. Despite the neglect of many of the buildings here, Spišská Kapitula is still a fully-functioning religious centre, although it is not always possible to see inside the cathedral, in whose interior are fourteenth-century frescoes depicting the coronation of the Hungarian King Charles Robert.

From Spišská Kapitula the road runs down into the centre of Spišské Podhradie itself. One can walk up to Spiš Castle from the centre of the town (it takes about 15 minutes); the road up to the castle is a turning off the main Poprad-Prešov road, a short distance beyond Spišské Podhradie. The castle ruins, best seen from Spišská Kapitula, are strung out along the top of a rocky plateau at a height of 634m (2,080ft), and they dominate the landscape for miles around. Because of its prime defensive position, the hill on which it stands has been occupied since the Stone Age by various tribes who built fortified settlements here. The present-day stone castle was founded in the thirteenth century; by 1450, over 2,000 people lived within its confines, including members of the nobility, their servants, and soldiers. Throughout the next few centuries it was owned by various aristocratic families, and it was partly rebuilt in Gothic and then in Renaissance style. The last military activity the castle saw was in 1710, when it was captured by the Imperial Army. Soon afterwards it was damaged by an extensive fire, and neglected; it was gradually allowed to turn into a ruin. Between 1969 and 1979, the castle was extensively restored, and was eventually opened to the public. To be seen in the castle are huge ramparts and towers, many rooms, and the remains of five courtyards and the chapel, which houses a small museum.

Just south of the castle is an archaeological site called **Dreveník**. There are many rock formations and unique plant life. A path leads round it, starting from just below the castle.

Slovak Paradise Near Hrabušice

The Slovak Paradise (Slovensky Raj) is an area of tiny streams, gushing waterfalls and narrow canyons, to the south-east of Poprad. The Slovak Paradise covers a large area, and it includes the Dobšina Ice Cave and Dedinky (see the beginning of the next chapter). The most interesting area, however, is that which includes the gorges near Hrabušice, only 15km (9 miles) to the south-east of Poprad. Here, half a dozen narrow gorges have been cut into the soft limestone of the area, by fast-flowing mountain streams which still flow through them. The gorges can be walked through by means of ladders, steel and wooden walkways, and chains, which are built into the sides of the vertical cliffs above the waterfalls. Often, walkers in the canyons are dwarfed by the towering cliffs above them, which in some places are 300m (984ft) high. There are dozens of possibilities for walking in this area, and those intending

to walk here should buy the map *Letná Turistická Mapa: Slovensky Raj*, number 23 in the *Edícia Turistickych Máp* series, which is available from many bookshops and hotel reception desks in Poprad and the Tatran resorts. If the map is hard to find, try looking in the excellent book shop in Poprad, just up from the Čedok office on Námestie Dukelskych Hrdinov, which should stock it. In fact, it is probably pointless trying to see the area without this map, since thorough advanced planning is needed before setting out on trips: many of the paths are one-way only, and are marked as such by arrows on the map. This means it is only possible to walk up the canyons. One cannot walk back down the canyons, and must return by another route that leads over the tops of the hills. The following description assumes that travellers are in possession of the aforementioned map. The main gorges to explore, which can easily be identified on the aformentioned map, are described below.

The **Hornád Gorge** (Prielom Hornádu) is the most popular part of this region to visit. It runs between Cingov, a short distance west of Spišská Nová Ves, and Podlesok, a short distance south-west of Hrabušice. Both places are chalet camps, not villages, and are accessible by road. However, the gorge itself that runs between them can only be seen on foot. A 16km (10 miles) blue-marked track runs the whole length of the gorge, over footbridges, steps, metal ladders and built walkways. This is not a one-way track, so it is possible to walk only part of the way along the gorge, and then turn back. Note that there is also a yellow-marked track linking Hrabušice with Čingov. This track runs parallel with the gorge, and above it, affording amazing views over it, especially from the viewpoint Tomášovsky Vyhlad. To walk the complete length of the blue-marked track takes 3 hours, the yellow track 2 hours.

From the aformentioned chalet camp at Podlesok it is possible to walk right into another beautiful gorge, the **Suchá Bela Gorge**, parts of which are ascended by means of ladders. This gorge can get crowded at busy periods, however. It is a one-way gorge; it takes 2 hours to reach the top from Podlesok, and one must return by a different route.

From Podlesok there is a green-marked track runing all the way over to the Dobšiná Ice Cave (see Chapter 8). This path provides access to the **Piecky Gorge**, and ,further on, the deepest gorge in the Slovak Paradise, **Velky Sokol**.

Deep in the hills, and accessible after a long walk, is the **Sokolia Dolina Gorge**, a walk along which reveals a number of high, isolated waterfalls, including the Zavojy Vodopád falls, the highest in the Slovak Paradise. The best way to approach this gorge is from Podlesok, via Kláštorisko and through the valley Tomášaská Belá.

Many paths in the area lead to or through Kláštorisko, an isolated chalet community, campsite and restaurant situated on a mountain meadow. Archaeologists are slowly excavating an old thirteenth-century monastery here, to which the native Slavs of the region fled during the Tartar invasions.

Central Slovakia

Approaches to Banská Bystrica

Banská Bystrica lies in the very centre of Slovakia, at the foot of the Low Tatras and overlooked on all sides by mountains. Because of its centrality, it is an important road and rail junction, and can be approached from a number of different directions.

Roads from the Váh Valley, to the north, approach central Slovakia by means of mountain passes over the Low Tatras, the highest of which is the **Čertovica Pass** (1,238m, 4,061ft) on the road between Poprad and Liptovsky Mikuláš, and Banská Bystrica. There are a few skitows in the minor winter resort situated at the summit of the pass. This road also passes the Bystrá Caves (see entry, under 'Low Tatras'). It is popular to approach Banská Bystrica from Ružomberok (53km, 33 miles) away by road. At the highest point on the this road, and mid-way between the two towns, is **Donovaly**, (960m, 3,149ft), another ski resort in the Low Tatras. There is a short chairlift up to Nová Hola (1,370m, 4,493ft) from here, and there is a limited amount of downhill skiing. Many walking tracks start from here. A monument in the village, outside the Sport Hotel, recalls the important role that it played in the Slovak National Uprising. The third road from the north is from Martin (65km, 40 miles), via Turčianské Teplice. A railway follows this road, but runs through a tunnel as the road goes over the pass (1,000m, 3,280ft). After winding down from the summit of the pass, the road passes the carpark for the **Harmanec Cave** (Harmanecká Jaskyňa), 16km (10 miles) before reaching Banská Bystrica (there is also a railway station by the cave entrance). It is a short walk up the path from the carpark to the entrance to the caves, and from the terrace at the entrance there is a good view of the Velká Fatra range. The length of the sightseeing circuit which the public is taken on is 720m (2,362ft), which leads visitors past small lakes and many limestone formations.

Most of those who are approaching from the south will be coming from Bratislava, 208km (129 miles) away. The road from Bratislava passes through Nitra (see Chapter 6) and just bypasses Zvolen (see below). This road continues from Banksá Bystrica, over the Čertovica Pass to Poprad and High Tatras.

Banská Bystrica

The early history of Banksá Bystrica is dominated by the iron, copper and silver ores that were mined near the town in medieval times. It has also earned itself an important place in the more recent history of Slovakia, because it was here that the Slovak National Uprising against the Nazi occupation broke out in 1944. The main points of interest in the town are around the colourful main square in its centre, Námestie SNP, which is dominated by a high clock tower (1522) and nearby, a seventeenth-century Jesuit church with four columns on its façade. On the same side of the square, Thurz's House, an old burgher's residence, now contains the museum of Central Slovakia, and an Ethnographical Museum which is better than most. Many other Renaissance and Gothic buildings line the square.

A square immediately beyond the clock tower contains a number of buildings that have been constructed where the town's medieval castle once stood. At the centre of this group of buildings is the Church of the Virgin Mary, founded in the thirteenth century. Inside is a wood-carved altar made in 1508 by Master Pavol of Levoča which sits in one of the side chapels of the church; at the centre of the work is a portrait of St Barbara, the patron saint of miners, obviously watching over the safety of the men to whom medieval Banská Bystrica owed its considerable wealth and importance. Next to it is the former Town Hall, an attractive building distinguishable by its Renaissance arches; it now houses an art gallery. Next to this is a rather shabby tower, one of the few remaining medieval bastions of the castle. The Church of the Holy Rood, the other side of St Mary's, is not so nice, but entering its cemetery allows one to see more of the old bastions and walls of the medieval castle.

Follow Horná Street, which continues up from the castle area and the main square, and take the first turning on the right, down an alley way between the houses. This brings one to a few more remaining parts of the medieval walls, and a distinctive building (it could almost be a space station of some sort) that was built in 1969 to house the museum of the Slovak National Uprising, which documents the history of the revolt which started in the town in 1944.

Excursions From Banská Bystrica

Banská Bystrica is an excellent base from which to see the Low Tatras. One can follow the itinerary described under the section 'Low Tatras' in reverse, past the Bystrá Caves and then up Bystrá Dolina to the chairlifts up to Chopok. The Harmenec Caves, described immediately above, are only 16km (10 miles) from Banská Bystrica, along the road to Martin.

The E66 which is dual carriageway, runs from Banská Bystrica to **Zvolen**, 20km (12 miles) to the south. A railway line also links the two towns. Zvolen, too, is an ancient settlement, with many medieval and Renaissance houses lining its square, but its principal attraction is the impressive castle, which is next to the railway station. It was originally built as a summer palace for the Hungarian king Louis the Great, in the fourteenth century. The fortification walls and bastions one sees today date from the sixteenth century. The castle now houses art collections of the Slovak National Gallery, comprising mainly lesser known medieval and Baroque European painters, but there is also a section concerned with Master Pavol of Levoča.

The E571 runs west from Zvolen to Žiar (17km, 10 miles). Half way along this road, a road runs south for 20km (12 miles) to **Banská Štiavnica**, which, like Banská Bystrica, is an old mining town, in an attractive setting amidst the hills of the Tiavnické Vrchy. In the Middle Ages, these hills yielded high quantities of silver ore and other minerals. The Gothic buildings on the town's main square, Tojičné Námestie, were once the homes of the German mineowners, while their workers lived in the old miners' cottages in the twisty lanes of the old part of the town. The vaults of town's castle (no public access) once contained stocks of metal from the nearby mines, safeguarding the town's wealth from any marauding Turks who might be passing. The town's Gothic and Baroque churches, and the mining museum (on the main square and on Klopačka Street) will provide interest for some, while the best appreciation of the attractive setting of Banská Štiavnica can be gained from the church of Štiavnica Kalávaria, situated on a hilltop overlooking the town. Incidentally, the first use in Europe of gunpowder for mining pruposes was made in the mines of Banská Štiavnica, in 1657.

Returning to the E571, one can continue to Žiar, from where road 50 brings one after 48km (30 miles) to Prievidza. A short distance west of Prievidza is the small town of **Bojnice**, and its very attractive, multi-turreted castle. The current building is the result of the reconstruction of a medieval castle at the turn of this century. The Hungarian aristocrat who owned the castle at this time was influenced by the architecture of French châteaux on the River Loire, and the present construction is a pleasing mixture of towers, spires and battlements. As well as an art gallery and a museum, the tour of the castle includes a look at a cave beneath it, where palaeolithic man once lived. Bojnice itself is a spa town, with a number of modern spa buildings. In the shadow of the castle there is a sizeable outdoor swimming pool, heated by water from the thermal springs.

Also in this area, west of Banská Bystrica, is **Kremnica**, the third of the central Slovak mining towns. Banská Bystrica's mines produced copper, those in Banská Štiavnica silver, but the mines here produced gold, and the town soon became rich through its mining activities. This town was once the Kutná Hora (see Chapter 3) of Slovakia, or rather Hungary, providing all the coins for the Hungarian and later the Austro-Hungarian empire, and although the town's appearance today gives little indication of its previous wealth, a well-fortified castle and bastions are an indication of the attention to which its medieval rulers paid to its security. The mines near Kremnica are the only ones in this part of Slovakia that are still active, although even the commemorative medals and coins they produce to honour worthy Czechoslovak citizens cannot compete in beauty or value with the exhibits in the Museum of Coins and Medals in the old Town Hall on the main square, which also exhibits examples of more recent Czech currency pieces. A bizzare oddity in Kremnica is a museum devoted to skiing, also on the main square. In Kremnica, as in Banská Štiavnica, Gothic burghers houses in the town's centre are a contrast to the miner's own cottages, which were built away from the central square. The town's castle, damaged considerably in the last war, has been closed for many years for restoration; its most noted feature is its chapel, much admired architecturally. Incidentally, almost only for the sake of historical continuity and tradition, a modern mint near Kremnica continues to manufacture Czechoslovakia's modern coinage.

Additional Information

Places of Interest

Banská Bystrica
Museum of the Slovak National Uprising
Open: 8am-6pm, daily except Monday

Art Gallery
Open: Tuesday to Friday 9am-5pm.
Weekends, 10am-4pm.

Ethnographical Museum
Open: weekdays, 8am-12noon, 1-4pm;
Sunday, 9am-12noon,
1-4pm; closed Saturday.

Banská Štiavnica
Mining Museum
On Tojičné Námestie

Open: daily except Monday, 10am-4pm.

Beckov
Beckov Castle
Near Nové Mesto nad Váhom
Closed for extensive restoration at time of research. Revised opening times unknown.

Bojnice
Bojnice Castle (Hrad Bojnice)
Open: April, October, weekends only,
9am-12noon, 1-4pm.
May to September, daily except Monday, 8am (9am September) -12noon, 1-5pm.

Bystrá
Bystrianská Cave
(Bystrianská Jaskyňa)
On road 72, north-west of Brezno
Open: 1 April to 15 May, 16 September
to 31 October, daily except Monday,
tours at 9am, 11am, 2pm.
16 May to 15
September, daily except Monday, tours
on the hour, every hour, 9am-4pm.

Čachtice
Čachtice Castle (Hrad Čachtice)
Access only on foot from village of
Čachtice, near Nové Mesto nad Váhom
Open access at all times.

Demänová Cave of Liberty
(Demänovská Jaskyňa Slobody)
In the Demänovská Dolina Valley,
between Liptovsky Milkuláš and Jasná
Open: 15 May to 16 September, daily
except Monday, tours on the hour, every
hour, 9am-4pm.
Rest of the year daily except Monday,
tours at 9am, 11am, 2pm.

Demänová Ice Cave
(Demänovská L'adová Jaskyňa)
In the Demänovská Dolina Valley,
between Liptovsky Mikuláš and Jasná
Open: 15 May to 16 September only,
daily except Monday, tours on the hour,
every hour, 9am-4pm.

Harmanec Cave
(Harmanecká Jaskyňa)
16km (10 miles) from Banská Bystrica,
on the road to Turčianské Teplice and
Martin.
Open: 1 April to 15 May, 16 September
to 31 October, daily except Monday,
tours at 9am, 11am, 2pm. 16 May to 15
September, daily except Monday, tours
at 10am, 11.30am, 1pm, 2.30pm, 4pm.

Kremnica
Museum of Coins and Medals, and *Ski
Museum*
Both on the main square
Open: daily except Monday, 7.30am-
3.30pm.

Levoča
Spiš Museum
In the Old Town Hall, next to St James'
Church.
Open: Tuesday to Sunday, 9am-12noon,
1-4pm.

St James' Church
On the main square, Mierové Námestie
Opening times as posted on door.
Closed Sunday morning, and all day
Monday.

Spišské Podhradie
Spiš Castle (Spissky Hrad)
Open: May to October only, daily except
Monday, 9am-5pm.

Tatranská Kotlina
Belianska Caves
(Belianska Jaskyňa)
20 minute walk up the path from the
north end of the village on road 67
Open: 15 May to 16 September, daily
except Monday, tours at 9.30am, 11am,
12.30pm, 2pm, 3.30pm.
Rest of the year: daily except Monday,
tours at 9.30am, 11am, 2.30pm.

Tatranská Lomnica
Tatra National Park Museum
On main road, below Grandhotel Praha
Open: daily, 8.30am-12noon, 1-5pm
(mornings only at weekends).

Trenčín
Trenčín Castle
Open: daily all year, 8am-4pm.

Trnava
West Slovak Museum
Staromestská Street
Open: daily except Monday, 9am-5pm.

Važec
Važec Caves (Važecká Jaskyňa)
Just off E50 (road 18), 28km (17 miles)
east of Liptovsky Mikuláš
Open: as for Bystrianská Jaskyňa.

Zvolen
Zvolen Castle (Art Gallery)
Open: 10am-5pm, daily except Monday.

Boating and Sailing

Orava Dam Lake, northern Slovakia,
north-east of Žilina on the Polish border.
Boating, fishing, watersports. Boats out
to an island in the lake, with a church
and museum on it, from Slanická Osada.

Liptovská Mara Lake, on the River Váh
west of Liptovsky Mikuláš.

Skiing

This region includes the best skiing areas in Czechoslovakia, and those which are most frequently visited by Westerners.

Malá Fatra
Vrátna (620m, 2,034ft): 1,500m (4,920ft) of downhill runs, 2 chairlifts, 12 skitows. Also cross country skitracks. Martinské Hole (1,200m, 3,936ft): 1,440m (4,592ft) of downhill runs, 1 chairlift, 12 skitows

Velká Fatra
Málinô (550m, 1,804ft): 1,350m (4,428ft) of downhill runs, 1 cable car, 3 skitows. Donovaly (860m, 2,821ft): 1,360m (4,461ft) downhill runs, 1 chairlift, 12 skitows.

Low Tatras
Jasná (950m, 3,116ft — north side of Mount Chopok): 2,005m (6,576ft) downhill runs, 6 chairlifts, 12 skitows. Bystrianska Dolina (600m, 1,968ft — south side of Mount Chopok) 2 chairlifts, 9 skitows.

High Tatras
Štrbské Pleso (1,350m, 4,428ft): 1,915m (6,281ft) downhill runs, 2 chairlifts, 4 skitows. Skijumps. Stary Smokovec (850m, 2,788ft): 1,480m (4,854ft) downhill runs, 1 funicular, 7 skitows. Tatranská Lomnica (850m, 2,788ft): 2,180m (7,150ft) downhill runs, 5 lifts, 5 skitows. Ždiar (800m, 2,624ft): 1,180m (3,870ft) downhill runs, 1 chairlift, 13 skitows.

Jasná and Štrbské Pleso are the two most important ski resorts in Czechoslovakia.

Seasons: from November/December to April/May in most cases.

Transport

ČSA-Czechoslovak Airlines: offices and airports at the following:

Piešťany
Nálepkova 1 ☎ 26184, 22950
Flights to Prague and Poprad-Tatry

Banská Bystrica - (Sliač)
Partyzánská Cesta 4
☎ (088) 41975
Flights from Sliač airport (south of Banská Bystrica) to Prague

Poprad
Hviezdoslavova 1
☎ (092) 24190, 23828
Flights from Poprad-Tatry airport to Prague and Bratislava.

Tourist Information Centres and Accommodation Offices

Čedok offices in most towns act as tourist and accommodation offices.

Banská Bystrica
Námestie V.I.Leniná 4
974 75-Banská Bystrica ☎ (088) 54471

Liptovsky Mikuláš
Námestie Osloboditelov 6
131 13-Liptovsky Mikuláš ☎ (0849) 22985

Poprad
Námestie Dukelskych Hrdinov 60
058 01-Poprad ☎ (092) 23287

Ružomberok
Ulica Cervenej Armády 1
034-50 Ružomberok ☎ (022) 22463

Stary Smokovec
On main street in town
060 12-Stary Smokovec ☎ (0969) 2417

Tatranská Lomnica
Lomnica Hotel
059 60-Tatranská Lomnica
☎ (0969) 967428

Žilina
Hodžova 9
011 09-Žilina ☎ (089) 23347

Zvolen
Námestie SNP 4
960 75 Zvolen ☎ (0855) 22561

Čedok offices in Žilina, Banská Bystrica and Stary Smokovec also offer one day/half day coach tours to places of interest in the surrounding area.

8

EASTERN SLOVAKIA

B oxed in on all four sides, by the massif of the Tatras in the west, and by the
Hungarian, Polish and Soviet borders to the south, north and east, Eastern
Slovakia is in some ways an isolated limb of Czechoslovakia, largely neglected
by Western tourists. Czechoslovakia does not, however, suddenly end at the
Tatras, and despite the proximity of the vast, bleak plains of the Soviet Ukraine
that lie not so very far to the East, the comparatively undiscovered attractions
of this area are numerous.

Here, more than anywhere in Czechoslovakia, the familiar preconceptions
of Eastern Europe become reality: many of the older women wear heavy skirts
and bury their faces beneath thick but often brightly coloured shawls; in
villages, these same women wash their family's clothes in the local mountain
streams; motorists must be prepared to become stuck behind a horse and cart
being driven to market and the people of rural Eastern Slovakia are largely
unaccustomed to tourists, and either look upon the visitor with suspicion or
curiosity. Nowhere more than the isolated rural areas boast such conditions
of poverty and backwardness. Only since World War II has the principal order
of society broken out of a patriarchal, peasant-dominated stagnation and in
some communities, society is still dominated by the same clans and rigid
traditionalism that has existed for centuries, seemingly overlooked by the
strong-armed socialist rulers in Bratislava or distant Prague.

Folklore customs still exist in some places, though they are more likely to
consist of traditional feasts in people's private homes, rather than costume
wearing and folk dancing for tourists. Many places are understandably ramshackle and appear to be suffering from neglect; the twentieth century, as well
as tourists, seems to have passed by Eastern Slovakia in many respects.

Those deciding to spend some time in this area will find their efforts are
rewarded. Travellers after interesting natural sites will find entertainment
above and below ground, in the many caves in the western part of the region,
and in the east, in the hills of the Vihorlatské Vrchy. In the north-eastern part
of the region, where Slovakia meets the Polish and Soviet borders at the top
of Mount Kremenec, old churches constructed entirely out of local wooden
timbers are scattered through valleys lined with tiny hamlets. All of this can
be enjoyed in a climate which boasts the highest number of sunshine hours in

the country. Away from natural attractions there is the usual clutch of historic towns and castles to divert the eyes of the visitor tired of mountains and meadows: Bardejov, Prešov and Košice, the region's capital, are all worthy destinations, while near Rožňava, are Betliar and Krásna Hôrka Castles.

Poprad To Košice

Poprad To Rožňava

It is 73km (45 miles) from Poprad to Rožňava by road 67, a scenic trip along which the visitor can stop off at a number of places of interest.

Leaving behind the rather dismal housing estates on the outskirts of Poprad, after 10km (6 miles) one comes to Hranovnica and the turn-off to Hrabušice (see Chapter 7). Continuing along the main road, however, one enters the Slovak Ore Mountains, a range of dark and slightly forbidding hills which occupy an area to the south-east of the High Tatras. After passing through the village of Vernár (14km, 9 miles on from Hranovnica) the road ascends a short, sharp pass over a limb of the Low Tatras and then comes down into the valley of the River Hnilec which rises close to here. The pass itself is over 1,060m (3,477ft) high. A junction is reached after the road reaches the valley from the pass, where a left turning is made. After a short distance the road crosses the boundary into the Slovak Paradise National Park and the car park and hotel-restaurant complex next to the entrance to the **Dobšina Ice Cave** (Dobšinská Ladová Jaskyňa) is reached.

The Dobšina Ice Cave is the only cave open to the public in the Slovak Paradise National Park, but it is one of the world's most extensive ice cave systems. It lies at an altitude of 970m (3,182ft) on the slopes of a limestone hill called Duca. The cave was formed by the action of the River Hnilec on the limestone rocks of this region. However, the lower sections of the river became blocked off, and favourable conditions then resulted for the formation of ice in the cave. The bottom floor of the cave is covered with ice 25m (82ft) thick; there are also other ice columns and waterfalls. The cave has been open to the public since its discovery in 1870 and in 1887 it became the first cave in the world to be illuminated by electric lighting. The total known length of the cave system is about 1,400m (4,592ft), but the circuit that the public walks is only 475m (1,558ft). Although the caves are at a fairly high altitude, there is a railway station very close to them (called Dobšinská Ladová Jaskyňa) on the very scenic line that runs between Banská Bystrica and Košice via Margecany. There are no rail connections from here to Poprad or Rožňava — the line takes a different route to the road. Do not confuse the Dobšina Ice Caves and the town of Dobšina which lies a fair distance to the south-east.

A short distance beyond the Dobšina Ice Cave, soon after the village of Stratena, a left-hand turning leads towards the village of Dedinky. After a short while this road skirts the side of a small artificial lake, called Palcmanská Maša, a very pleasant spot which in summer is popular with swimmers and windsurfers. Just before the road enters the village a track on the right leads to the bottom station of a chair lift *(lanovká)* up to the Geravy Karst Plateau at an altitude of 1,040m (3,411ft). There is skiing here in winter and a couple of ski lifts have been built near the top station.

Back on the main Poprad-Rožňava road, one should continue on to the town of Dobšina, over another pass. At Dobšina the road enters the valley of the River Slaná which becomes increasingly wider as one continues southwards.

Nineteen kilometres (12 miles) beyond Dobšina is the village of **Betliar**, where, on the left hand side, set back a little from the main road, is Betliar Château, the present apprearance of which dates from 1880 and which houses a museum of interior design, and other collections of crystal, porcelaine, rare furniture, weapons and hunting trophies. It was closed at the time of writing for an extensive period of renovation. The château was a hunting lodge of the local aristocratic family, the Andrassys, who were once the biggest industrial and feudal magnates in Hungary. The castle is built over the remains of a smaller, Gothic castle that was established here in the fifteenth century. The château is surrounded by a pleasant park with a couple of lakes and other aristocratic folly-type buildings. Six kilometres (4 miles) beyond Betliar the town of Rožňava is reached.

Rožňava And The Slovak Karst

The town of **Rožňava** is uninspiring, but it is an excellent base from which to see the Slovak Karst, with its caves and gorges. There are a few hotels here. Rožňava grew up as a gold mining town in the Middle Ages. Those who have some time to spend in the town may care to visit the mining museum on Šafárikova Street, and see the Renaissance observation tower on the town's main square. There is also a small Gothic cathedral in the town; its altarpiece shows scenes from the working life of the old gold miners who created this town's medieval prosperity.

The numerous excursions that can be made from Rožňava include Betliar Château, to the north; Krásna Hôrka Castle, Jasov Caves and the gorge of Zádielska dolina to the East; and the three caves described in this section, all of which are part of the Slovak Karst Protected Landscape Region, which roughly covers an area to the south and east of Rožňava. The limestone in this area is up to 500m (1,640ft) thick, and water flowing through this rock has created a large number of underground caves with their fascinating stalactite and stalagmite forms that are a result of millennia of geological evolution. In contrast to the Slovak Paradise to the north, the attractions of the Slovak Karst lie mainly underground. Four of the caves have been opened to the public; three of them are within easy excursion distance from Rožňava, and are presented in this section. The map entitled *Slovensky Kras:Domica* may prove a good investment, even if there is less walking to be done in this area than in the Slovak Paradise.

From Rožňava road 50 (E571) leads south towards Plešivec, Šafárikovo and Rimavská Sobota. The second village one passes through, travelling along this

road, is Slavec. After the village there is a turning off to the left, to the village
of Silica. Along this road on the right is **Gombasec Cave** (Gombasecká
Jaskyňa). This cave was discovered in 1951 and is famous for its slender white
'quills' that are anything up to 3m (10ft) in length, but only a few millimetres
wide. The length of the tour of these caves is 300m (984ft).

Returning to the main road one must continue south to the small town of
Plešivec; from the major junction in the centre of this town, a road leads left
towards Dlha Ves and **Domica Cave** (Jaskyňa Domica) which is reached after
a short drive up a rather bleak valley. The Domica-Baradla cave system is
21km (13 miles) in length and is one of the fifteen longest cave systems in the

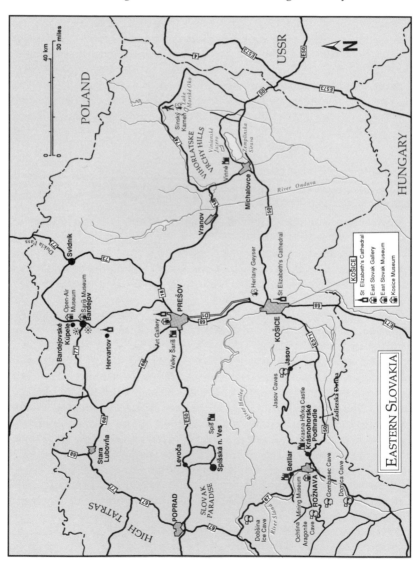

world. In fact, the majority of the cave system lies under Hungarian territory, but nevertheless, the length of the tour taken on the Slovak side is about 2km (1 mile) in length, which normally includes a boat ride on the underground River Styx, which hollowed out the cave on its three levels. On occasions, low water levels in the River Styx may mean this boat trip cannot be made. A number of archaeological finds have been made in the cave, including painted ceramics, from 5,000 years ago when it was inhabited by prehistoric man.

To reach the **Ochtina Aragonite Cave** (Ochtynská Aragonitová Jaskyňa) one must head in a different direction to the caves mentioned above. From Rožňava, take the minor road leading west towards Štítnik and Jelšava. After the village of Štítnik, 13km (9 miles) from Rožňava, this road heads along a steep, narrow valley. At the highest point of this road, about 8km (5 miles) from Štítnik, is the car park for the caves, which are inaccessible by road; it is a walk of less than a mile to the entrance, up a fairly steep path. The length of the tour is 240m (787ft). There are many pretty rock features including the small aragonite 'flowers' which cling to the rock like limpets.

Rožňava To Košice

It is 69km (43 miles) from Rožňava to Košice, along road 50 (E571). There are a number of interesting things to see along this road.

Five kilometres (3 miles) from Roznava the road rounds a slight curve and **Krásna Hôrka Castle** can be seen on the left hand side, sitting atop a hill that rises above the small village of Krásnohorské Podhradie. Motorists must turn off the main road and drive through the village to reach the castle. The first castle was built on this site in 1320; later reconstructions turned it into a Renaissance fortress against the Turks who always threatened to extend their vast empire into Slovakia. From the sixteenth century the castle was the seat of the Andrássy family (see under 'Betliar Château', above) and since 1910 the castle has housed the Andrassy Museum.

Back on the main road, immediately after the village of Krásnohorské Podhradie, is the **Andrássy Mausoleum**, built in 1904 and reputedly the most beautiful art-nouveau building in Slovakia. The mausoleum is a small, simple domed structure, set back from the road in its own gardens, just past a big motel and in sight of the castle where its deceased incumbents lived. The interior is a riot of marble and gold; those who do not decide to stop off at the castle should not miss a quick look in here.

The next village after Krásnohorské Podhradie is Lipovník and from here the road ascends **Jablonovské Pass**, which crosses over a low arm of the Slovak Ore mountains. There are excellent views to the west as one ascends the pass, which encompass Rožňava and the dominant hillock on which Krásna Hôrka castle sits. The descent on the east side is also interesting. The road now runs along the flat-bottomed valley of the River Turňa, with its steep sides; the ridge of hills on the right mark the border with Hungary.

A few miles further on along the road is the **Zádielska Dolina Gorge,**one of the most interesting sights of the Slovak Karst area. Access to the gorge is from a car park in the village of Zádiel, which the main road along the valley of the River Turňa just bypasses. Zádiel (to the immediate north of the road) and Dvorníky (to the immediate south) really form one settlement. There is a road linking the two villages, which runs under the main road. There is also a railway station at Dvorníky on the Rožňava-Košice railway line. The gorge can only be seen on foot, by walking through it along the red-marked track which leads from the carpark in Zádiel along a metalled road which cannot be used by private motorists. The entrance to the gorge, which is visible from the main road, leads into a steep, narrow valley leading off the main wide valley of the River Turňa. The gorge itself is 3km (2 miles) long and in some places is only 10m (33ft) wide with soaring, vertical limestone walls up to 400m (1,312ft) in height. The River Blatnica whose eroding actions formed the gorge still flows down the middle of it. It takes an hour to walk up the gorge.

The road continues beyond Zádiel-Divorníky, and soon passes the small ruins of **Turňa Castle** on the left hand side, above the road on a vineyard-covered hillside (access to the castle is difficult; the best view of it is from the road). Ten kilometres (6 miles) further on from the castle is Moldava nad Bodvou. Those not wishing to visit the last cave of the Slovak Karst region should simply continue on to Košice, 22km (14 miles) on along the main road. However, at Moldava nad Bodvou there is a left turning which leads to the town of Jasov, 9km (6 miles) to the north. At Jasov is **Jasov Cave** (Jasovská Jaskyňa) hollowed out by the underground River Bodva. Archaeological finds attest to the fact that this cave was inhabited in the Stone Age, and the cave itself used to be in the hands of the monks of Jasov Monastery. The cave is seen on a tour 620m (2,034ft) in length. The monastery in the village is considered to be the most impressive Baroque structures in Slovakia; though founded in the twelfth century, its present buildings all date from the eighteenth century. The monastery is set in a huge park. From Jasov one does not have to head back to the main road to reach Košice; Košice is 28km (17 miles) from Jasov along a minor road.

A railway line links Rožňava and Košice. Lipovník Station should be used for Krásna Hôrka Castle. Unfortunately, the railway goes through a tunnel under Jablonovské Pass, so rail travellers do not get the views of those using the road. Dvorníky-Zádiel station is convenient for the gorge: the red-marked track up through the gorge actually starts at this station.

❄ Košice

The town of Košice is the capital of the Eastern Slovakia, and is the region's principal transport centre. This means that most people visiting the region are likely to find themselves at least passing through Košice and, most probably, staying there. Košice is so accessible and is on so many transport routes that it is difficult for travellers in Eastern Slovakia to avoid passing through it. It is a stop on the north-south international rail route between Cracow (Poland) and Budapest. There are through trains running east to Moscow via Kiev. Through trains run west to Poprad (frequent; $1^1/_2$ hours), Prague ($10^1/_2$ hours, some overnight trains with sleeper or couchette cars), Cheb and Karlovy Vary (once a day, overnight; 19 hours), Bratislava (via Poprad and Žilina; frequent, 8 hours), Brno and many other places in Czechoslovakia. By road, Košice is 422km (262 miles) from Bratislava, 473km (293 miles) from Brno and 667km (414 miles) from Prague. The E50 from Prague via Brno, Trenčín, Poprad and Prešov runs through Košice and then continues east through Michalovce to Kiev and Moscow. The E71 is a fast route that runs south from Košice to Budapest. Some people may want to fly to Košice, which is well served by internal flights from Prague and Bratislava.

The Spiš Chronicle, one of the oldest documents recording the history of Eastern Slovakia, tells that a monastery was founded at Košice in 1216; other, less easily authenticated records tell of the present day site of the city being inhabited by Slavic peoples as long ago as 400BC. Whatever its origins, the town's importance began to grow in the fourteenth century, when the first ramparts surrounding the town were constructed. By 1400 Košice was one of the most important cities in the Hungarian empire after Buda (now part of Budapest, the capital of Hungary), and was (and sometimes still is) known by its Hungarian name, Kassa. The town played an important part in repelling the Turks from Hungarian territory, and in fact it became the capital of Hungary for a short while in its own right after the fall of Buda to the Turks.

The character of the town changed in the nineteenth century when industry arrived, including a steel works, and during this time there were increasing demands from the town's citizens to be released from the control of an increasingly brutal Hungarian government. During World War II the town was actually occupied by Hungarian forces. In 1945, the town was one of the first to be liberated from Nazi control by the Russian Red Army as it swept westwards through Czechoslovakia; later in that year it was briefly the capital of a newly-liberated Czechoslovakia before Prague was freed and was made the capital. Tremendous growth since World War II has meant the population has swelled making it the largest city in Slovakia after Bratislava.

Košice is one of the most important steel-making towns in Czechoslovakia after Ostrava in Moravia, and the emphasis of the town's economy on industry is strong; nevertheless, there is much here to interest the visitor. At the centre of the town is a long, elongated square, called Námestie Slobody, lined with buildings that used to house offices of the Hungarian administration. In the middle of the square is **St Elizabeth's Cathedral**, the biggest church in Slovakia, built between 1382 and 1497. Both the exterior, with its exhuberant Gothic detailing, and the interior are worth seeing. In May and June the organ in this church is used for the Košice International Organ Festival. In a crypt on the left hand side of this church is the tomb of Ferenc Rakoczi, a Transylvanian prince who led Košice's struggle against the ruling Hungarian Habsburgs in the eighteenth century. The ceiling and high altar of the cathedral date from the fifteenth century. Next to the cathedral is its belfry, called the Urban Tower, built in the sixteenth century but reconstructed in 1628, with the arcade around the bottom dating from the 1940s. In the arcade are gravestones, with German inscriptions, from the cemetery that used to surround the cathedral.

The building was damaged in a fire in 1966 and extensively rebuilt. It houses a museum of metal working. On the other side of the cathedral is St Michael's Chapel. The attractive building of the State Theatre dating from the nineteenth century is also an obvious feature of the square. A pleasant area of greenery and fountains separates the cathedral and the theatre.

Beyond the theatre, on the right, on the corner of Adyho Street and the main square, is a **Jesuit Church** dating from the the seventeenth century. Walking down Adyho Street brings one to the buildings of the Košice Museum and the Katova Bastion, part of the defences from the medieval era which also houses a museum. A little way beyond these buildings, walking along Hrnchiarska Street and then turning left along Gen Petrova Street, brings one to **Jacob's Palace** (Jacabov Palác), an interesting looking pseudo-Gothic mini-palace built by a rich Hungarian aristocrat at the beginning of this century. The fact that Edvard Beneš, the first president of Czechoslovakia after World War I, lived in this house is recorded on a plaque on the wall. The interior of this building is not open to the public.

There are a number of museums in Košice. On the main square, at number 72, is the art gallery **Vychodoslovenská Galéria**, which exhibits twentieth-century paintings and sculpture by Slovak and Hungarian artists. Just up from this, walking away from the theatre and cathedral, one comes to the **Technical Museum**, on the same side of the square. This museum, like that in the Urban Tower, in the centre of the square next to the cathedral, concentrates on the wrought ironwork that has been traditionally made in this region. Here the square simply narrows into a road, but walking on up this road brings one

Krásna Hôrka Castle

to the square Maratónu Mieru and the **East Slovak Museum** (Vychodoslovenské Múzeum), with displays relating to the archaeology and history of Eastern Slovakia, and also the Košice Gold Treasure, where there is a hoard of over 3,000 gold coins dating from between 1400 and 1700. Another part of the same museum is at 10, Pri Miklušova Väznici Street, approached from the main square along Adyho Street. From the sixteenth century these two houses were the location of the Mikloš Prison (Miklušova Väznica), and along with displays relating to the history of Kosice there are medieval torture chambers and cells dating from this time. Next to this building in the Katova Bastion on Hrnciarska Street is a zoological museum.

Eighteen kilometres (12 miles) north-east of Košice is the geyser at **Herlany**. The village is reached by taking the E50 towards Michalovce and turning left (north) after 17km (10^1/$_2$ miles), on the minor road leading towards Vranov nad Toplou. The geyser gushes every 32 to 35 hours for a period of about 20 minutes and the water jet is anything up to 40m (131ft) high. One should enquire at the Čedok office in Košice (in the Hotel Slovan on the southern end of main square), to find out when it will be active. Unfortunately, the staff in the office can often only give a vague time or sometimes simply do not know. Those staying in a hotel in Košice, could ask the receptionist of the hotel to ring the number 116 and listen to the recorded information (in Slovak only) about the weather conditions in the region, which should also contain information about when the geyser is next due to be active.

Košice is excellently placed for a number of day-excursions, such as to Jasov Cave and the Zádielska Dolina Gorge, or Prešov or even Zemplínska Šírava.

Itineraries From Košice

Košice To Bardejov

Geographically in the centre of the East Slovakian region, **Prešov** is a pleasant market town and is also a good base from which to see many places of interest in Eastern Slovakia. It is 36km (22 miles) due north of Košice along the E50 road (also D1 motorway). There are a number of hotels and in and around the town. The town is an important industrial centre, particuarly in the branches of engineering and food. Prešov is the cultural centre of the Rusyns in Eastern Slovakia, and bears witness to this in its architecture and history. It is also the centre of an important wheat producing area, and many agricultural markets are held here.

The town's main square is called Slovenskej Republiky Rád. There are three interesting churches in Prešov, built in three different styles and home to three different faiths. On the square next door to Čedok is the principal church of the Uniate religion, known as the Grecko-Katolická Katedrále, where eastern Orthodox iconostas decorate the inside of a typically Baroque Catholic church building. In the middle of the square is the Gothic Church of St Nicholas, dating from the fourteenth century. On Svatoplukova, a few blocks down from the square towards the railway station, is the seventeenth-century Evangelical Church. Back on the main square is the town's art gallery, featuring works of Slovak art. There are other fine old buildings in the town in the vicinity of the square.

 The large ruined castle of **Velky Šariš Sitš** on top of a high hill 6km (4 miles) to the north-west of Prešov. There is a good view from the top. The castle dates from the thirteenth century and was burned out in a fire in 1687. The castle ruins can be approached from the village of Velky Šariš, which is a turning off the main road 68 which runs north of Prešov. Note that 30km (19 miles) along road 18 (E50) that runs west from Prešov is Spiš Castle, and further beyond this, the historical town of Levoča; both were described in Chapter 7.

Continuing, however, in a northerly direction, 31km (19 miles) from Presov is the small town of **Bardejov**, approached by taking road 18 from Prešov and after 8km (5 miles) turning off to the left (north) at the village of Kapušany onto a more minor road.

The town was founded in the fourteenth century and still retains its original medieval ground plan, and there are some buildings that remain from the fifteenth and sixteenth centuries. Around the old town are fairly well-preserved medieval walls. At two points there are bridges over the old moat, guarded by bastions. In the middle of the town's colourful sloping central square, called Námestie Osloboditelov, is the interesting building of the Old Town Hall, built between 1505 and 1511, now housing the Šariš Museum with its interesting collection of religious icons from the fifteenth and sixteenth centuries taken from the Uniate churches of the surrounding area. Near to the old town hall is the Gothic Church of St Egidius (St Giles) from the fifteenth century, in which there are eleven Gothic folding altars, all dating from the years 1460 to 1510 and still with their original paintings and sculptures. The bronze baptismal font dates from the fifteenth century. Along the square, and in the streets surrounding it, there are a number of medieval and Renaissance burghers houses. These buildings all date from the time when Bardejov was an important stop on trade routes between Poland and Russia. Little new industrial or residential development has taken place here, and Bardejov is a pleasant place to wander in.

Road 77 runs north of Bardejov towards Svidník. Just after leaving the town, on the left is a turning which leads to **Bardejovské Kúpele**, a small spa, known for its treatment of digestive and muscular disorders. The spa buildings are modern but it is a relaxed place; it may be preferable to stay here rather than Bardejov, 6km (3¹/₂ miles) away, as the two hotels in the latter town are rather uninspiring concrete-box affairs. There is an open-air museum (*skansen*) of folk architecture (many old wooden houses are on view), and an eighteenth century church, in Bardejovské Kúpele. There are buses from Košice to Bardejov via Prešov.

North and east of Bardejov is an area of low, isolated hills called the Low Beskyds (Nízke Beskydy), famous for the isolated, rural Rusyn communities in which old, domed, wooden Uniate churches, many of which are centuries old, still stand. There are some examples in folk museums in the area (such as the one at Bardejovské Kúpele, above, or in the town of Svidník), but those with their own transport and sufficient time to spend travelling around this relatively un-frequented region can find other churches in many of the villages in the Beskyds. Most churches are kept locked, but those who manage to view the interior of one of these wooden buildings will find it bristling with orthodox decoration, including iconostas and medieval icon paintings. Villages near Bardejov with noted examples of this unique form of rural architecture include Hervartov, Tročany and Lukov, but there are many more all over this part of Eastern Slovakia.

The **Dukla Pass** is the principal pass over the Low Beskyds and is a crossing point between Czechoslovakia and Poland. The road up to the pass runs up from the town of Svidník. Those who manage to journey this far east can see the enormous memorial to the Soviet dead, just a short distance before the border. There is a large open-air museum between the villages of Višny Komarnik and Krajná Polana, on the road leading up to the pass.

Košice To The Vihoraltské Vrchy

Few visitors reach Eastern Slovakia to begin with; even fewer will travel further east beyond Košice and Prešov. Some of those that do will be heading for the Vyšné Nemecké-Užgorod frontier post on the E50 road east of Michalovce, the only border crossing between Czechoslovakia and the Soviet Union. However, for those that do decide to spend a couple more days in Eastern Slovakia, the destination of the Zemplínska Šírava lake and the Vihorlatské Vrchy hills which rise up from its northern shores may prove a relaxing change after visiting Košice or Prešov. The lake and hills are fairly close to Košice and can be seen in a couple of day's excursions from Košice or Prešov, though it is probably preferable to stay in the region itself. The main centre of the region is the uninspiring town of Michalovce, near the western shores of Zemplínska Šírava.

Road 50 (E50) runs from Košice to Michalovce, 60km (37 miles) to the east. After passing through the small town of Svinica, the road goes over a low range of hills called the Slanské Vrchy via the **Dargov Pass**. In 1944 this pass was the scene of heavy fighting between the Soviet Red Army and the occupying Nazi forces, during which 22,000 Red Army soldiers were killed. There is a huge Victory Memorial by the road side and a rose garden next to it.

In **Michalovce** there are three hotels. Although it is not a place to linger, the Zemplín Museum, concerned with the area, is next to the bus station, and the Čedok office for this region is in the town's main street. Along the northern shores of the Zemplínska Šírava lake there are more hotels and camp sites.

Zemplínska Šírava, just beyond Michalovce, is a large resevoir, covering an area of nearly 35sq km. Those who are not staying in Michalovce can simply travel through the town and onto the road that runs along its northern shore, linking all the resorts. The shores of the southern part of the lake are inaccessible; all the resorts are on the northern and western side. The chief resort is Hôrka; other resorts include Biela Hora (on the western shore), and Medvedia

Hora and Kamenec which are beyond Hôrka on the northern shore. There is little difference between the resorts: all are pretty soulless and grey. Tourist cruise ships ply between the resorts, and it is possible to rent small boats, swim and sun bathe on the beaches. Beaches are, of course, a rarity in Czechoslovakia, and the area is crowded in high summer but dead for the rest of the year.

The small village of **Vinné** is immediately north of the lakeside town and resort of Hôrka. It is reached by a turning off the aforementioned main road which runs along the northern shore of the lake. From the church in the middle of the village there is a marked track to the ruins of Vinné Castle (Viniansky Hrad) which are situated on a hill above the village, inaccessible by road. It takes half an hour or so to reach the castle, up a very steep slope and along a path which is not properly marked (in theory, one should follow the blue markers almost all the way up to the castle, and then the yellow markers up the last slope). The ruins are more extensive than they appear from the bottom of the hill, and are eerily neglected and overgrown with trees that seem in some places to actually sprout from the castle walls; there are good views from some parts of the castle, however.

A road continues on from Vinné towards Humenné. The next village beyond Vinné, continuing in a northerly direction and travelling in the away from Zemplínska Šírava, is Chemko Strážske, with its associated **Lake**

*The north doorway,
Košice Cathedral*

Vinianské Jazero. This is a much nicer lake than Zemplínska Šírava, though it is far smaller — in comparison to the former lake, it is little more than a large pond. It is much more pleasant to swim here than at Zemplínska Šírava and there is the usual collection of boats to hire and narrow beaches from which to sunbathe and swim. It is pleasantly situated in the low hills of the Vihorlatské Vrchy. By the bus stop on the southern shores of the lake is the start of another, longer walking track to Vinné Castle ($1^1/_2$ hours, yellow markers). The Vihorlatské Vrchy are a pleasant range of low volcanic hills that lie immediately to the north of Zemplínska Šírava; their southern slopes, rising above the northern shores of the lakes, are covered with vineyards. They are really another part of the Carpathians — a long, rambling mountain range that includes the Slovak Ore and High Tatra Mountains to the west, which then drifts off east into the Ukraine, curving round in a great arc to head south. By far the nicest part of the hills is **Lake Morské Oko**, set in a beautiful, isolated position surrounded by low hills and overlooked by a rocky peak called Sninsky Kameň. It is reached by travelling along the road that runs along the northern shore of the lake from Michalovce, through the resorts of Hôrka, Klokočov, and Kusín to Jovsa, at the far north-eastern end of the lake; then through the village of Poruba and at the next junction taking a left-turn towards Remetské Hámre. The road continues through Remetské Hámre and terminates in a car park for the lake 9km (6 miles) from this village, from where the lake itself is a short walk. Those using the suggested road atlas *Autoatlas CSFR* should note that although the village of Remetské Hámre and the lake of Morské Oko 8km (5 miles) to the north are both clearly marked on the map, it appears that there is no road between them; this map is wrong and it is easy for cars to use the road north of Remetské Hámre — in fact, many buses, and large trucks carrying logs use this road. It is a pleasant journey along the scenic valley of the River Okna to the parking area, where there are refreshments on sale in season. There is no swimming or boating on the lake itself, as it is in a nature reserve but it is a beautiful spot. The fact that it is in a nature reserve has unfortunately not stopped large-scale tree felling in the whole area.

The rock outcrop **Sninsky Kameň**, 1,005m (3,296ft) and with a spectacular view over the whole of the Vihorlat region. The Zemplínska Šírava lake is situated above Lake Morské Oko to the north. It is interesting to walk up to it following the blue marked track from the southern end of Morské Oko, via the pass sedlo tri table (821m, 2,693ft). One can walk to the top of this distinctive promontary. It takes $1^1/_2$ hours to walk from Morské Oko to Sninsky Kameň.

Sninsky Kameň and Morské Oko are both about 13km (8 miles) or so from the heavily guarded border with the Soviet Union. One can often hear or see military activity in this area, though the attractions mentioned above should stay open at all times. There is a detailed walking and touring map of the region, entitled *Vihorlatské Vrchy-Zemplínska Šírava*, number 29 in the series *Edícia Turistickych Máp*, but it is not very easy to find. Keep looking for the map in bookshops in Košice or Michalovce, although it may be much easier to find it in bookshops in Bratislava, for those visiting this city and intending to journey on to this region.

Additional Information

Places of Interest

Bardejovské Kúpele
Skansen (Open-Air Museum)
Open: daily except Monday, 8.15am-4.15pm, closed in winter.

Dobšina Ice Cave
On road 67 between Vernár and Dobšina.
Open: 16 May to 15 September only, daily except Monday, tours at 9am, 11am, 1pm, 3pm.

Domica Cave
On road running east from Plešivec to the Hungarian border; 20km (12 miles) due south of Rožňava Open: 16 May to 15 September, daily except Monday, tours at 9am, 10.30am, 12noon, 2pm, 3.30pm. 16 September to 15 May, daily except Monday, tours at 9am, 11am, 2pm.

Gombasec Cave
On road between road 50 and the village of Silica, 12km (7 miles) south-west of Rožňava.
Open: 1 April to 15 May, 16 September to 31 October, daily except Monday, tours at 9am, 11am, 2pm. 16 May to 15 September, daily except Monday, tours on the hour, every hour, 9am to 4pm.

Jasov
Jasov Cave. 25km (15$^1/_2$ miles) west of Košice. Open: as for Gombasec Cave.

Košice
Vychodoslovenská Galéria
Corner of the main square and Šmeralova Street. Open: Tuesday to Saturday, 10am-6pm; Sunday, 10am-2pm.

Košice Museum
10, Ulica Pri Miklušovej Väznici, and also in the Urban Tower, main square Open: daily except Monday, 9am-5pm (to 1pm on Sundays).

East Slovak Museum
Námesti Maratónu Mieru
Open: daily except Monday, 9am-5pm, (to 1pm on Sunday).

Technical Museum
Námestie Slobody. Open: 8am-5pm (1pm on Sundays). Closed Mondays.

Krásna Hôrka Castle
East of Rožňava, on main Rožňava-Košice road. Open: April to September, daily except Monday, 8am-4.30pm October to March, daily except Monday, 9am-2.30pm.

Ochtina Aragonite Cave
On road between Štítnik and Jelšava Open: as for Gombasec Cave.

Prešov
Art Gallery
On main square. Open: daily except Monday, 10am-6pm (1pm at weekends).

Rožňava
Mining Museum (Banícke Múzeum), Šafárikovo 43. Open: daily except Monday, 9am-4pm (1pm on Sunday).

Turna Castle
Access only on foot from Turnianske Podhradie. Open:castle ruins all times.

Velky Šariš Sitš Castle and Vinné Castle
Open: access at all times.

Transport

ČSA - Czechoslovak Airlines
Pribinova 4, Košice ☎ (095) 22578, 22577
Flights from Košice to Bratislava and Prague.

Tourist Information Centres and Accommodation Offices

There is a Čedok office in most towns which deals with accommodation:

Košice
Rooseveltova 1, 040 01 Košice
☎ (095) 23121-3

Michalovce
Námestie Osloboditelov 12
071 01 Michalovce ☎ (0946) 21455

Prešov
Slovenskej Republicky Rád 1
080 01 Prešov ☎ (091) 24040

Rožňava
Námestie Baníkov 22
048 01 Rožňava ☎ (0942) 2343

CZECHOSLOVAKIA FACT FILE

Accidents and Emergencies

For procedures involving road accidents and break downs, see under 'Driving in Czechoslovakia'.

The following telephone numbers apply all over the country:
Police 158
Fire 150
Ambulance 155

The police are known as Vařejná Bezpečnost (VB) and have offices in the centre of most towns, and also in many main railway stations, and in Prague, in metro stations (the latter dealing with crimes or other difficulties involving public transport). Police headquarters in Prague is at 14, Konvitská Street, Prague-1

Accommodation

In many places in Czechoslovakia, it may be hard to get hotel accommodation. If possible, accommodation should be booked in advance. Čedok offices abroad will supply lists of hotels in towns or selected areas. They will book a room in the more expensive hotels; to book a room in a cheaper hotel, you must write to the institution yourself. Hotels are classed from A* de luxe to C, or from 5 to 1 stars. The more expensive hotels require the bill to be paid in Western currency, or by credit card. Some C hotels close in winter, except in large cities or mountain areas, which are busy all year round.

In London there are a few recently-founded agencies which specialise in arranging accommodation for people travelling to Czechoslovakia, in flats, cottages and private rooms, either bed and breakfast or self-catering, in cities and in the countryside, which is normally much cheaper than the expensive hotels which Čedok book. Intending visitors from North America may also want to use their services, or find out if there are similar organisations in their own countries. One such agency is the Czechbook Agency, 52 St John's Park, London SE3 7JP ☎ (081) 853 1168.

If you arrive in a town without having booked a room in advance, go to the town's Čedok office to arrange a room. They have details of which hotel rooms are available. They also own some hotels (the Čedok Interhotel chain). There is a Čedok office in most towns in the country, normally on the main square or street. The addresses of Čedok offices in principal towns are given in the Additional Information section at the end of each chapter. See also under 'Tourist Information' in this Fact File. If you see an hotel you can go and check in (but not in Prague; see below). Campsites (often Autokemping — car and tent/caravan sites) are found in many places. They come in two categories, A and B. Some are owned by Čedok. All are extremely cheap, but the facilities are normally very poor; there is rarely hot running water. Campsites are normally open only between May and September. Many of the larger ones have more West European-style luxuries, and are open longer. Information about these can be obtained from Čedok offices inside and outside Czechoslovakia. Many campsites (not just the larger ones) have bungaloes (called *chata*) which can be rented by those without a tent.

There are only seven youth hostels (called 'Junior Hotels') in Czechoslovakia, which can only be booked through the main office in Prague. Youth hostels are run by Cestovní Kancelář Mládeže, known as CKM (for main office in Prague, see below, at the end of this section). They are normally booked out by groups, but those who manage to get a place will find them very acceptable (they are better than some hotels). There are Junior Hotels at Prague, Mariánské Lázně, Karlovy Vary, Bratislava, Jasná (in the Low Tatras), Horny Smokovec (in the High Tatras) and Banská Bystrica. There is no age limit. Those who can show an IYHF card will pay a cheaper price, though a card is not essential to use Junior Hotels. In July and August only, university dormitories in a number of towns and cities (including Prague) are opened up for use by travellers. Their location changes every year. They can not be booked in advance. They must be booked on the day and paid for at the town's main CKM office, who will tell you the location of the dormitories (Čedok or other information centres will always be able to provide you with the address of the local CKM office).

Since 1989 people in private houses have been renting out their rooms to foreigners. Look for the German sign, Zimmer Frei (Rooms Free) hung outside houses. The system of private rooms is well established in Prague, Brno and Bratislava, but only recently has the option begun to appear in smaller towns and villages and other out-of-the-way places. The villages on the Prague-Karlovy Vary road, for example, have many private rooms to hire in this way. Many people may want to be paid in Western cash; if you can only pay in crowns, it may cost you more. Many Čedok offices will provide you with a room in this way, particulary if all the hotel rooms in a town are full. However, some Čedok offices would rather have tourists stay in their own hotels, so they may not tell tourists of any vacancies there are in private rooms. A general rule is, in cities private rooms are rented out through Čedok, in the countryside they are arranged independently — but there are always exceptions.

Other accommodation possibilities are motels (of which there are few), and stone-built huts high in the mountains, which you must walk to. It is also wise to book these in advance. The main places where this system operates is in the High Tatras (book through Slovakoturist's office in Novy Smokovec); elsewhere, book through the region's main Čedok office.

Prague: Do not bother going directly to hotels in Prague, as you will be told they are full up for weeks. Apart from hotels and private accommodation, three boats permanently moured on the Vltava, called *Botels*, are used as hotels. Accommodation in private houses and cheaper hotels may be a long way from the city centre (though public transport is very convenient and reliable, however far out one is). The minimum stay in private accommodation is normally 3 nights. If you arrive in Prague without pre-arranged accommodation, go to one of the accommodation agencies, through which the city's rooms are arranged:

Čedok Hotel Reservation Service
5 Panska Street
Prague-1
Metro: Náměstí Republiky or Mustek.
☎ (02) 222 70 04 (02) 222 56 57
Open: Monday to Friday, 9am-8pm; weekends, 8.30am-2pm.
They deal with expensive hotels, and some private accommodation.

Pragotur
U Obecního domu 2
Prague-1
Metro: Náměstí Republiky.
☎ (02) 31 72 81
Open: Monday to Friday, 7.30am-9pm; Saturday, 8am-1pm,
1.30pm-8pm; Sunday, 8am-3.15pm.
They deal with cheaper hotels and campsites, and private accommodation.

There are also accommodation offices at Ruzyně airport and the railway stations. Many private accommodation agencies have been established since 1989, which tend to deal more with private rooms. Try, for example:

Toptour
Rybna 3
Prague-1
☎ (02) 32 10 77
Open: weekdays, 9am-8pm; weekends, 11am-7pm.

The main youth hostel, and main office of the country's Youth Hostel Association, is at Žitná 12, Prague-2 (Metro: Karlovo Náměstí). The youth hostel here is permanently full, but ČKM normally operate very basic dormitory accommodation in other parts of the city, which must be arranged at this office. Write to them at:

ČKM
Žitná 12
12 105 Praha-2
☎ (02) 29 45 87

Climate

The day-to-day weather in Czechoslovakia is generally changeable, as it is in most of northern Europe. However, the climate is 'continental' in character, with warm summers and cold winters. In Prague and Bratislava in particular, it can often get uncomfortably hot in July and August, with afternoon temperatures sometimes in the mid-30's (°C, 86 °F), and uncomfortably cold in January and February, when often the temperature in Prague will not rise above freezing, even in the afternoon. Spring or early summer (May to early June) are often considered the best months to visit Prague. During autumn everywhere in the country is typically cold and damp. In mid-winter the weather is more stable, with clear skies but often bitterly cold temperatures. On average, the Danube Valley and the area around Zemplínska Šírava in Eastern Slovakia are the warmest areas. Always bring rain wear in any season, as rainfall totals everywhere are high. Climate details for mountain regions are given in the main text.

Communications

Post
Posting letters and parcels abroad is generally reliable; no special rules exist for sending parcels abroad, but always take them to a post office *(pošta)* for weighing. Everything should be sent *letecky* (air mail). Post boxes are orange and blue. Mail to Europe takes 3 to 5 days, 7 to 10 days to North America. Stamps *(znamka)* are sold in hotels, and at shops which also sell postcards. The best place to look for a post office in any town is normally next to the main railway station. Main post offices in the largest cities are open 24 hours a day, including the main post office in Prague, at Jindřišská 14, Prague-1 (just off Wenceslas Square). Others open from early morning until 5pm or 6pm Monday to Saturday and close completely on Sundays. There are normally seperate queues for seperate sevices in post offices, so try not to stand in the wrong one. To send a letter poste restante, write the name of the recipient, post restante, pošta-1, then the name of the town. This means it will be held at the particular town's main post office. Get the sender to write the recipients' surname in block letters, to avoid any confusion when the letter is collected or held by the post office.

Telephones
There are coin-operated public telephones *(telefon)* in the street, and, in metro stations in Prague, but they cannot be used to call outside the country. The way to use the phone is described in the phone box in pictures, and sometimes in English, although many may still encounter difficulties and may need to go to hotels or post offices even to make internal or local calls, where telephone numbers can also be looked up by receptionists or clerks. Telephone abroad from most post offices, or from any hotel, regardless of whether or not you are staying there although there is a surcharge. Write down the number for the receptionist or post office clerk to dial, then pay him/her after the call; no coins are needed to feed into a machine. Telephoning abroad is very expensive. Direct dialling to callers outside the country is unlikely to be encountered, since the dialling is normally done by the hotel receptionist or post office clerk. However, for use in the VERY FEW public phone boxes from which international calls can be made, or for other purposes, dialling codes from Czechoslovakia are: UK 0044; USA & Canada 001; Australia 0061.

Currency and Credit Cards

The unit of currency used in Czechoslovakia is the Korun, abbreviated to Kčs and often referred to by its anglicised name, the 'Crown'. The Czech crown is a very small unit of currency, and there are 100 Hellers to the crown. There are notes for 10, 20, 50, 100, 500, and 1,000 Kčs; coins for 5, 10, 20, 50 hellers and 1, 2 and 5 kčs. The exchange rate of the Czech crown changes more than that of Western currencies, but once inside the country it is pointless 'shopping around' for the best exchange rate—it is normally the same everywhere.

It is not yet possible to buy Czech crowns from Western banks although this regulation may change in the near future. Foreign bank notes — pounds, or, even more usefully, German Marks or US dollars — are often needed to pay for souvenirs (in the street), or for private accommodation in people's homes. On leaving Czechoslovakia, you will normally be allowed to change a limited amout of crowns back into Western currency (you will normally be given deutchmarks, Austrian schillings or dollars for it). But do not automatically assume this will be the case; do not change more money then you need, or you might find yourself having to bring virtually useless Czech crowns back home with you.

There should be no difficulty exchanging travellers cheques; bring them in sterling, dollars or German marks. Banks are difficult to spot and often do not advertise themselves as such, though in some tourist areas they may have the sign 'Směárna', 'Wechselstube' (German) or 'Bureau de Change' outside their door. The few occasions where exchange offices exist in their own right are at main railway stations, airports and important tourist attractions. Some of these may only change cash. Most hotels will change cash but only a few will change travellers cheques, and will charge a large surcharge for this service. Bear in mind that the exchange offices at many roads and rail border posts will not change traveller's cheques, only cash. By far the easiest place to change money or traveller's cheques is at any Čedok office. Opening times of Čedok exchange facilties vary, but are normally 9am-4pm weekdays (possible break at 12noon of 1 or $1/_2$ hour for lunch), and 9am-12noon on Saturdays. The address of the Čedok office for each major town is given in the Additional Information section after each chapter. Keep the exchange receipts for presentation at hotels, customs posts etc, to prove you have changed money legally.

Credit cards are not widely accepted in Czechoslovakia but institutions that do accept them will take all the major ones. Good hotels take them, as do some car rental companies, ČSA airlines, Tuzex shops and main Čedok offices for services such as Čedok tours or buying international rail tickets.

Do not change money on the Black Market in the street. It is illegal, does the Czechoslovak economy no favours, and the chances of being cheated (eg by being given out-of-date bank notes) are high.

Customs Regulations

Gifts can normally be taken into Czechoslovakia duty free. However, there are tight regulations on what you can take out. It is forbidden to buy and export antiques, foodstuffs, furs, clothes, linen, leather goods, footwear, jewellery, tyres, electrical goods, and gas appliances. Goods bought at Tuzex shops are exempt from export duty but keep receipts to prove you paid for them. Other goods (eg, crystal, alcoholic drinks) should be declared at customs on departure, but the general rule is, you can take goods out duty free up to a value of 50 per cent of the total amount of money you changed into crowns (there are different regulations for those visiting Czechoslovakia for only one or two days). Further information on the complex and ever-changing customs regulations can be sought from Čedok. Do not 'forget' to declare any amount of crystal, etc at the border, as you could be charged with attempting to smuggle it out. When entering the country, you may be asked to declare expensive items (eg cameras, tape recorders, Western currency) on a sheet of paper, for presentation when you leave, so that it can be checked you have sold none of them on the Black Market, but this regulation normally applies only to those who need visas to enter the country.

Driving in Czechoslovakia

Those considering driving in Czechoslovakia or taking a car into the country are strongly advised to contact motoring organisations in their own countries for up-to-date advice on matters such as insurance, emergency and breakdown procedures, etc. The head office of the country's motoring organisation, which can provide up-to-date advice and information:

Autoturist
Opletova 29
Praha-1
☎ (2) 224828

Driving Conditions

The roads in Czechoslovakia are generally good and have less traffic on them than roads in Western Europe. A motorway network is gradually being built up; the principal motorway that has already been built links the three biggest cities, Prague, Brno and Bratislava. Motorways are toll-free. Most main roads have a number; motorways are prefaced with the letter D. Many roads have two numbers as they are also part of the European network of roads, and are prefaced with the letter E. Signposting is generally very good. The road number and distance in km is given for each destination marked on a signpost. Most mountain roads are cleared of snow in winter.

Prague has a congested city centre, where many streets are closed to traffic and many others are one-way, and its complex network of flyovers and fast modern highways in the suburbs can be a nightmare for uninitated drivers, especially during the rush hour (early morning and mid-afternoon). It is difficult to find anywhere to park. The city has a fabulous public transport system, and most places are within walking distance in any case; cars are a liability in Prague, and should be left in hotel garages or parking lots.

Documents Needed

Driving licences valid in all European and most other countries are valid in Czechoslovakia. While it is not strictly necessary for motorists to be in possession of a green card or an International Driver's Licence, it would be foolish not to have both, and they are easily obtainable from national motoring organisations in the UK, USA and other countries. Those who do not have a green card must buy insurance at the border on entry. The driver must carry the car's registration document. A driver who is not the owner of the car he is driving must have the written permission of the owner, countersigned by a motoring organisation. Cars, caravans and trailers must all display an international identification sticker. By law, all motorists must also carry a red warning triangle, a set of replacement bulbs and a first aid kit with them.

Motoring Rules And Regulations

Drive on the right. It is illegal to drive with any amount of alcohol in the blood. Children under 12 cannot travel in the front passenger seat. Seatbelts must always be worn. Always carry your driving licence and car documents with you when you are driving. Do not enter bus lanes. Be very wary of trams in cities, which travel fairly fast and may suddenly appear from unexpected directions. If a tram stops in the middle of the road and there is no safety area, remain stationary to allow the tram passengers to get off and cross the road. Use headlights at dusk, night, and during poor visibility caused by bad weather. Do not stop before the tops of gradients, near pedestrian crossings, tram lines or level crossings, at crossroads or on bridges. Always slow right down for level crossings, as the road surface can be very uneven here. The speed limits are 110kph (68mph) on motorways; 90kph (56mph) on other roads and 60kph (37mph) in built up areas. The speed limit for cars towing caravans or trailers is 80kph (50mph). Motorists must be in possession of a red warning triangle and must use it in the case of emergencies or breakdowns. The maximum speed limit for motorcyclists is 80kph (50mph), and those driving motorcycles which can travel faster than 40kph (25mph) must wear a crash helmet (as must their passengers). Parking should not be a problem, except in Prague, where few streets are open to traffic in any case. Car parks are indicated by a 'P' sign. The police tow away illegally-parked cars and will fine motorists on the spot if they commit any of the offences described above.

Fuel

Fuel stations are much less common than in Western countries. They are often signposted in towns. A list of the addresses of fuel stations is included in the suggested road atlas, *Autoatlas ČSFR*, and on many city and town maps (see 'Maps'). In theory, Westerners cannot buy fuel from the pumps with Czech crowns; fuel must be bought with special coupons (*Poukázka Na Benzin*), available from main Čedok offices, some border posts, some motoring organisations outside Czechoslovakia, Tuzex shops, and many banks in Czechoslovakia and their associated offices abroad (eg, Zivnostenska Bank, 18, King William Street, London EC4N 7BY ☎ [071] 283 3333). However, most filling stations will supply motorists with fuel, for Czech crowns or, even better, some hard currency (cash). It is advisable to pay for fuel with pre-purchased coupons. Buying fuel with coupons is often cheaper than with Czech crowns and may mean queues are avoided at filling stations. Diesel fuel is called NAFTA, and filling stations supplying this fuel are even less common. The purchase of diesel fuel requires special coupons, which motorists driving this type of car are advised to purchase in advance before entering the country. Diesel can only be purchased using these coupons. Wherever they are bought, coupons can normally only be paid for in hard currency. Čedok offices can supply a list of the small but growing number of garages in the country which sell unleaded fuel known as 'natural' or 'bezolovnaty'. There are very few garages in Slovakia which offer this service ouside Bratislava.

Breakdowns

Breakdowns can be a real problem. There are emergency telephones on motorways; otherwise, an up-to-date list of emergency telephone numbers of the breakdown service (*Silničí Služba*) of Autoturist, and repair garages, can normally be supplied at frontier posts, garages, police stations, or at the main Autoturist office which deals with breakdowns, at Opletalova Ulice 21, Prague-1 ☎ (02) 224906. In theory, the breakdown number over the whole country is ☎ 154. Motorists are strongly urged to take out full motor insurance from motoring organisations before they leave home. Spare parts for many Western models may need to be imported. Car repair garages are listed in the suggested road atlas, *Autoatlas ČSFR*.

Car Hire

There are a number of car rental companies in Czechoslovakia, the main one being Pragocar, with offices in many towns and cities; in Brno and some other towns in Moravia, cars can be hired from Brnocar. Good hotels in many towns will often make arrangements for cars to be hired through the local Pragocar office. These organisations often allow drivers to drop their cars off in other countries. Hertz and Avis operate from Prague (Ruzyně airport), and cars from this office can be reserved at Hertz and Avis offices abroad. The main office of Pragocar is at 42, Štěpánská Street, Prague-1 ☎ (02) 352825, 352809. They also have an office at the Hotel Intercontinental and at Prague-Ruzyně airport. They will normally allow motorists to reserve cars at other hiring offices throughout the country, or at least supply a list of these offices. Another car rental company to try in Prague is 'Budgetcar', with offices in central Prague (at the main ČSA-Czechoslovak Airlines office, 1 Revolucni Street) and at Ruzyně airport. It is usually more expensive to hire West European models rather than East European models (mainly Ladas and Škodas).

Renting a car is just about the one thing in Czechoslovakia that is expensive by Western standards. An option for those travelling to the country overland is simply to hire a car in Austria or Germany, where hiring rates are much less, and drive it into Czechoslovakia from there.

Road Signs

A few Czech road signs:
Jednosměrny provoz — one way; *Nevstupujte* — no entry; *Objíždka* — diversion; *Pozor* — attention; *Na silnici se pracuje* — road works; *Nebezpečí* — danger; *Vchod* — entrance; *Vychod* — exit.

Embassies

British Embassy
14 Thanovská Street
Prague-1
☎ (02) 533347, (02) 533340, (02) 533370

American Embassy
15 Tržiště Street
Prague-1
☎ (02) 536641-8

Canadian Embassy
6 Mickiewiczova Street
Prague-6
☎ (02) 326941

Czechoslovakian Embassies and Consulates in Western cities

Uk & Republic of Ireland
28, Kensington Palace Gardens
London W8 4OX
☎ (071) 727 3966

Canada
50, Rideau Terrace
Ottawa
Ontario K1M 2A1
☎ 514 849 4495

USA
3900 Linnean Avenue N.W.
Washington DC 20008
☎ 202 363 6315

Australia
169 Military Road
Dover Heights
Sydney NSW 2030
☎ 02 371 8878

Entry Formalities

Citizens of the United States, the United Kingdom and Canada do not need visas to visit Czechoslovakia. British citizens are advised that a one-year British Visitors Passport is not valid for travel to Czechoslovakia, and that they must be in possession of a full passport. Australian citizens still need a visa, though this regulation may well be dropped in the near future — contact the embassy in Sydney for up to date details. Passports must be valid for at least 3 months from the date of entry, regardless of how long you intend to stay in the country. The maximum length of stay in Czechoslovakia is 3 months (6 months for British citizens only). Once inside the country, visas can be extended by the local police, or more preferably, at the main passport and visa office at Olsanská 2, Žižkov, Prague.

Essential Things To Take

Most medical and food supplies that visitors will need can be obtained in the country, but it is very wise to bring all regularly needed items and basic medical or first ail items from home, since availability of supplies in Czechoslovakia may break down at the crucial time. A chemist is a *lekárna* (Czech) or *lekáreň* (Slovak). Those who are planning to walk in the mountains should bring proper shoes and other equipment, eg cagoule, first aid kit, water bottles, etc, from their home country. Tap water is officially safe to drink, though often prone to alarming discolouration, and many may feel safer buying the mineral water that is readily available; other soft drinks are usually very sweet. The electric current varies according to where you are. Bring a universal adaptor for all electric appliances.

Bring all photographic needs from home. Although the availability of Western films and equipment is getting better, its supply can be rather erratic, and outside Prague you will be very lucky to find anything. Make sure that film bought in Czechoslovakia, which is often locally (or East European or Soviet) made, can be processed in the West (film processing normally takes a long time in Czechoslovakia, although there are a few shops in Prague which offer express processing). Very few museums or galleries allow visitors to take photographs, with or without a flash (a notable exception is the National Museum of Technology in Prague). Photography inside churches is usually allowed, although it is often very gloomy, so use a fast film (up to ASA 1000). Bear in mind that the weather can often be dull and grey, as well as sunny.

Facilities for The Disabled

Disabled people were never catered for in terms of access to public buildings and hotels, travel on public transport, etc in Czechoslovakia and it is likely to be a long time before any serious consideration towards people with disabilities is made by planners in the country.

Illness and Health Care

Visitors to Czechoslovakia should take out a comprehensive insurance policy, which includes medical treatment, before they enter the country. Foreign nationals have the right to free emergency health care in Czechoslovakia, but insurance will nevertheless allow citizens to full financial support (if needed) and facilities which include flying the ill or injured party back home for attention. Some useful addresses in Prague are listed below (elsewhere contact Čedok or your hotel as a first step to getting medical attention):

Medical Services For Foreign Visitors
Faculty Polyclinic
Karlovovo Námesti (Charles Square) 32
Prague-2

Emergency Dental Services
Vladislavova 22
Prague-1
☎ (02) 261374

Dispensing Chemists With Emergency Service
Na Příkope 7
Prague-1
☎ (02) 220081

Rabies is present in Czechoslovakia, as it is in all countries of continental Europe. Do not approach any strange animal. If bitten by any type of animal, wash the wound thoroughly with soap and water, and apply alcohol spirit if it is available. Note the type of animal and the address of its owner, and go to the nearest police station to report the incident before getting proper medical attention from a doctor or a hospital.

Language

Two languages are spoken in Czechoslovakia, Czech (in Bohemia and Moravia) and Slovak (in Slovakia). The two languages are very closely related Slavik languages and though written in Roman script (like English) the sounds that many of the letters make are unfamiliar to English speakers. There is also a bewildering number of accents and speech marks above many letters. Some words also seem to consist of strings of unpronouncable consonants, with no vowels to give the words any obvious sound.

Although the incidence of English being spoken is increasing a phrase book is absolutely essential for anyone visiting Czechoslovakia. Čedok offices in London and New York sell Czech phrase books. Slovaks understand Czech so you can use Czech phrase books all over the country. English-Czech and English-Slovak language dictionaries are available cheaply in Czechoslovakia.

Most Čedok offices will have at least one member of staff who speaks English, but, except in Prague, Brno, Bratislava, Karlovy Vary and the High Tatras, you can rarely expect staff of hotels or restaurants to speak English. German is the language of tourism and is spoken by many people who come into contact with tourists as part of their jobs. Russian is the third language, with English fourth. The incidence of German and English being spoken declines the further east one travels.

One word you hear all the time is *prossím* — literally 'I ask', but used to indicate a variety of different meanings like 'hello', 'please', 'next please', or simply to get someone's attention. Remember that in every word, the stress is always on the first syllable. Vowels are always short, as in rot or rat, never as in rote or rate. Some useful Czech phrases are:

Yes *Ano (A-no)*
No *Ne (Neh)*
Good morning *Dobre jitro (DOB-reh YIT-ro)*
Hello (formal) *Dobry den (DOB-ree DEN)*
Hello (familiar) *Ahoj (A-hoy)*
Goodbye *Sbohem (SBO-hem)*
Please *Prossím (PRO-seem)*
Thank you *Děkuji (DYE-koo-yi)*
How much? *Kolik to stoji? (KO-lik to STO-yee)*
Hotel *Hotel (HO-tel)*
Street *Ulice (U-lit-se)*
Square *Námesti (NAHM-nyeh-styee)*
Restaurant *Restaurace (REST-au-rat-se)*
My name is *Jmenuji se... (MEN-u-yee se...)*
Château *Zamek (ZAH-mek)*
Castle *Hrad (HRAD)*

Days of the week:	Czech	Slovak
Monday	*Pondeli*	*Pondelok*
Tuesday	*Utery*	*Utorok*
Wednesday	*Streda*	*Streda*
Thursday	*Ctvrtek*	*Sturtok*
Friday	*Patek*	*Piatok*

| Saturday | *Sobota* | *Sobota* |
| Sunday | *Nedele* | *Nedela* |

Maps

Maps in Czechoslovakia are available at *Knihy* (book shops). Some maps may be difficult to get hold of, so if, while you are travelling, you see a map of an area you intend to visit later on in your holiday, buy it then rather than when you get to the area itself, where it may be unobtainable or far less easy to obtain. There is an excellent map shop in Prague, which sells maps of all parts of the country, at the Mustek end of Na Příkope (Old Town side of the street).

A number of fold-out sheet maps of Czechoslovakia are available from outside the country, but these will often not be detailed enough to find many of the places mentioned in this book. Highly recommended for motorists is the *Autoatlas ČSFR*, available in book shops and some Čedok offices in Czechoslovakia. This covers the whole country in book form, with information and map keys in English. Other useful information includes street maps of various towns and cities, the addresses, facilities and opening hours of filling stations, the addresses of car repair shops and garages, and the addresses of camp sites which accept cars.

For more detailed maps of certain areas, there is an excellent series of maps called *Poznáváme Československo* (Getting To Know Czechoslovakia). Fourteen of these fold-out maps cover the whole country. Included with the maps is a good section describing places of interest to tourists in English, and detailed street plans of towns in the region the map covers. There is no 'practical' information on addresses of useful facilities, hotels etc.

There is a street map available for virtually every town in Czechoslovakia. A street-map is called a *Plán Města*. Listed on the back are the addresses of post offices, tourist offices, restaurants, hotels, sporting facilities, car repair shops etc. Information and map keys are given in English.

It is pointless trying to find one's way around Prague's medieval streets without a decent map. There are three maps available: *Praha Plán Středu Města* is a map of the city centre, and is vital for sightseeing. It includes Vyšehrad and Troja. There is another map of the whole of Prague, which covers the central area in less detail, and is much less useful. There is also a special map of Prague for motorists, *Praha pro Motoristy*, showing which streets are pedestrianised, the one-way system, detailed plans of complicated road junctions, and which roads lead out of Prague to other places in Czechoslovakia.

For walking maps, see the section on walking. Motorists are also likely to find walking maps useful as they are the most detailed maps available, showing minor roads linking small hamlets, etc.

Most houses in buildings in Czechoslovakia have two numbers on them. Ignore the red number, which is the building's registration number in municipal records. The blue number is the building's street number, and address.

A lot of streets in Czechoslovakia are being renamed. In most towns and cities, the main street or square was named after Marx, Engels, Lenin etc and the names of these are only gradually being changed. Therefore do not always expect streets to still carry the same names as they do on out-of-date maps or in this book.

Measurements

The metric system is used in Czechoslovakia. Conversions are:
1 kilogram (1,000 grams) = 2.12lb
1 litre = $1^3/_4$ pints
$4^1/_2$ litres = 1 gallon
8km = 5 miles

Opening Hours

The opening hours of the main places of interest to tourists are given in the Additional Information section after each chapter. Bear in mind that an attraction may close for restoration or rebuilding work, so check first with the nearest Čedok office as to whether an attraction is open. Virtually everything is shut on a Monday, and attractions outside large cities also close from October/November to April/May.

Most churches are only open on Sundays, when they are used for mass. However, tourists wishing to see the inside of a church could try asking around for a key at a religious or priest's house. This rule does not apply in the largest cities, when churches are normally open during the day.

Chairlifts and cable cars normally do not operate on one day a week (usually Monday; occasionally Tuesday) and normally shut down entirely during April/May and October/November (this does not apply in the High Tatras, where lifts operate all year). Ski-lifts, as opposed to chairlifts, operate only when there is snow on the ground.

Most shops and tourist attractions close on national holidays: 1 January, Easter Monday, 1 May, 5 May, 9 May, 25 & 26 December.

Outdoor Activities

Cycling
Czechoslovakia is a good country for touring by bicycle, as there is such a variety of scenery in such a small area. However, it is not possible to hire bicycles anywhere. Cyclists should note that freelance camping is prohibited.

Skiing
Some skiing areas in Czechoslovakia are becoming popular with Western visitors. The two most notable resorts are Jasná in the Low Tatras, and Štrbské Pleso in the High Tatras. Čedok (London) Ltd and a number of British holiday companies now offer package skiing holidays to these places. The Krkonoše Mountains in Bohemnia are also popular, and have the longest skiing season. However, the having to wait for lifts and relatively poor conditions in these mountains are notorious. The skiing season in most places is December/January to March/April. Skiing maps, showing the ski runs, are available for many skiing areas.

Walking

There are 40,000km (25,000 miles) of marked paths and tracks in Czechoslovakia. All paths are colour coded; for example, a blue-marked track will be indicated as such on track marker posts (which are at track junctions, in towns, at road sides, and at important track destinations), by blue markers along its length, and by a blue line drawn on a special walking map. Distances on track marker posts are given in kilometres in Bohemia and Moravia, and in hours and minutes in Slovakia. The colour-code of any particular track is indicated by a mark, which is a horizontal line showing its colour, with horizontal white lines painted above and below it. These marks appear every 200m (656ft) or so along a track, painted on rocks, trees, fence posts, buildings, etc, and are repainted every 3 years (2 years in mountain areas). Walking maps can be bought in most book shops. The keys to the maps are often in English. If not then a dictionary may be needed to decipher them. There are also a number of nature trails, although the information they present, usually on boards along the path, is inevitably in Czech or Slovak. The most popular area for walking is the High Tatras.

Public Conveniences

Public toilets are rare, but can often be found at tourist attractions and at metro or railway stations. They are indicated 'WC'; men = *Muži* or *Pánn*, women = *Ženy* or *Dámy*. Hygiene standards leave a lot to be desired. A minimal payment is often required to use these facilities.

Public Transport

The public transport system in Czechoslovakia is in some ways better than that in many Western countries. Ticketing and reservation facilities at bus and train stations in main centres are computerised, but elsewhere the system is very ancient. Virtually all bus and train stations have a manned left luggage office, but the luggage lockers are often broken or hard to use.

Within Cities

Taxis can be found at taxi ranks, and outside stations or hotels, in most cities and towns. Buses and, in many cases, trams, are the main way of getting around in cities. Often, visitors will not need to make use of these facilities, since the central area of a city or town, where all the major sights and hotels are situated, is normally small enough to walk round. It is rarely possible to buy a ticket on the tram or bus. In most cases, tickets must be bought at PNS (newspaper) stands, some hotel reception desks, cafés, large railway or bus stations, etc, though sometimes there are automatic ticket selling machines next to bus or tram stops, in the centre of cities. Cancel the ticket in the punching machine on the bus or tram. Always carry a good supply of tickets. In virtually every city, there is a flat fare (ie one ticket) to travel any distance; use a new ticket if you change tram or bus. Tram and bus routes often change, but are shown on city and town maps. The following cities have trams: Prague, Brno, Bratislava, Plzeň, Most, Ostrava, Olomouc, Liberec and Košice.

Prague

There are no buses in the centre of Prague, as it is so congested. There are only buses in the suburbs. The main way of getting around in the the the centre is by tram (use the rules explained above) or metro (subway or underground railway). The tram system is very extensive. At tram stops, a blue number on a white background indicates day-time tram routes; at night, all the tram routes change, and there is a limited (ie once every 40 minutes) night tram service on most routes, indicated by white numbers on a blue background at tram stops. Trams run to timetables, which are posted at stops. The metro system is excellent and is gradually being extended. There is a flat fare (ie one ticket) to travel any distance on the metro. Use tram tickets, or buy tickets from the orange dispenser in every metro station (these tickets can also be used on trams and buses). Tickets must be validated by stamping them in the other orange machines at the entrance to every station. It is possible to change metro lines without using another ticket. The metro runs from 5am to 12 midnight. Metro stations are indicated by green 'M' signs in the street.

Between Cities

Air

ČSA (Czechoslovak Airlines) runs a reasonably extensive internal air service. Fares can be paid for in Czech crowns, and are very reasonable. There are airports at Prague, Bratislava, Ostrava, Karlovy Vary, Pieštany, Sliač (for Banska Bystrica), Poprad (for the High Tatras), and Košce. There is only a very limited service between Prague and Brno. Addresses of ČSA offices in towns with airports have been given in the Additional Information sections after each chapter.

Prague

Prague's main airport, Praha-Ruzyně, is 20km (12 miles) west of the city centre. Apart from taxis into the city, there is a ČSA bus to the River Vltava terminal at 25, Revolucní Street, in central Prague, next to the Vltava, and there are a few buses between the main hotels and the airport.
The main office in Prague is at:
ČSA - Czechoslovak Airlines
Revolucní 1, Prague-1
Metro: Náměstí Republiky
☎ (02) 31 73 95

Train

The railway system, run by ČSD (Czechoslovak Railways), is extensive. Trains are frequent and reliable, but are often not very fast. The rail services in Slovakia are less good than those in Bohemia and Moravia. Note that international trains are often late, as they travel long distances and can get delayed at borders (many trains on the main Prague-Brno-Bratislava line are international ones running between Berlin and other East European capitals). Trains are either *Rychlik* (express), shown in timetables in red, or *Osobní* (normal), shown in black. Some *Osobní* trains are railcars and are breathtakingly slow. A supplement must be paid at the ticket office to travel on express trains. You do not need to pay a supplement if your ticket was purchased outside Czechoslovakia. If you get on a train without a ticket, you must pay a small fine as well as the cost of the ticket. An R in a box by a train number means that you must have a seat reservation to travel on that train. An R without a box means reservation is reccommended, rather than obligatory. If you get on the train without one, you will have to pay a fine. Posted timetables showing departures are marked Odjezd (Czech) or Odchod (Slovak), those showing arrivals are marked Příjezd or Príchod.

Timetables are difficult to understand. Those planning to do a lot of travelling by train should buy the ČSD timetable, which has a section in English on how to use it. It is available from bookshops and stations. Most hotels and Čedok offices will have a timetable you can borrow. There are information *(informace)* offices at all stations, though the staff in these places are unlikely to speak English. Try writing down the place you want to go to, and pointing at your watch. Better still, ask at a Čedok office. Some Čedok offices will sell long-distance train tickets. Many east-west trains carry couchettes (sleeping berths) or sleeping cars. These cost a fraction of the price they do in Western Europe and are just as good. Tickets for these trains can often be bought at Čedok offices, but in summer reserve as far in advance as possible wherever you buy them from. Note that it is forbidden to smoke on any domestic train service in Czechoslovakia. Remember to ask for reductions on the already very cheap fares: children under 12 and those over 60 can normally travel for half price.

Prague

The main station in Prague is Hlavní Nádraži in the New Town, *Metro:* Hlavní Nádraži. Those travelling between Prague and Britain (via Nürnberg) will use this station. The staff in the information office here speak English. The second station (many trains to Brno and Slovakia use this one) is Praha-Nádraži Holešovice, *Metro:* Holešovice. Tannoy announcements here are often given in English! Other stations are Praha-Masarykovo Nádraži (previously Praha-Střed), on Hybernská Street in the very centre of Prague (*Metro:* Náměstí Republiky), and Praha-Smíchovské Nádraži (*Metro:* Smíchovské Nádraži) in the south-western part of the Lesser Quarter.

Bus

The bus service is also very extensive, and is run by ČSAD. Buses are faster, less frequent, more expensive and less comfortable than trains. Virtually every village is linked by bus to the nearest large town, several times a day. Towns are also linked by an extensive network of good intercity buses (coaches). Bus stations are normally next to railway stations. There are also information offices in bus stations, but it is better to enquire at a Čedok office. Some busy intercity routes (eg Prague-Karlovy Vary) may require you to buy tickets in advance and reserve a seat. In fact, those intending to travel by any of the fast, long-distance intercity coaches operated by ČSAD should always book in advance if possible, particularly services operating at weekends, in summer, or which depart early in the morning. The main bus station in Prague is Florenc (*Metro:* Florenc), from where it is possible to catch a bus to almost any town in the country. Information officers here speak English. Those intending to travel by bus in Czechoslovakia should buy the main bus timetable, which gives a translation of what all the timetable symbols mean in English without knowing which bus travel is virtually impossible.

Restaurants

Restaurants and other eating establishments have a class *(skupina)*, 1 (most expensive) to IV. Many class IV places to eat are stand-up cafés or bars. The quality of service is variable, but it is normally pretty lousy. A few restaurants are closed on Mondays. The best bet for a very good restaurant is often at a hotel. It is often necessary to book a table in advance at good restaurants. Tipping in restaurants, or rounding up the bill, is appreciated. Smoking is not allowed in most eating establishments. Vegetarians will find that they have a hard time finding anything to eat in restaurants. The concept of being a vegetarian is simply unknown in Czechoslovakia, and vegetarians may find themselves permanently dining out on a very limited number of dishes.

Restaurace   Restaurant
Samoobsluha   Stand-up cafeteria
Hospoda/hostinec   Pub
Pivnice   Beer hall (food sometimes available)
Vinárna   Wine bar (ditto)
Cukrárna or Kavárna   Café, selling cakes, coffee, sweet drinks and snacks, familiar to those who have travelled in Austria.

Shopping

Shops are open from 6/8am to 6/8pm, with a break for lunch (normally at 12noon) for 1 to 2 (and sometimes even 3) hours. Most shops are closed on Saturday afternoon, and virtually all are closed all day Sunday. A few are also closed all or part of Monday. Some may be open later into the evening on Thursdays. Banks and post offices are normally open 8am to 2pm, weekdays only.

A *Potraviny* is a supermarket or general grocery store; a *drogeria* is a chemists; a *kniha* is a bookshop. The biggest chain of department stores is called 'Prior'. The number of people in a shop at any one time is often controlled, which is why there are sometimes queues to get in them.

Tuzex shops, which are found in most large towns and tourist centres, only accept hard currency, credit cards, or 'Tuzex vouchers' which must be bought with hard currency at banks, Čedok offices, etc. They sell many quality Czechoslovak goods, and many imported goods too. Porcelaine, embroidery and other fancy textiles and leather goods, the ubiquitous Czech crystal, carved wooden ornaments and toys, costume jewellery and antiques are all good souvenirs, but unless you buy them at a Tuzex shop (and keep the receipt to prove you have done so), you may find yourself having to pay a big export tax on these goods to take them out of the country.

Tourist Information

Outside Czechoslovakia

Tourist information outside Czechoslovakia is handled by the organisation Čedok — the Czechoslovak State Travel Office. On a general level, they can give out information on what to see, up-to-date information on driving and other documents, and on customs regulations etc; other more specific areas in which they can help are:-

Supplying lists of hotels, campsites and other accommodation facilities in the area you intend to visit, and, if necessary, booking it for you (they can normally only book the better class hotels).

Supplying information about, and booking, a variety of package tours to Czechoslovakia, some of which also take in visits to Austria, the USSR and other East European countries. This includes grand 2-week coach tours, and also skiing holidays.

Selling motoring maps and atlases of Czechoslovakia, and Czech phrase books.

Supplying information about specialist holidays in Czechoslovakia: Skiing holidays; hunting, shooting and fishing trips, which must be organised before you travel to Czechoslovakia; spa treatment holidays in Karlovy Vary, Františkovy Lazné, Mariánské Lázně, and other spas, which must also be arranged before you travel to Czechoslovakia.

Some specialist activity holidays are outside the scope of Čedok, but they will tell you where you can find out about them; options include small group holidays involved in advanced climbing or mountaineering, rafting and canoeing, and hill or mountain trekking.

The main Čedok offices abroad are:

Čedok (London) Ltd	Čedok
17-18 Old Bond Street	10 East 40th Street
London W1X 4RB	New York, N.Y. 10157
☎ (071) 629 6058	☎ 212 689 9720

There are no Čedok offices in Canada or Australia.

In Czechoslovakia

Tourism in Czechoslovakia is only slowly becoming more orientated towards catering for the needs of the individual traveller — the country has always been much more geared towards package and group tourism. There are very few tourist information offices as such. Čedok is the main travel bureau in the country; they will help with travel arrangements, and can often advise on things like local events, etc, but as for providing information on what there is to see they are often very unhelpful. Čedok offices in the main tourist centres also run day-long or half-day tours to local places of interest, normally by coach, and also walking tours of some towns, with an English-speaking guide. Information on these is given in the 'Additional Information' sections at the end of the chapters. These tours normally operate from mid-May to mid-September only. Čedok is mostly useful as an accommodation office and for changing money (see relevant sections). There is a Čedok office in virtually every town in the country, and in small towns as well if they are popular with tourists. They are normally located on the town's main street or square. Most offices open 8am-12noon, and 1-5pm (4pm in winter), and on Saturdays 8am-12noon, though this can often vary slightly. Virtually all Čedok offices will have someone who speaks English. Other tourist and travel bureau, often even less useful, include CKM (for young people and students), Rekrea, and Slovakotourist (in Slovakia).

Bookshops are often better sources of information on what to see in any given area. They often stock multi-lingual maps or guides of the surrounding region, which will have a certain amount of information in English.

Prague

The principal Čedok office in Czechoslovakia, and a source of tourist information about both the city and the country, is at 18, Na Příkopě Street, Prague-1 (Monday to Thursday, 8.15am-4.15pm, Friday 8.15am-3.45pm, Saturday 8.15am-1pm [until 12noon October to May], Sunday closed). The services they offer, apart from general help and assistance to foreign tourists, include the sale of rail and bus tickets to destinations within Czechoslovakia and abroad, and the running of day or half-day coach tours to many places near Prague (eg Karlštejn Castle, Melník, Kutná Hora, Karlovy Vary, Hluboká Castle, etc), and walking and other sightseeing tours of Prague. N.B. There is no accommodation office here (see under 'Accommodation').

The best source of information specifically concerned with Prague is the Prague Information Service (PIS), next door to the above office at 20, Na Příkopě Street (Monday to Friday, 8am-8pm [7pm November to March], Saturday 8am-12noon, Sunday closed); other offices at Hlavní Nádraži (main railway station), Hradčanská Metro Station, and opposite the Astronomical Clock on Staroměstské Náměstí (Old Town Square) at number 22. It offers a similar service to Čedok; guides can be hired by individuals wanting to see Prague, also excellent advice on theatre and entertainment scene, booking theatre tickets etc, but again no accommodation service.

Travelling to Czechoslovakia

By Air

ČSA-Czechoslovak airlines operates services between London, Montreal and New York, and Prague-Ruzyně airport. National carriers of many other countries also fly to to Prague. Tickets can be booked through ČSA to other destinations in Czechoslovakia, but a change of plane is necessary in Prague.

ČSA-Czechoslovak Airlines	ČSA-Czechoslovak Airlines
12a Margaret Street	2020 Rue Université
London W1N 7LF	Montreal H3A 2A5
☎ (071) 255 1898	☎ 514 844 4200

ČSA-Czechoslovak Airlines
545 5th Avenue, New York N.Y. 10017, ☎ 212 682 5833

By Train

Prague is linked to the main West European rail network via a number of frontier crossing points. Most visitors coming from Britain will use the frontier post at Cheb-Schirnding on the Nürnberg (Nuremberg)-Plzeň-Prague line. The main route across Europe from Britain is Bruxelles (Brussels)-Aachen-Köln (Cologne)-Frankfurt-Würzburg-Nürnburg. Many rail travellers will need to change trains at Köln (Cologne), allowing for a good opportunity to see that city's fabulous Gothic cathedral which is literally right outside the entrance to the city's main railway station. International train services link Prague directly with Zürich, Munich, Paris, Berlin, Vienna, Warsaw, Budapest, Bucharest, Sofia, Moscow and other cities. International rail services also link Brno, Bratislava, Karlovy Vary and other cities in Czechoslovakia with cities in Western Europe, and, more frequently, Eastern Europe.

Inter-rail and Eurotrain cards are valid for travel in Czechoslovakia. Rail tickets bought in Czechoslovakia to destinations in Western Europe can only be purchased at Čedok offices and must be paid for in hard currency or by credit card. Tickets to destinations in Eastern Europe can be bought at railway stations with Czech crowns.

By Car

Prague is about 1,300km (800 miles) by road from London. From the English Channel (Dover-Ostend is the best ferry route) there are a multitude of different routes motorists can take, through Belgium and Germany. The best one is probably Bruxelles-Köln-Limburg-Frankfurt-Würzburg-Nürnberg. Then come off the *autobahn* and take the main road from Nürnberg to Prague, crossing the border into Czechoslovakia at Weidhaus-Rozvadov and travelling through Stříbo and Plzen.

A good place to stop off or spend the night on the road or rail journey between London and Prague is the Baroque city of Würzburg in Bavaria, which the *autobahn* skirts past and the railway passes through. A very short diversion off the German *autobahn*, which would not significantly increase the time taken on this journey, could take motorists travelling between London and Prague along the scenic Rhein Valley between Bonn and Mainz (via Koblenz). Rail routes between Prague and London pass along this valley anyway.

Bear in mind that new road and rail crossings between Czechoslovakia and Austria and Germany are gradually being opened (or re-opened). However, some minor road border crossings marked on maps are exclusively for the use of Czech and German or Austrian citizens. Čedok offices can supply lists detailing the current situation.

By Coach

There are direct coach services from London to Prague, which take about 23 hours. One of the best companies to use is Kingscourt Express, 35 Kingscourt Road, London SW16 1JA ☎ (081) 769 9229, but there are other companies which operate this route.

INDEX